MANAGING
THE HUMAN
SERVICE
ORGANIZATION

SOURCEBOOKS FOR IMPROVING HUMAN SERVICES

Edited by Richard Steiner, *State University of New York at Albany*

Volume 1: Managing the Human Service Organization *by Richard Steiner*

Subsequent volumes will explore other problems of interest to human services professionals—including planning, management, and service delivery.

Published in cooperation with the School of Social Welfare, State University of New York at Albany

MANAGING THE HUMAN SERVICE ORGANIZATION

From Survival to Achievement

Richard Steiner

SAGE Publications / Beverly Hills / London

For information address

SAGE PUBLICATIONS, INC.
275 South Beverly Drive
Beverly Hills, California 90212

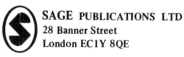

SAGE PUBLICATIONS LTD
28 Banner Street
London EC1Y 8QE

Printed in the United States of America

Library of Congress Cataloging in Publication Data

Steiner, Richard.
    Managing the human service organization.

    (Sourcebooks for improving human services; v. 1)
    Bibliography: p. 233
    1. Social work administration. 2. Public welfare
administration. I. Title. II. Series.
HV41.S783   658'.91'361   77-2150
ISBN 0-8039-0849-0
ISBN 0-8039-0850-4 pbk.

FIRST PRINTING

CONTENTS

PREFACE

This series has been prompted not only by the tremendous growth within the human services, but also by increased interest from students and practitioners in making the system more responsive and productive. The human services have been allocated an ever-rising proportion of public-sector domestic resources. Inevitably, policy makers, professionals in the field, and academicians have turned their attention toward the results obtained with these resources. However, there is wide concern about the ability of these organizations to achieve far-reaching, but socially necessary, goals, and about whether the human services have an achievement motivation, a desire to be performance-oriented in terms of effectiveness and efficiency.

Given our federal system of government and of mixed economy, the major avenues for improving the management, planning, and delivery of human services involve intergovernmental and public/private relationships. While nationalization of a delivery mechanism is under serious consideration, current trends show a concerted effort toward strengthening state and local delivery capability. The states and the localities are the governmental units most concerned with direct service delivery. It is in these units that the success of human service programs is ultimately determined and where public and private resources are put to work on some of today's most pressing human problems.

These realities were recognized with the 1974 enactment of Title XX of the Federal Social Security Act, requiring state and local involvement in comprehensive human service planning. Yet, this legislation also illustrates the continuing tensions within the intergovernmental system; it further illustrates the need for greater local autonomy and the requirement for national standards which, though broadened, continue to impose severe restraints on effective local management, on planning, and on delivery.

7

Keeping this context in mind, it is plain to see that human service organizations are in a somewhat untenable position. On the one hand, they must be responsive and responsible to a local constituency for the delivery of services and accountable for expenditures. On the other hand, the same organizations are at the end of a chain of command which stretches from county to state to the federal government. In essence, human service organizations are puppets, and when they make a mistake in the eyes of the public, it is not the puppet master who is the target of the ire, but rather, the hapless "dummy."

If a child throws a ball through a window, you do not punish the ball; the ball is merely a vehicle and not the initiator of the misdeed. Along these same lines, the federal and state government often underestimate local impacts of mandated service and maintenance. It is within such a system that the human service organization, its managers, and its employees must operate. Consequently, the current series on human services management, planning, and delivery will focus on issues of both national and local concern; it will focus on improving integration, management, and services within and between organizations charged with the responsibility for public welfare. Each volume will highlight a different aspect of the system.

This volume emphasizes the role and importance of the human service organization in the overall delivery mechanism. Through various means, it attempts to demonstrate how the human service organization can move from a management philosophy based on survival to a management strategy that emphasizes achievement. A future volume in this series concerns planning and the planning process, which is critical for the development of sound human service programs. Behind current policy changes regarding federal aid to localities stand pragmatism and accountability. In the aftermath of these policy changes appears a primary common requirement—planning. Consequently, the purpose of the planning volume is to focus on common planning requirements in terms of definition, process, technique, and applicability in an effort to assist those who must organize and conduct the planning process competently and in full recognition of available alternatives and opportunities. In addition, it will also address the application of the planning process in a human service setting, taking into consideration the particular constraints and opportunities that exist in service planning and in programming.

Another volume will emphasize the individual and the managerial dimensions of management activity. Today's human service executive should be multidimensional. Not only must the manager possess a high

MANAGING THE HUMAN SERVICE ORGANIZATION

SOURCEBOOKS FOR IMPROVING HUMAN SERVICES

·II●II●II●II●II●II●II●II●II●II●II●II●II●II●II●II●II●II●II●II●II●II●II●II●II●II●II●II●II●II●II·

Edited by Richard Steiner, *State University of New York at Albany*

Volume 1: Managing the Human Service Organization *by Richard Steiner*

Subsequent volumes will explore other problems of interest to human services professionals—including planning, management, and service delivery.

Published in cooperation with the School of Social Welfare, State University of New York at Albany

II●II●II●II●II●II●II●II●II●II●II●II●II●II●II●II●II●II●II●II●II●II●II●II●II●II●II●II●II●II●II●II

MANAGING THE HUMAN SERVICE ORGANIZATION

From Survival to Achievement

Richard Steiner

SAGE Publications / Beverly Hills / London

For information address

SAGE PUBLICATIONS, INC.
275 South Beverly Drive
Beverly Hills, California 90212

SAGE PUBLICATIONS LTD
28 Banner Street
London EC1Y 8QE

Printed in the United States of America

Library of Congress Cataloging in Publication Data

Steiner, Richard.
   Managing the human service organization.

   (Sourcebooks for improving human services; v. 1)
   Bibliography: p. 233
   1. Social work administration. 2. Public welfare
administration. I. Title. II. Series.
HV41.S783   658'.91'361   77-2150
ISBN 0-8039-0849-0
ISBN 0-8039-0850-4 pbk.

FIRST PRINTING

CONTENTS

PREFACE

This series has been prompted not only by the tremendous growth within the human services, but also by increased interest from students and practitioners in making the system more responsive and productive. The human services have been allocated an ever-rising proportion of public-sector domestic resources. Inevitably, policy makers, professionals in the field, and academicians have turned their attention toward the results obtained with these resources. However, there is wide concern about the ability of these organizations to achieve far-reaching, but socially necessary, goals, and about whether the human services have an achievement motivation, a desire to be performance-oriented in terms of effectiveness and efficiency.

Given our federal system of government and of mixed economy, the major avenues for improving the management, planning, and delivery of human services involve intergovernmental and public/private relationships. While nationalization of a delivery mechanism is under serious consideration, current trends show a concerted effort toward strengthening state and local delivery capability. The states and the localities are the governmental units most concerned with direct service delivery. It is in these units that the success of human service programs is ultimately determined and where public and private resources are put to work on some of today's most pressing human problems.

These realities were recognized with the 1974 enactment of Title XX of the Federal Social Security Act, requiring state and local involvement in comprehensive human service planning. Yet, this legislation also illustrates the continuing tensions within the intergovernmental system; it further illustrates the need for greater local autonomy and the requirement for national standards which, though broadened, continue to impose severe restraints on effective local management, on planning, and on delivery.

7

Keeping this context in mind, it is plain to see that human service organizations are in a somewhat untenable position. On the one hand, they must be responsive and responsible to a local constituency for the delivery of services and accountable for expenditures. On the other hand, the same organizations are at the end of a chain of command which stretches from county to state to the federal government. In essence, human service organizations are puppets, and when they make a mistake in the eyes of the public, it is not the puppet master who is the target of the ire, but rather, the hapless "dummy."

If a child throws a ball through a window, you do not punish the ball; the ball is merely a vehicle and not the initiator of the misdeed. Along these same lines, the federal and state government often underestimate local impacts of mandated service and maintenance. It is within such a system that the human service organization, its managers, and its employees must operate. Consequently, the current series on human services management, planning, and delivery will focus on issues of both national and local concern; it will focus on improving integration, management, and services within and between organizations charged with the responsibility for public welfare. Each volume will highlight a different aspect of the system.

This volume emphasizes the role and importance of the human service organization in the overall delivery mechanism. Through various means, it attempts to demonstrate how the human service organization can move from a management philosophy based on survival to a management strategy that emphasizes achievement. A future volume in this series concerns planning and the planning process, which is critical for the development of sound human service programs. Behind current policy changes regarding federal aid to localities stand pragmatism and accountability. In the aftermath of these policy changes appears a primary common requirement—planning. Consequently, the purpose of the planning volume is to focus on common planning requirements in terms of definition, process, technique, and applicability in an effort to assist those who must organize and conduct the planning process competently and in full recognition of available alternatives and opportunities. In addition, it will also address the application of the planning process in a human service setting, taking into consideration the particular constraints and opportunities that exist in service planning and in programming.

Another volume will emphasize the individual and the managerial dimensions of management activity. Today's human service executive should be multidimensional. Not only must the manager possess a high degree of technological, administrative, and managerial competence, but he also must be a leader—one who can motivate employees, enhance their capabilities, and spur creativity. The human service worker, however, has many legitimate, competing claims on time both on and off the job. There seem to be new and emerging value systems which are no doubt caused by our fast-changing social, political, and economic systems. Human service executives must squarely face the problems involved in managing and in leading today's people. Such issues become even more magnified when one considers that, although social problems are increasing, the available dollars and manpower probably will be held constant or will be decreased. Thus, this book not only will consider the question of motivating employees to develop a self-actualized desire to obtain "management's goals," but also will consider the issue of increasing worker productivity.

Finally, other volumes in the series will concentrate on some very real and pressing delivery problems. There will be a clear demonstration of how good management, sound organizations, and competent individuals can be integrated to make for high levels of delivery performance.

A unique combination of analytic resources has been mobilized for the preparation of these volumes. The core contributors have been drawn from the professional faculty and professional staff of the School of Social Welfare, University at Albany. Each volume will present new and interesting perspectives on some of the techniques and technologies available for solving some of our immediate and long-range human service problems and concerns.

We intend to make this series relevant, readable, interesting, and useful to all established practitioners and for those who contemplate a human service career. It is our hope they will attend each volume critically, with an eye to internalizing those suggestions and ideas which are meaningful and challenge those ideas they do not either understand or cherish.

Every individual—student or practitioner—has some very real and different perspectives which might significantly differ from that of the several authors. Rather than being a sign of discord, this is indicative of serious reader intent. If this series can generate a willingness to question the system as it is, if it can force readers to ask what can be done better, and if it can then act as a catalyst for change, it has met its goals. All the lofty rhetoric, notwithstanding, if the aforementioned is accomplished, this is a compliment of the highest calibre.

Richard Steiner, Editor
Noreen Judge, Assistant Editor

MANAGING FOR ACHIEVEMENT IN THE HUMAN

SERVICES, OR, WHERE HAVE WE GONE WRONG?

INTRODUCTION

Chapter 1 provides a general outline for Volume One. Since the human service system has grown at an accelerated rate, so have the demands made of it and the number and breadth of its critics. Chapter 1 begins with a discussion of what this rapid growth means for the human service manager and organization. The main focus of Volume One is the human service system from an organizational perspective.

The discussion of human service organizations begins with a brief overview of the factors, relationships, and, in general, processes of organizational systems. It is followed by a more extensive overview of similarities and differences between private-sector profit-oriented and publicly funded human service organizations. The overview concentrates on the differences between the two. A number of human service management and organizational problems stems from this discussion of differences. Eight such problems and the subsequent chapter devoted to each are listed at the end of Chapter 1. This list serves both as a delineation of some human service problem areas and a guide to discussion for the entire volume.

GROWING TO ACHIEVE, NOT MERELY TO SURVIVE

In just two words, if one were to characterize the human service delivery system during the past forty years, the words one uses would have to be growth and complexity. The shift from basically localized, small, voluntary efforts to help a few "unfortunates" among us has blossomed into gargantuan delivery systems which provide a massive range of services to almost every man, woman, and child in the country. This seemingly endless organizational growth and maze of administrative laws, rules, and regulations that serve to confuse, rather than clarify access and eligibility are seriously being questioned by the public and politicians alike. When anyone brings up the subject of human services, a common expression of frustration is that there has to be a better way.

Organizations from the Health, Education, and Welfare (HEW) to the local county agency are under constant attack. No longer are the critics isolated malcontents who abhor "giveaways" and vehemently support free enterprise. Rather, those people who express serious concern come from all spectrums of society and political thought. Human service organizations are being blamed for everything from institutionalization of the very problems they seek to correct, to the massive budget deficits that afflect all governmental levels. The criticism mounts, yet the system survives. However, does it survive because benefits outweigh deficits or because, in the final analysis, service organizations are so apathetic and shortsighted that improvement is not available? In most cases, it seems reasonable to assume that the targets for disapproval are not the final objectives, but the systems designed to achieve them. Obviously, human service providers can no longer afford to ignore the rumblings of a public that, rightly or wrongly, views the service organization as wasteful, poorly administered, and an economical drain.

Perhaps we are in this dilemma because survival—not service—has become the primary organizational objective. Such drastic displacement of legitimate objectives has had a forceful impact both on the perceptions of performance and the organization's ability to deliver programs. Organizational survival, as the only measurable outcome, is no longer an acceptable goal. Survival for its own sake is an admirable self-defense reaction, but the only beneficiaries of it are the fortunate few who receive weekly pay checks. This circumstance is not sufficient justification for the funding of massive programs, as the lesson of the Office of Economic Opportunity (OEO)[1] has taught us. Rather, survival of a human service organization must be based on the following goals: (1) accepting the obligations of public responsibility and responsiveness; (2) developing productive mechanisms for serving human needs; (3) admitting the necessity for being held accountable for both failures and successes; (4) finding ways of integrating the service into, rather than dominating, the community.

Unfortunately, before organizational performance can actually be achieved, two simultaneous actions must occur. First, the human service manager must achieve a state of excellence heretofore unknown in the context of service organizations. The manager is the individual upon whose shoulders rests the ultimate responsibility for making the human service delivery mechanism a productive, socially enriching, nondraining vehicle.

In most organizational situations, the manager is both blessed and cursed. Managers are blessed with clientele and resources because without either one there is no need for the organization or the administrator. On the other hand, the administrator is cursed with limited delivery technology, change resistant organizations, and an increasingly hostile public environment. In looking for improvement in service delivery, a great deal of emphasis should be placed on developing, educating, training, enriching, and broadening one of the most important, but least appreciated, organizational resources—the human being. This approach is not to say, of course, that "super" managers will make "super" organizations. Quite the contrary, this stage is where the second element in the formula enters the picture. In other words, top-flight managers are sufficient, but not necessary, causative factors of productive human service organizations.

The organization itself must be prepared to accept the motivated, effective, and achieving manager. Human service organizations must be designed to facilitate change and adaptibility in order to reduce unneeded procedures and processes, to fully utilize individual potential, and to ensure that internal administrative systems support, rather than dominate, service operations to focus on objectives, tasks, and outcomes. Productive human service delivery mechanisms are those in which managers and organizations not only coexist, but also enter into totally integrated symbiotic relationships. If performance is to be achieved, neither the managers nor the organization can exist in isolation.

Think of an analogous situation which occurs in the racing world. To win a race requires a combination of factors, including a highly skilled driver; a well-designed, mechanically superior racing machine; and a skillful, coordinated pit crew. Take the world's top drivers and provide them with an inferior or defective vehicle, and there is no chance of that machine's being competitive, or even its winning the race. On the other hand, take the most highly advanced racing machine available, place it in the hands of a rank amateur, and the end result will likely be the same. Even if one could match a world-class driver with a high-performance vehicle, all would be for naught if the pit crew consisted of bumbling fools.

The human service delivery mechanism operates in much the same way. The best, brightest executives available will not be able to turn around the system, at least not by themselves, regardless of their supposed superhuman qualities. Likewise, human service organizations alone, no matter how eloquent their design, will not be able to have a significant impact on the delivery system. If there is any hope of improving human service delivery, it is predicated on integrating the effective manager into a streamlined organization supported by task-oriented work teams. There is no substitute, no magic formula, no legislative trick, and no political rhetoric that can change this reality. Recombine, consolidate, cut, add—it does not matter; nothing short of total integration is demanded among management, organization, and worker to achieve a human service delivery structure worthy of our people and our country.

Consequently, this book's main focus is the development of a detailed appreciation and understanding of the human service organization and its inherent strengths, weaknesses, problems, and prospects. Future works in this series (*Sourcebooks for Improving Human Services*) will specifically concentrate on the manager's function. However, as a first step, it is crucial that both students and practitioners alike prepare to be onlookers. All too often we are deluged with detail and unable to adequately perceive what goes on around us. Treat this book as an opportunity to obtain an overview of how and why human service organizations are the way they are. Human service organizations did not evolve in isolation. They are products of the people that manage them, work in them, support them, and use them. What follows is a play-by-play description of how these organizations operate. Admittedly, it is a highly personalized analysis, yet it might spark some independent thought and analysis from those who have intimate knowledge of how the game is played.

What is an Organization?

The concept of organization is simple to generalize abstractly, yet difficult to specify, since the entire concept of how an organization functions revolves around a complex of highly particular sets of relationships. Consequently, rather than play the "definition game," it might prove more worthwhile to operationalize the concept of what an organization is, how it functions, and what it produces. Organizational performance is dependent upon how, in what manner and proportion, it is able to integrate available delivery technology, staff capability and motivation, structure, management styles, communication links, and environmental constraints. Some of these organizational factors are under direct control of the administrator. Other factors can be imparted through the influence process. Still, others are completely outside the scope and control of the administrator. Diagrammatically, then, as displayed in Figure 1-1, an organization consists of these factors.

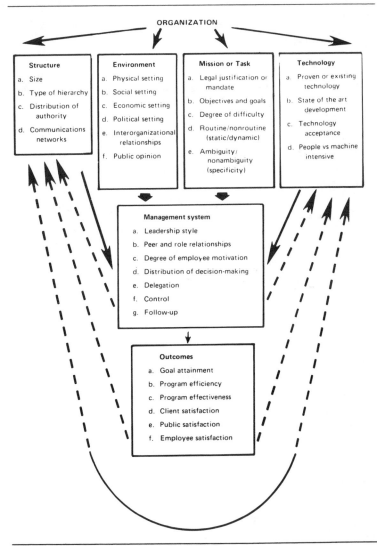

Figure 1.1: ORGANIZATIONAL FACTORS

An organization, therefore, can be seen as a system of interacting and interlinking elements or structural components that seek to accomplish specific objectives by utilizing identifiable technology and operations within a broader environmental framework. Organizations accomplish their purposes by manipulating resources, processes, or goals. These terms become easily translatable into inputs → thruputs → outputs. The purpose of any organization, including human service agencies, is to deliver a specified product or service. It is accomplished in the manner displayed in Figure 1-2.

The basic assumption of this model is that assigned resources, such as money, time, people, technology, and equipment are converted by the administrative functions to attain specific goals and objectives which have a beneficial social impact. All described factors are interdependent.

Typically, in the hierarchy of allocated resources, money assumes paramount importance. Money is the mechanism whereby the organization purchases services, people's time, technology, and equipment. In some cases, the human resources have internalized the needed technologies, while, in others, the technology has to be developed or purchased outside the system and brought into the organizational setting. With both, the staff has to be trained to adequately utilize the technology and equipment needed to deliver the mandated services.

The process mechanisms, such as organizational structure, management systems, and procedures, exist to support the administrative functions of planning, decision-making, directing, controlling, coordinating, and evaluating. Organizational structure, in turn, determines the type, place, and role of interaction involving management of budget, personnel, and information, and the measurement systems needed to make the organization a productive operating unit.

Output is the organizational end product. The administrative and management goal is to produce a service which meets standards in quality and quantity. Service production is met through a variety of programmatic activities with the assistance of numerous people and support systems.

The primary function of a human service organization is to turn legislative mandates into program reality. This apparently simple statement is the bane of almost every human service administrator at all government levels. One often wonders, "Why can't we seem to get a handle on the behemoth called the welfare system?" After all, Xerox, IBM, General Motors, Exxon, and numerous other private-sector operations seem to have successfully harnessed the organizational monster. What makes these organizations appear to function so productively compared to human service agencies?

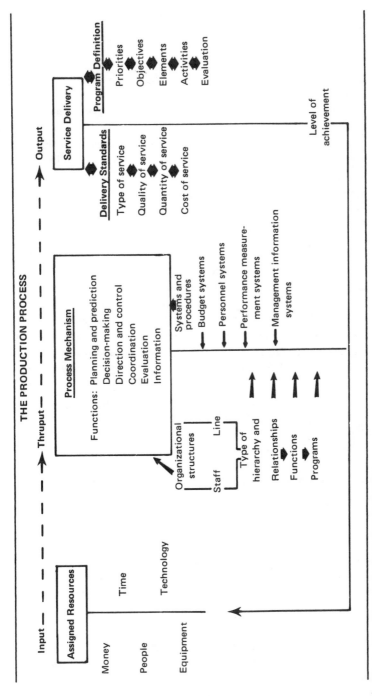

Figure 1.2: THE PRODUCTION PROCESS

17

PUBLIC AND PRIVATE ORGANIZATIONAL
SIMILARITIES AND DIFFERENCES

Until now discussion has centered on "organization" as a generic concept, but one wonders whether it is practical or fruitful to lump together all classes and types of organizations as if they were without distinguishing characteristics. In other words, maybe there is a need to look at human service organizations as separate and distinct operational entities. Is there a lesson to be learned from managers outside the human service milieu, or are they working in an entirely different environment? Before directly examining this proposition, it might first be worthwhile to point out that for every private-sector success story there are massive failures, such as Grants, Penn Central, and Lockheed. Even industrial giants like Xerox, General Electric, and RCA took severe financial beatings in their attempts to develop sophisticated computer lines. These tales are not being told to denegrate, but to lay to rest the myth of private-sector infallibility held by many welfare-sector administrators. Few among us can be classified as "super managers" who are able to leap legislative roadblocks in a single bound. Nevertheless, human service organizations have to be managed, regardless of the task's impossibility or legislative ambiguity. It is left up to mortals to turn dreams into social reality. Our degree of success depends on many far-ranging organizational and environmental factors, some of which will be discussed in Chapter 1.

Perhaps we can obtain a handle by first examining some differences and similarities found between the private-sector, profit-centered organization and the publicly funded human service agency.

Organizations, as generic systems, have much in common. The basic models described in Figures 1-1 and 1-2 remain unchanged. As Perrow[2] points out, every organization must accomplish four tasks:

1. Secure capital inputs sufficient to establish itself and to expand when the need arises.

2. Secure acceptance of basic activity legitimization.

3. Marshal the necessary human skills.

4. Coordinate the activities of its members and the relations of the organization with other organizations and with clients or consumers.

Even more specifically, all organizations have a structure—formal and informal—which details work flows, sets divisions of work responsibility, defines work rules, and describes interactive relationships among employees. Similarly, organizations must be prepared to make accurate decisions around a type of specific, contextual framework. They must have a communication process through which organizational members can relay, transmit, and send information. Concurrently, the organizations must be capable of processing, analyzing, gathering, making sense of this information, and integrating it into the decision-making structure. Also, systems, procedures, processes, and policies have to be specifically spelled out to ensure performance uniformity and production of common program outputs. There has to be a mechanism for managing human resources and financial and physical resources of the organization. Finally, all organizational productivity depends on the quality of exhibited managerial leadership, together with a high level of employee motivation, in order to facilitate commitment to the operation and its objectives. These are only some of the common elements.

Perhaps, if a true understanding of the human service organization and its special place in the study of managing for performance is to be achieved, it would be worthwhile to concentrate on organizational differences. Differences that will be discussed include: financial resources, utilization of time, technology, worker values, tasks, social responsibility, decision-making, administrative process, organizational flexibility, measurement of output, and accountability.

Financial Resources

The best place to start the analysis is up front where an immediate, apparent difference between private-sector, or profit-making, organizations and human service organizations can be ascertained. In terms of assigned resources, private-sector organizations directly obtain financial support either from the investment or from the consumer-serviced market. Consequently, a direct relationship is achieved between consumption and control, or between needed service and its delivery. In the private, industrial sector the individual who benefits from the service usually pays not only the full cost of its production, but also an additional amount to allow for a profit margin. On the other hand, in the human services, it is not typically the consumer or the direct beneficiary who pays for the service—money is usually provided by a secondary or public resource. The implications for the delivery of human services based on this factor alone are immense.

For instance, in the private sector, the marketing mechanism helps to refine and balance the products produced and to define their relative worth and degree of consumption. Ford Motor Company introduces the Edsel and invests hundreds of millions doing so. The public shuns the car; hence, the Edsel disappears. If there is no ready market for the product, there is no profit. If there is no profit, the product either is modified in style or is removed from the inventory. The meat boycott and recent economic stagnation also graphically illustrate this point. As meat prices rose because of increases in costs to farmers and ranchers, the consumption of beef fell. As consumption declined, a surplus of meat became available; hence, prices were lowered. Overstocked automobile dealers sometimes find it to their advantage to reduce prices, and thereby take a temporary loss on each unit sold in order to reduce inventory. Similarly, the style, size, and mechanical characteristics of the automobile have changed to meet new consumer demands arising from not only the rise in price but also from the shortage of gas. What is being demonstrated is that, for all intents and purposes, the private sector is sensitive to shifts in consumer tastes, needs, desires, and complaints.

The human services, however, do not react in a similar manner. The explanation is obvious. Most payments for services are made either through third-party payments or through fixed budgets which bear little or no relationship to client or community needs. Take, for instance, the school system where attendance is in rapid decline. The private model would call for a reduction in services or costs, yet school services and their concurrent costs are on the increase. We have more hospital beds than needed, yet new hospitals are being built which stretch scarce human and fiscal resources almost beyond the breaking point. Similarly, drug therapy has allowed the emptying of mental institutions and schools for the retarded, yet we are building new institutions or maintaining old ones to house a nonexistent population. In the heyday of the war on poverty, we had community action agencies funded by the OEO; the neighborhood health centers funded by HEW; Model Cities programs funded by the Department of Housing and Urban Development (HUD); labor programs funded by the Department of Labor; and a plethora of local and state agencies all competing for the same clients. The biggest problem for such agencies was not delivering services, but finding clients. In some ways, attempts are being made to remedy this lack of relationship between consumption and control by interposing a planning process.

It is the need for profit in the private sector that drives the organization to strive for consumer acceptance, while in the public human services, it is the need for survival. Survival often does not depend on who is serviced, but on who pays the bills, and these two are not often the same. Consequently, who pays for the service is a major distinguishing characteristic between profit-centered and human service organizations.

Time Utilization

Time utilization is another obvious difference. Private-sector enterprises usually have strict time constraints placed both on personnel and production units. For example, the production of an automobile is a highly interdependent process in which all workers, foremen, and engineers have to adjust to the precise pace of the production line rather than have the production mechanism conform to the workers' schedule. In most cases, human service organizations place less emphasis on the time imperative. Assembly lines might have cars rolling off every eleven minutes, but in a professional-helping situation, treatment might last one week or ten years. Even in more highly controlled situations, such as in determining social service eligibility, there can be wide variation in the time it takes to process specific applications. Similarly, the fact that a professional might not be available at a particular hour, or that more than the normally allotted time with a client is spent, will not irreparably damage the production schedule because of limited interdependence and flexibility in the output process. Also, the product—in this case, a treated client—bends to the time constraints of the professional. Think in terms of the doctor-patient relationship. Who among us has not spent considerable time impatiently waiting for the physician to see us. While most resent these delays, we realize the need for matching individual attention to the severity of the problem. In the social services, it is the client who determines the need, based on analysis of problems, on the type of treatments performed, and on their duration.

The old adage that no two cases are exactly alike then leads us into the time problem. In the private sector, organizations can highly structure and allocate time as a resource, while in the human services, such abilities do not exist. The reason for this phenomenon is the uniformity of the output unit. In the human services, there is limited product uniformity because of the varying nature and severity of problems. Hence, time management is a definite problem. On the other hand, the hallmark of assembly-line production is uniformity; hence, there is the need to control scheduling and time utilization.

Technology

The type and degree of sophisticated technology applied to the service or production process is also a point of variance between profit-centered and human service organizations. It would probably be a kindness to say that human service technology (as in the case of all the social sciences) is in a rudimentary stage of development. After all, unlike producing automobiles, we just do not know how to crank out well-adjusted, independent, cured people. If it were only as simple as making cars! Treatment is often dependent on the individualized competency of the professional who is responsible for its delivery. Where overall treatment modalities exist, there is still wide variance in application. In short, there is yet no single technology that would allow the service practitioner to reduce to zero the present uncertainty of the nature of human and social behavior. In other words, while practitioners can "act on" clients, there is no way of predicting just how successful the treatment will be. Consequently, rather than having one agreed-to technology which can reduce all uncertainty about the nature of man, human service organizations are forced to manage many varied technologies and still do not have the assurance that they will work.

Think of the havoc wrought if every steel worker could decide on how much alloy, iron ore, and coke should be mixed to produce each batch of steel. There would be no uniformity in product; hence, it would be difficult, if not impossible, to predict the product's uses. Fortunately, steel technology is highly developed, and we do not often run into this predicament. Similarly, while we have four major automobile manufacturers, with each producing cars of various styles and sizes, the basic production technology remains constant, with most parts being totally interchangeable. Private-sector service industries, such as the massive insurance business, have a highly defined technology in terms of marketing, actuarial science, investment strategies, and electronic data processing. Unfortunately, in the human service professions and the agencies designed to deliver this assistance, such an identifiable technology does not exist. This reality not only partially accounts for the spotty record of accomplishment in human services delivery, but also for the great difficulty encountered in managing the system.

Worker Characteristics

Compared to social service agencies, the types of workers attracted to private-sector, profit-oriented organizations, probably differ—if not in terms of overall quality, in their specific knowledges, skills, values, and exhibited behaviors. Assumptions in each of these areas could be made about the capabilities of private vs human managers if one were inclined to view the management process consisting of these competencies: (a) analytic and decision-making skills; (b) individual/group/organizational dynamics; and (c) administrative/management process skills.

One could probably make the prediction that the strength of professional human service managers, because of their education, training, and value sets, lies in the area of individual and group dynamics. Consequently, human service managers tend to heavily emphasize human transactions and their impact on the organization and the individual. Such attitudes, if they do exist, would push human service administrators toward the human relations approach to management. On the other hand, weaknesses in the abilities of human service managers would most likely appear in areas concerned with administrative procedures and with applications of analytic tools to the decision-making process. Deficiencies might also arise when dealing with organizational dynamics and change, since this procedure involves interactions between the administrative-analytic processes.

The opposite would probably be true for private-sector managers. Because of their education, training, and values, one would expect managers to show strength in the application of analytic tools—operations research, for example—in solving highly technical problems and in the handling of administrative/management procedures. Weaknesses could probably be discerned in the areas of individual and group dynamics. These gaps and differences in knowledge, skills, values, and behaviors are continually being narrowed by the cross-fertilization between public- and private-sector management, in addition to the upsurge in post-entry management development.

Tasks

While individual management differences and capabilities tend to be only differences in degree, some striking comparisons can be made by looking at the nature of the tasks the work force performs. A cardinal principle of private-sector production is specialization and routinization. Each employee is expected to contribute a highly defined piece-of-the-action to the completed product. Job tasks are broken down into the simplest possible component parts. Hence, there is little ambiguity. When there is little ambiguity, there is high specificity, resulting in the production of a uniformly completed product that meets high standards of quality control. While attempts at specialization have been made in the social services (as with the case of separation of services), most task situations still remain highly ambiguous. There is a lack of both uniformity and quality control in program output when this circumstance occurs. Perhaps this is the nature of the beast, but there must be some logical way to deal with this problem.

Human service agencies have uniquely resisted new types of organizational technologies which are designed to attack the problem of multiple services and high job ambiguity, such as the linking-pin concept or the matrix organization. Along the same lines, the human service work force also tends to be highly professionalized compared to the more bureaucratic structure of private-sector organizations. Both these modes, the professional and bureaucratic, have advantages and disadvantages. Many theorists believe that bureaucratization is at the heart of both worker and client dissatisfaction. Bureaucracy itself promotes specificity of expertness, while it also strictly limits areas of responsibility. As an organization grows in size and power through the adoption of more efficient methods and procedures, it becomes more bureaucratic in structure out of necessity. Relationships with the staff and public become more depersonalized and categorized when this situation occurs. Nevertheless, bureaucracy allows for a complete chain of command accountability, reduces ambiguity, and provides for objective determination of client needs—up to a point.

A professional organizational orientation, on the other hand, can likewise lead to staff and client dissatisfaction. It is true that professionals, such as social workers, take a more personal approach to the client, with their decisions supposedly being based on the needs of the client rather than the practitioners or the organizations. Nevertheless, professionals typically organize themselves into very powerful peer associations for self-control. The rules of professional conduct, behavior, and surveillance are external to the organization. Consequently, loyalties can become divided among the organization, the profession, and the client, at times causing not only confusion but also misdirected efforts. Finally, private-sector organizations tend to be technology-intensive because the methodologies are there, while the human services are labor-intensive because the methodologies are lacking or are totally absent.

Social Responsibility

For the most part, this discussion has centered on input characteristics, such as money, manpower, time, and technology. What about process functions, such as planning, coordinating, controlling, and decision-making systems, and others? It should be quite evident that all organizations, in order to achieve to some level of sophistication, must process or organize the inputs to ensure that a product is produced. What does differ among organizations is the type of raw materials acted upon, the values, and the data base used to make decisions.

In private-sector organizations most decisions have increased profitability as their basic framework. A product is only the means to generate profit; hence, there is little discussion or effort expended detailing the social benefits of the "hula hoop." Consequently, data are focused on issues of product marketability and acceptance rather than on the product's ability to advance social progress. For the most part, the raw material used in the production process is physical in nature: steel, wood, aluminum, and so forth. Even in the context of private-sector, profit-oriented service organizations, such as proprietary hospitals, patients are a means to an end (profit). Because of this limited scope, the administrative process tends to be somewhat simplified since outputs are more easily measurable and standards are more highly developed. The private sector can refuse to take on nonprofitable tasks because it values profit. Such a refusal by the human service organization would be contrary to public or client benefit.

We do not say that all private-sector organizations are robbers and cutthroats and that human service organizations wear halos, but that private-sector survival depends on staying in the black. A sense of public responsibility is there, but only to the extent that it assists and does not interfere with the organization's primary mission—to make money.

Consequently, by placing full responsibility on the human service organization for solutions to virtually insoluble social problems, we not only guarantee a sense of helplessness, but also immensely increase the difficulty of administration.

Decision-Making

Other comparisons can be found in the decision-making process. Decisions in the human services tend to be slower and more highly ritualized than in profit-oriented organizations. In the private sector, decisions tend to be of a technological nature; have an adequate, supportive data base; and to be arrived at quickly by using some form of sophisticated, analytic structure. However, in the human services there is the value set that decisions must be arrived at by consensus and compromise, with as much group involvement as is possible. Such openness, while admirable, does serve to considerably slow down the process to the point where its utility as a potential solution becomes devalued. Similarly, the information data base is much more amorphous and less specific than that typically found in private-sector situations. In addition, many of the questions and problems which arise in the human services are not readily amenable to sophisticated analysis, since they are much more complex, wider in scope, and have far-ranging social and political implications. It is relatively easy to predict the impact of increasing average automobile gas mileage from fourteen to eighteen miles per gallon than it is to anticipate the social and monetary implications of a proposed family assistance plan or a guaranteed annual wage.

Administrative Process

Private-sector organizations tend to value technique and technology, whereas human service organizations value process and procedure. Such variation in ideology can be summed up by the often-expressed private-sector attitude of "I don't care how you do it as long as it gets done" vs the human services attitude of "Do it by the book." Similarly, in the private sector, great credence is placed on the planning process, both internally and in external marketing considerations, while the human services treat planning as a necessary evil—something that has been mandated but has little organizational utility.

Organizational Flexibility

Other striking differences can be found in the area of flexibility, where private-sector operations, less encumbered by legal control and court mandates, can more readily adapt to new, changing situations. For instance, if a particular product is too difficult to manufacture and is not making a profit, it can be withdrawn without much hulabaloo. However, just try to cut out one of the more costly, marginally useful welfare provisions, such as "Thirty plus a third," and you will hear a human voice cry so loud that it will have repercussions in the White House. Similarly, if it is more efficient to consolidate one or more operations, private-sector organizations can do it. If consolidation is a possibility, then so is expansion. New locations can be opened, new plants built, and new markets conquered. Human service organizations, particularly public ones, have a much more limited scope of involvement. They cannot let market conditions or cost factors determine their product mix, for they are often legally obligated to deliver a wide range of services, regardless of cost and of potential usefulness, or they will be politically hampered by employees and clientele. Likewise, it is often impossible to achieve organizational efficiency through merger, growth, and consolidation, because geographical limits are often predetermined by law or tradition.

Information Flow

In law, if not reality, human service organizations are forced to conduct much of their organizational business under public scrutiny. New emphasis has been placed on access to public information by the enactment of so-called "sunshine laws." Nevertheless, such mandates often come in conflict with the professional's value of client confidentiality. On the other hand, private-sector organizations are not typically under similar obligation to release to the public what they consider administratively confidential information. Consequently, treatment of information flow to the public is at major variance between the two organizational settings.

Output Measurement

The objective of the organizational process, whether it is private or human service, is output. Perhaps it is here that differences are most evident. The private-sector organization, knowing what it is about (making a profit), is able to measure its relative success to achieve this end. Things like "social relevance" and the "public good," while important considerations, are not what private-sector successes are made of. It is easy to determine through the use of any good accounting system whether the private-sector operation has attained the desired ends, because there are obvious standards of acceptable performance in both quality and quantity. How do you measure the success of human service organizations in meeting their objectives, assuming, of course, that the organization actually knows what it is in business for? Just what value do you place on a rehabilitated addict's food-stamp provision, or sanitary place of residence for an elderly client? Is it possible to place both social and monetary values on these items? Quite obviously, social service objectives are not only more difficult to develop, but also to measure, since there is no easy way to visualize success or failure in the accomplishment of a specific organizational task.

This statement is not saying that a methodology for measuring the organizational performance does not exist, as we will demonstrate in Chapter 9. In many ways, it is unfair to compare private-sector with human service organizations on the output factor, since it does not take into account political and economic reality. Many politicians conceive the human service delivery mechanism to be an instrument of economic policy. They also perceive this organizational segment to be an employer of the last resort, acting like a sponge willing to sop up the spilled milk after all the kittens have had their fill. The logic of such programs, while having noble ends, does pose some major limiting factors for the effective operation of a human service system.

For example, when the human service agency acts as the employer of last resort, it forces or injects into the organizational human-resources cadre a large group of employees who lack both the technical and the interpersonal skills needed to make a highly complex system perform. Second, it causes the organization to shift its focus from output-oriented criteria, such as helping a client, to such internal considerations as ameliorating disputes and grievances caused by the inflow of new people. Organizations now have to be concerned with provide employees with basic training and skills and, at the same time, develop logistical support facilities. Therefore, what comes about is a noticeable, misdirected shift of resources from client to employee in terms of time, money, and manpower. Additionally, there comes a point when the organization is no longer successfully able to cope with the "client-employees" within its boundaries. Trying not to appear overly harsh, there comes a point when any organization, no matter how previously productive, will collapse under the weight of its own incompetence if forced to accept more than its share of what is commonly called "excess baggage." It takes an amazing amount of organizational effort to train and adequately integrate a new employee. If the flow becomes a torrent because of economic policy, then the organization is doomed on two counts: inability to operate administratively and failure to meet output performance standards. Such an occurrence spells disaster, as can be readily demonstrated in the case of community-action agencies sponsored by the OEO and the HUD-funded Model Cities program. While such activity is a common occurrence in the human service sector, private organizations are usually not forced into situations where they act as employers of last resort. Typically, if this is a desired end, government will offer monetary and economic incentives to hire this class of employees rather than mandate their hiring.

Accountability Factor

In addition, private-sector utilization of high technology allows the production of standardized and uniform outputs. Because these standards for production exist, it becomes possible to impose quality-control criteria, thereby keeping the product uniform. In the human services, however, because of the ambiguity of the production situation, it is much more difficult to develop quality-control mechanisms. Hence, there is wide variability in the end product.

This phenomenon is at the root of the accountability problem. Because human service managers cannot relate expenditures to results or output, the public assumes that the programs are ineffective. The simple fact is human service managers often have no idea of their impact. Private-sector managers, on the other hand, find it easy to demonstrate success through a simple bookkeeping process. Also, the public assumes that private-sector managers are not squandering public dollars and, therefore, has higher esteem for them. More about public perceptions of social service agencies and workers is covered in subsequent chapters. At any rate, there are obvious differences between managing in the private, or profit-making, sector compared to managing the public human service organizations. Perhaps we should reserve value and normative judgments about which sector is more readily accomplishing the assigned tasks. Needless to say, both have their strengths and weaknesses.

A primary purpose of this book is to identify areas of potential improvement and to suggest certain techniques and methodologies which the management of human service organizations, through prior application, have found to be valuable. While these varied techniques can be utilized in multiple situations, either private or public, their method of direct application differs because of a range of factors: problems to be solved, costs, time restraints, type of organization, employee skills, and others. In order to appreciate certain organizational distinctions, it is essential to develop a clear understanding of what a human service organization is, what it does, how it does it, and where and why it differs compared to a typical private-sector operation.

If one agrees with the premise that the kinds of management and organizational skills needed to run a human service agency are somewhat different from those needed to operate a private-sector enterprise, then we can get down to the basic business at hand—developing an appreciation not only of problems to be overcome, but also of types of solutions which can be implemented to ameliorate some of the very real organizational problems the human service administrator faces. Before detailing some of the more common problems human service organizations face, it might be worthwhile to summarize the previous discussion which focuses on the comparative analysis of public and private organizations shown in Figure 1-3. From this review, we might gain a clearer understanding of why some of the criticisms in the next section are being leveled at the welfare delivery system.

Social Service Management and Organization Problems

The first crucial step in developing acceptable alternatives for solutions to the problems is to define and expose the management and organizational problems the welfare delivery system faces. If the problems are not accurately identified, then little likelihood exists for the discovery of mechanisms to deal with their ramifications. Nevertheless, it is a rare problem that comes with ready-made answers. There is no premixed, predirected, and factory-prepared formulation that will allow what is commonly called a "fix." Do not deceive yourselves into thinking that a "cookbook" of solutions exists. Indeed, it is usually unclear whether there is a single problem or several, oftentimes with many perplexing elements interrelated in complicated and obscure patterns. Consequently, we must cut through this "monster maze" and identify,

	Private Sector	Public Human Services
INPUT	**Assigned Resources:** Directly from consumers or investment market	Third-party payment or through taxation
	Time Utilization: Tends to be highly fixed, conforming to engineered work schedules. Organization controls scheduling, with worker bending to time-production constraints	High variability in allocation of time to produce. Professional sets scheduling with client (product), bending to time constraints of work force
	Technology: Utilize sophisticated state of the art technology	Rudimentary technological base
	Nature of Management Work Force: Strength exhibited in analytic and administrative areas	Strengths exhibited in process and interactive dimensions of management
	Nature of Task: High degrees of specialization and routinization	Highly ambiguous and undefined
	Organizational Structure: Tend toward tall bureaucratic organizations with emphasis on production needs	Mixture of bureaucratic and professional modes, with emphasis on client needs
	Social Benefit: Limited concern with potentiality of social benefit—mission to make a profit	High concern for social benefit
PROCESS	**Decision-Making:** Rapid, based on broad data base—highly technological in nature	Slower, more highly ritualized, emphasizing consensus and compromise, utilizing less well-developed data base
	Administrative Process: Value technique over process—"Get the job done"	Value process over technique—"Do it by the book"
	Organizational Flexibility: High amount of adaptiveness due to limited mandates	Typically inflexible and slow to change due to mandated responsibilities
	Access to Information: Public has limited rights	Public rights protected through "sunshine laws"
	Measurement: Clear and obvious standards of successful performance possible	More difficult but still possible to measure performance
OUTPUT	**Output Benefits:** Benefits designed to accrue directly to consumer with secondary economic social impact	Outputs utilized as an instrument of social and economic benefit
	Accountability: Because standards more easily developed, high degree of accountability possible	More difficult to establish standards because of variability of end product
	Type of Output: Tends to be uniform, with high degree of quality control built-in	Tends toward high variability with limited degree of quality control possible

Figure 1.3: SUMMARY COMPARATIVE ANALYSIS

30

define, and analyze the obstructing elements. It is out of this web of interlocking elements that we can make clear definitions of relevant problems.

Many human service managers have the intuitive, generalized feeling that things are not well, but rarely take the necessary step to develop formalized problem statements or to ask the proper questions of the who, what, where, when, and how variety that would help identify human service delivery problems. Such questioning must lead to further problem clarification and might suggest other areas to be investigated. additional information to be gathered, and new relationships to be analyzed. Problem statements can serve to clarify the objectives to be achieved, difficulties to be overcome, resources available, constraints circumscribing implementation of acceptable solutions, and criteria used to judge the acceptability of proposed solutions. Consequently, problem statements can only come after a substantial understanding of the total problem situation has been achieved. Before listing some of the more common complaints about the operation of the human service delivery system, it might be worthwhile to point out once again that to a degree all organizations experience similar types of dislocations.

It might be beneficial at this juncture to enumerate some of the more commonly heard complaints, especially as they relate to the delivery of human services. The list might be entitled, "Why Human Service Organizations Don't Work." Nevertheless, while this problem agenda is somewhat limited, it is not intended that it serve as one gigantic "bitching" session, but that it form the basis and act as a general guide to this volume. Each chapter focuses on the mentioned dislocations and discusses in detail some of the techniques available to address that particular problem area.

The following list shows complaints which are commonly lodged against human service organizations:

I. In general, human service organizations are ill-managed, inefficient, ineffective, wasteful, while they, at the same time, consume an ever-larger share of our financial and human resources. This general inefficiency complaint has been broken down into four areas each of which is discussed in Chapters 2 to 5.

   A. Human service managers are poorly chosen, lack confidence, not suited to managerial responsibilities, and fail to improve organizational efficiency and productivity. Chapter 2 focuses on the failures in current techniques of management selection and possible alternatives.

   B. The ongoing human service organization fails to renew its valuable human resources, update methods for encouraging employees, and provide a mechanism for promoting individual growth within the organization. Chapter 3 focuses on the issues of management development and opportunities for individual growth to produce increased overall organizational effectiveness.

C. Organizational structures and procedures designed to cope with predictable, simplistic, and routine problems are becoming inadequate to deal with escalating demands of new, more complex social problems. This situation is a failure to update and provide a capacity for the organization to adapt to change in order to increase overall organizational effectiveness. Chapter 4 concerns the development of organizational problem-solving perspectives and techniques to establish an adaptive human service organization.

D. Chapter 5 continues the emphasis on organizational structure and procedures by addressing the specific complaint that current approaches to human service delivery are ill-conceived, poorly coordinated, and cumbersome to administer. Chapter 5 also discusses change through the organizational-development process, with special emphasis on structural changes, as possible remedial alternatives to these structural complaints.

II. The intergovernmental approach (federal, state, local) to the delivery of human services generates a maze of counterproductive, confusing and contradictory administrative, judicial, and legislative laws, rules, regulations, and guidelines that serve to confuse and create conflict. These, in turn, produce a situation of limited teamwork, lack of integration, and even more conflict. Chapter 6 discusses the identification of conflict, the delineation of common human service conflict situations, and possible resolution techniques.

III. The human service manager has failed through lack of interest to legitimize and rationalize to a skeptical public the reasons for expenditure of public funds; there is an unwillingness to respond to the public's need for greater participation in the decision- making and delivery process; and charges that service techniques are dehumanizaing, inconsistent, ill-organized, insensitive, and incomplete have not been answered. Chapter 7 focuses on the issue of communicating with, informing, and interacting with the public, whether they are taxpayer or client.

IV. To continue in the same vein, Chapter 8 deals with the most talked about, but least-understood, organizational complaint— the lack of good internal communications. There is a general tendency for human service managers to slight this important linking mechanism in their overall responsibilities and a failure to build in an effective communication mechanism and view it as a total process from sender to receiver. To increase an understanding of internal communications, Chapter 8 describes the communication process and discusses the management of human service organization communication systems and ways to improve interorganizational communications.

V. There is a general failure to respond to proven needs as indicated by discrepancies between professed objectives and actual performance. Chapter 9 emphasizes performance measurement and available methods for evaluating human service program performance.

This list is neither complete nor final and does not represent the total spectrum of problems faced by human service organizations and their managers. In actuality, each problem statement or complaint area is composed of a multitude of organizational difficulties which have their roots in a myriad of causative, interrelated factors. Although many of these problems are results of systemic malfunctions, they are not totally unsolvable. Consequently, some areas of relief will also be suggested in each chapter. This guide might not be the cookbook we have all been looking for, but at least it is the first step to help identify the crucial ingredients.

NOTES

1. Kenneth Clark and Jeanette Hopkins, *A Relevant War Against Poverty* (New York: Harper and Row, 1968).

Daniel Moynihan, *Maximum Feasible Misunderstanding* (New York: Free Press, 1969).

Louis Zurcher, *Poverty Warriors* (Austin: University of Texas Press, 1970).

2. Charles Perrow, "The Analysis of Goals in Complex Organizations," in *Human Service Organizations,* Yeheskel Hasenfeld and Richard English, eds. (Ann Arbor: University of Michigan Press, 1974), pp. 127-128.

Chapter 2

SELECTING TO ACHIEVE

INTRODUCTION

Chapter 2 discusses a far-reaching program for increasing efficiency and effectiveness in human service organizations. The focus here is on methods for selecting and identifying those with human service management potential. A discussion of selection methods in the public sector naturally must begin with the civil service, an historical perspective of it, and the failure of its techniques.

Although civil service selection techniques have failed, the principle behind them, the merit principle remains a valid one. Two additional techniques are suggested to assist in making the merit principle more fact than fiction. There is a brief discussion of selection through a lottery system. However, the main emphasis in Chapter 2 is placed on the assessment center as an alternative selection-development technique. Chapter 2 ends with a description of the assessment center approach, a study of its acceptance as compared with other techniques, and a discussion of implementing it in the public sector.

SELECTING GOOD MANAGERS

One of the most commonly heard criticisms of the human service delivery system is that it is ill-managed, wasteful, and inefficient. Despite the merit of this type of "broad-brush" charge, it is incumbent upon those working within the human service structure to assess individual and collective culpability for this state of affairs. Oftentimes, managers, rather than to admit any responsibility for the productivity of their organizations, point to a lack of funds, shortage of staff, unrealistic objectives, or political interference as root causes for the unmanageability of service mechanisms. Perhaps, there is an unwillingness to even believe that the fault might be elsewhere—that is, with the management cadre itself. After all, it is only human nature not to want to see our own shortcomings.

Today's human service manager, if he is to improve organizational productivity, must possess a high degree of technological, administrative, interpersonal, and managerial competence. Similarly, he must be a leader and innovator, too—one who can motivate employees, enhance their capabilities, and spur creativity and risk-taking. In general, the successful human service manager is one who sets standards of excellence and reaches them, thus setting such acts as a role model for those supervised. Is this ideal achievable? Can we expect an ever higher degree of administrative and organizational competence on the part of the human service manager?

A comprehensive program for increasing efficiency and effectiveness of our human service organizations demands a three-pronged attack: (1) a mechanism for ensuring the selection and placement into key managerial positions of only the most qualified individuals; (2) a sophisticated program of management development, employee-assessment and manpower planning to increase the productivity of the in-place manager; (3) organization development and renewal that focuses on change strategies and team building. Unfortunately, and all too often, organizations put forth cosmetic efforts rather than serious attempts to implement the preceding three processes. This state of affairs cannot be attributed to fiendish attempts at sabotaging the delivery system; rather, most organizations fail to take corrective or developmental actions because they do not know how. That is why Chapters 2 to 5 will each be devoted to these three approaches in an effort to outline some useful, practical, and implementable techniques that human service organizations could readily bring on-line with proper incentives. In addition, these discussions will serve to bring human service managers up-to-date on the strengths and weaknesses of currently available strategies.

Chapter 2 begins with all the overall discussion of organizational effectiveness and efficiency and selection and placement techniques. Chapter 3 logically moves the discussion beyond management selection to management-development strategies. Finally, in Chapters 4 and 5 the focus is on the effectiveness improvement in terms of overall organization change efforts. Chapter 4 outlines organizational diagnosis, analysis, and change-implementation techniques. Chapter 5 specifically covers organizational development (OD) as a technique and uses structural reorganization to illustrate effectiveness change in organizations.

THE CIVIL SERVICE SYSTEM AND PUBLIC HUMAN SERVICES

Every year the higher education system and professional schools of social work graduate eager young students ready and willing to work in the human services. Most of those who secure jobs—whether in the public or private sectors—are competent, motivated, and highly idealistic about their ability to contribute to the organization. However, economic and social conditions have led to a precipitous decline in the number of openings available in the more prestigious private human service delivery sectors. This situation has forced many aspirants to consider local public human service agencies, as alternate employers where jobs, although not plentiful, are still available. In fact, many individuals who previously would have found employment in the private sector are being lured into public human services by relatively high starting salaries, excellent fringe benefits, impressive job titles, and the anticipation of rapid promotion based on sound accomplishments and contribution to the public good. Today's public human service manager has some very clear expectations of the job environment: (1) work that is important to the public, society, and organization; (2) work which presents an opportunity to learn and grow as an individual; (3) work which makes the manager part of the decision-making and delivery process; (4) work that enables the manager to demonstrate skills that lead to career and promotional opportunities.

The reality is that highly motivated people come into the public human services ready and willing to contribute to the system, but within two years, they are transformed into tired, old bureaucrats. This metamorphosis occurs because public employees quickly learn that hard work and good performance are not necessarily rewarded by increased pay, greater responsibility, and promotion. Why should they knock themselves out when the system is rigged against them? In short, there is no payoff for productive performance. Truly, some employees are output-oriented simply because of personal standards, but no one, no matter how dedicated, can maintain top-quality performance without some form of recognition. Put yourself in the shoes of an average first-line supervisor and think of the toll it takes on him in terms of lowered morale when he sees blatantly incompetent or mediocre employees being selected and advanced over more qualified individuals. Usually, after enduring about two years of frustration and perceiving no future relief, the employee settles into a routine that causes him the least-possible psychological conflict with the work system. In other words, he cops out and accepts the lowered group performance norms. There is little excitement left in the job and work becomes boring and mundane. It becomes something to be faced and tolerated, but not enjoyed. Thus begins a thirty-year cycle which continues until retirement. This attitude often has been verbalized by public employees who openly admitted in an informal survey that they are being utilized to only some 60 percent of their capacity. Think of it—workers are dissatisfied not because they are overworked, but because there is not enough to do and they are just bored. If the public sector could capture just a portion of that missing 40 percent, the gains in productivity and cost savings would be enormous.

What is the cause of this sorry state of affairs in the publicly operated human services? Many people have accused the selection mechanism as it is administered under civil service guidelines. It is well known that civil service systems everywhere are under assault, being blamed for everything from institutionalization of incompetence to budget overruns. Obviously, government no longer can afford to ignore a public that, rightly or wrongly, views the human service worker to be coddled, exclusive, underworked, and overpaid. These intuitive feelings about the government employee, in fact, may not be too far from reality. In a recent Harris Poll in which the public was asked to rate the productivity of various occupational groupings, government workers fared poorly. When asked who had below average productivity, the civil servant won, garnering 39 percent of the vote. This situation is apparently one honor that government executives will find difficult, or nearly impossible, to give away. With 24 percent, the only group coming even close was repairmen, and we all know how productive they can be.[1]

Much of the criticism leveled at selection procedures in the public sector has its roots in civil service's responsibility for staffing of organizations through the administration of an employee-selection mechanism of limited validity. It is here that the tale of woe begins. Anyone wishing to enter a public agency or to seek promotion must at some point come in contact with the hydra-headed civil service testing monster.

No one is advocating total abolition of civil service. It should be recalled that civil service laws were initiated in response to an over-abused patronage system. An individual's merit or qualifications—not party affiliation—was to be the one and only criterion for hiring a public servant. Around this credo, enacted by Congress in 1883, was built a patchwork of laws, regulations, court decisions, and rules that local civil service systems are daily attempting to implement. In theory, the merit principle has noble ends–the placement or promotion of the most capable individual into available government social service positions. However, the fact of the matter is that we presently lack the technology, fortitude, commitment, and desire to make it work within its present form. The result is establishment of a selection process in the public human services that is unable to successfully match the most qualified candidate to available positions or to ensure that good performance is rewarded with promotion. There are two basic reasons for this circumstance. First, such concepts come directly into conflict with the merit system, which seeks to promote the best "test-taker" rather than the most capable employee. Second, organizational-personnel systems are neither physically nor psychologically prepared to institute comprehensive employee-appraisal systems. The civil service system, by its very nature, has been said to reduce worker productivity; attract the security-minded rather than output-oriented; foster boredom, low morale, high absenteeism; and prevent lateral entry; consequently, it cries out for change.

THE TECHNIQUE HAS FAILED, NOT THE SYSTEM–THE WAY IT IS

A principal civil service activity is the staffing of local services by responding to personnel needs of various operating agencies with job-related selection methods. Unfortunately, whether it is by circumstances or design, the civil service mechanism does not carry out its stated purpose. It would perhaps be of some value to briefly describe the shortcomings of the present system prior to suggestions for improvement.

The basic fault in the civil service selection mechanism is a job-related examination system that exists in theory, not in reality. These so-called "job-related methods" are euphemisms for an examination which usually takes one of two forms–a written test or an oral board.

The written test as a selection device is perhaps the most used and abused selection mechanism. Both layman and expert readily recognize the inherent, fatal flaws of the paper and pencil test; for example, job-relatedness is difficult or almost impossible to achieve. In fact, there are very few cases where the validity of written tests have been proven. Paper and pencil tests are also unidimensional in outlook since they attempt to measure only certain areas of competence, such as written and cognitive skills–not performance capability. Similarly, quantitative scores and rankings lose meaning because they fail to take individual differences into account.

Even more surprising, Savas and Ginsburg[2] uncovered data that show written examinations actually discriminate against those applicants who are most qualified. Across all skill levels, Savas and Ginsburg discovered that candidates with low-passing grades on tests were more likely to be hired rather than those with higher marks. They attributed this situation to the long delay between testing and date of final appointment. The mean delay between testing and hiring averaged out to be seven months. Delays were often caused by administrative procedures, lawsuits, challenges, and appeals. Consequently, the longer the time between testing and hiring, the lower one had to go down the list to find people willing to accept appointment. In addition, when it came to filling any other than entry-level positions by "open" competitive examination, it was found that any insider (one already employed by that unit of government) who passed the exam was offered the position before it was offered to others. In other words, it was conclusively demonstrated that employees presently working in agencies with vacancies were promoted over those outside the agency, even when the outsider scored higher on the exam. The researchers' evidence shows that the insider was selected over the highest ranked outsider, even though insiders averaged fourteen points below outsiders.

Although using the oral board as a selection mechanism is an improvement over the written test, it still has many shortcomings; for instance, the oral board includes a greater range of performance dimensions, but there is no real attempt made to cover them all. Also, many panels are hurriedly created and oftentimes lack structure and coherence. In many cases, there is no formal method for recording behavioral observations and insights. Also, there is an inability on the part of the board members to calibrate their findings. Problems such as these frequently arise from a lack of training and an inadequate amount of time allotted to planning interviews and discussing results. Board members themselves are, at times, distrustful of the process. Many people perceive the process to be unreliable because they have little say in what dimensions or questions are selected. Similarly, there is the problem of bias. Interviewers with insufficient training tend to quickly reach a conclusion about the worth of an individual candidate, and follow-up questions are often designed to reinforce initial candidate expectations. Also, as is the case with written tests, it is difficult to establish job-relatedness with oral boards.

Once the examination process is completed, individuals are placed on eligibility lists according to a final adjusted average. This score can be raised or lowered for members of minority groups or for those with veterans' credits. Typically, only the top three candidates can be considered for selection or promotion.

It is highly unlikely that someone scoring 99 on an examination of questionable validity will perform better on the job than someone scoring 95. Unfortunately, those who make selection decisions seldom know how to integrate test results with other pertinent data. Overreliance on examinations only gives the illusion of objectivity in employee selection. It might appear cavalier for someone outside the civil service system to easily denigrate such a venerable institution. Nevertheless, it is not the concept of merit on "objectivity in the selection of people to fill jobs" which is being challenged, but the mechanism created to do so. As many have pointed out, civil service is a system where technique has triumphed over purpose.

Such findings have serious implications for the civil service system as we know it. First, it appears that the system created as a public guardian to ensure that government positions are filled by the most capable applicants is failing. Second, the system is helping to perpetuate a government elite—if not in terms of qualifications, in terms of salary, fringe benefits, and security. This circumstance is plainly demonstrated by the blatant way the selection process is rigged to discriminate against those people applying for positions from outside government. There appears to be a general policy of favoring its own personnel and discouraging lateral entry.

These are damning charges. It is not the merit principle which has failed but the technique needed to carry it out. It is a fact of life that we just do not possess the ability to economically discriminate between the potentially strong and the weak employee. We know, however, that written and oral exams are not satisfactory evaluations. Evaluations of previous work experience and supervisory ratings are perhaps better indicators of potential success on the job. Nevertheless, techniques short of performance-based evaluations, such as the assessment center, will be unsatisfactory.

Since written civil service examinations are not good predictors of on-the-job performance, then a perfectly feasible alternative would be to abolish them. No particular genius is needed to draw this conclusion. Until now, civil service systems have been devoting much time and energy relying on an examination system that does not work—the final result of which is a "Rube Goldberg" device of immense proportions and little value. Such typical behavior has forced the civil service system into a corner from which it might not emerge. Basically, there appear to be two options open: civil service can fight like hell to justify existing procedures (in which case it must be prepared to receive constant setbacks at the hands of the courts), or it can adapt to the new situation.

SOME NEW TECHNIQUES—THE WAY IT COULD BE

Rather than continually tamper with the examination process, it has been suggested that the process be replaced by a lottery mechanism, an assessment center, or a combination of the two. Such an approach is favored because of several factors: First, civil service systems must operate an actual, rather than a "name only," merit-selection process. Political patronage and the conditions which brought about the first merit laws are still present. Abolishment of the merit principle would only lead to gross abuse of the bureaucracy by the party which happens to be in power. No one really wants this situation. There is a recognition of the need to have certain positions under political control, but to have the entire administrative structure subject to political checkoff would surely lead to chaos. Second, the courts and prospective employees are successfully challenging existing tests in ever-increasing numbers. This test and challenge syndrome can lead to long delays in filling vacant positions and to eventual bureaucratic paralysis—if it has not already occurred. Third, there is a tremendous pool of applicants and an ever-decreasing number of available government positions. Many of these highly qualified individuals want long-term government human service careers, as opposed to several years ago when private-sector employment was the rage. Consequently, eligible lists have too many active names with too few vacancies to be filled. Fourth, it is difficult, if not impossible, to discriminate among prospective employees. Any effective testing device must be able to select those who have potential from those who do not. Our present examination process lacks this crucial ability. Fifth, the number of available candidates seems to be of uniformly high quality—that is, in terms of observable characteristics, such as grades and aptitude. The homogeneous nature of the applicant group makes it even more difficult to screen potential employees. Take, for example, the case of a state social service organization which has five entry-level professional vacancies for management interns with over 300 applicants. A typical candidate profile might show 30 percent having averages between 3.5 and 4.0 (4.0 = A) and graduate record exams in the ninety-fifth percentile and above. Who does the state accept and who does it reject? The lower scoring 70 percent can be immediately eliminated but what about the ninety that remain? Do we then start making selection discriminations based on ethnic background, age, sex, looks, income, schools attended, or what? When the two basic indicators of college average and performance on graduate examinations no longer allow you to make discriminatory choices and predictions about future performance, then the only logical alternative is to let random selection be your guide. Since this population is high quality, with all in the applicant pool meeting minimum job requirement, fairness would almost dictate a lottery approach.

This problem is precisely the same many civil service systems face in their selection of candidates for entry-level management jobs. We are overloaded with applicants meeting minimum job standards. In selecting from the available population, we know how to apply a measuring instrument that can be called either imperfect or totally useless, depending on your perspective. Perhaps the best approach would be to do away with all this harmful game-playing and admit that existing testing procedures do not allow for adequate selection of the most qualified individuals from an applicant pool. We can get on with the important task of designing a system that will objectively place qualified candidates into the proper jobs once this admission is made. Unless civil service systems are willing to get involved with a complex assessment center process, then a job-lottery approach might be a viable alternative.

HOW ABOUT A LOTTERY?

A lottery-selection system would help to simplify and reduce the costs of filling social service positions. It would also cut down on much of the delay in developing, testing, and selecting personnel for vacant positions. Major civil service functions, such as examinations, certain staffing services, the need for test validation, and the complex function of recordkeeping associated with maintaining and updating eligible lists, and all their concurrent costs, could be eliminated.

The proposed lottery-selection system would work something like this. A job vacancy would be posted for an entry-level professional position. Basic qualifications for applicants would be set. The job opening would be announced to the public and applications would be solicited. Once the deadline for their receipt has passed, there would be an initial screening to separate those who meet minimum requirements (college degree, grade point average, experience) from those who do not. The remaining candidates would then either be directly available for the job lottery or additional screening mechanisms would be applied to further reduce numbers. By the civil service's using valid, acceptable performance tests, for instance, it could require applicants to demonstrate adequate verbal and written communication skills. The type of performance test used, of course, would depend on the nature of the job and the actual duties associated with it. Performance-based measurements are more acceptable screening devices than written and oral examinations, simply because they evaluate actual behavior in job-related activities rather than relying solely on what a candidate says he would or would not do. For example, there is a world of difference between asking a candidate fireman to describe the hand and foothold to be used in climbing a ladder and having the individual actually demonstrate competence on the ladder.

After all "legitimate" screening devices have been employed, the lottery is held. As we recognize the need for certain management prerogatives and flexibility in selecting employees, then there is no reason to have a one-to-one relationship between lottery selection and the vacancy. That is, for each available position ten candidates can be drawn, with discretion left up to the hiring agency for final selection. In reality, this situation means replacing the present civil service rule of three with a rule of ten—not an easy task in itself. There should be no great difficulty in managing and maintaining a lottery-selection system.

Give It a Chance—It Might Work

As with the implementation of any new idea or concept, there are always limitations to be worked out. For example, the lottery was not designed to replace the myriad of civil service tests given at all levels. Rather, it can be most economically employed in certain situations: first, as a replacement for a series of exams in selected entry-level job areas where the pool of qualified applicants is expected to be high; second, where more sophisticated and acceptable techniques, such as assessment centers, cannot be practically utilized; third, in situations where probationary periods and review systems are routinely used to weed out unproductive employees prior to granting permanent status.

As a word of caution, the system—no matter how appealing—should not be implemented without, at least, a trial period, and to the author's knowledge, there has been no previous testing of this concept. In addition, it is crucial that, once implemented, a serious attempt must be made to evaluate its results by comparing outcome with more traditional mechanisms, such as the written test.

Civil service is presently in the most unenviable position of having almost no friends. The agencies supposedly served spend much of their time devising ways to circumvent the process in order to maintain operational abilities and to serve current job-holders. Legislatures keep chipping away at civil service department allocations. The public is disenchanted with the long delays, overly complex application procedures, lack of information, discourteous handling, exclusionary policies, and unrealistic tests. The time has come for civil service to reevaluate its role and function within the overall context of the public management system. Continued apathy toward management preferences, public need, and constant resistance to change and innovation will inevitably lead to increased public dissatisfaction with existing personnel systems. The human resource management system demands and requires a selection device that would engender confidence and trust. In this respect, the lottery mechanism at least warrants a try. Its implementation would not eliminate the existing personnel process, but would provide a valuable tool to upgrade the selection mechanism. Resisting such needed change will inevitably lead to an even greater degeneration of the merit principles fought so hard to secure.

An Assessment Center Approach?

The lottery mechanism as proposed is a short-term solution to the problem of selection among large homogeneous pools of qualified candidates for entry-level positions. It does not, however, satisfy the need for a practical, valid way to identify the potentially productive organizational employee, whether at the selection or promotion stage. The recognition of a need for such a device in the public sector sparked interest either in developing or adapting an existing procedure to the requirements of public organizations. The search is on for a sophisticated, yet accurate, and easily administered selection-development tool.

After reviewing a myriad of possibilities, this author's attentions were focused on a technique called the assessment center. Little doubt was raised over the validity of the process, since the center has been used successfully for many years as a selection-development mechanism in the private sector. Basic questions, however, remained as to the worth of the technique within the context of the public personnel system. Two crucial issues would have to be resolved before any serious consideration could be given to full-scale implementation of such a technique in the public sector. First, would this process be perceived as a valid assessment procedure when compared with other standard selection-development modalities? Second, if this were the case, would existing assessment technologies be so modified that the assessment center would be economically feasible within the public context? It was with these questions in mind that a pilot test of the assessment center was recently conducted by bringing together public employees from local, state, and federal government. What follows is an analysis of findings of this pilot effort. Results are being reported at some length because of their practical implications for selection and development procedures within the human services.

The concept—if not the term—"assessment center" might be new to most, even though its antecedents date back to World War I. Originally designed by both the British and Germans as a method for selecting operatives for special missions across enemy lines, the concept has been expanded to play a less glamorous but equally important role in the selection and development of managerial potential. Assessment center technology was highly refined during the 1950s at American Telephone & Telegraph (AT&T), and it was there that its merit as a selection and development instrument was first realized.

As originally conceived, an assessment center is a multifunctional mechanism. First, it can aid an organization in the critical selection process by providing a mechanism for objectively identifying and determining immediate management potential. This fact is based upon research findings indicating the center to be highly valid in terms of predicting managerial performance. Second, the center serves as a means for identifying and developing individualized executive improvement strategies. The center, by focusing on traits and characteristics associated with management functions, is able to chart areas of strength and weakness. When this is done, a highly personalized career-development plan can be proposed. Third, the assessment center can be thought of as a training vehicle. Research indicates that participants view the assessment process as a learning experience. This outcome is logical because most assessment materials and assessor training techniques are based on tried-and-true training methodology. Fourth, the assessment center can have a positive influence on morale, job expectations, and motivation. Candidates view the center as a means for fairly and objectively evaluating their worth and ability to perform. No longer is the appraisal process clouded by "politics" and unstructured and indefensible selection interview procedures. Finally, the center can be used as a highly accurate means for evaluating executive development or for other training programs.[3]

The assessment center works through a complex set of interactions between participant behavior and observer reactions. Simply put, it is built on two basic components: first, around a common, standardized series of exercises, simulations, and games which approximate actual management functions; second, around trained assessors who observe behavior and performance and record their observations according to a predetermined format. Evaluations are then based on performance in situations simulating the level of the position for which a candidate is being considered rather than solely on evaluation of current job performance or interviews. In this particular pilot test in the state of New York, the exercises were developed and constructed with the senior government manager in mind. Included in the series of simulations were one in-basket exercise, two leaderless group exercises, and an individual problem analysis exercise with a presentation of findings. In order to reduce potential observer bias, participants were viewed by different assessors during the two and one-half days they were present.

After candidates completed the exercises, they were debriefed and sent home. The assessor teams then met to discuss and evaluate each individual's performance in three major areas: (1) management skills; (2) decision-making abilities; and (3) interpersonal relations. They prepared a narrative report for every exercise, outlining strengths and weaknesses by category and dimension. First, individually and then as a group, the assessors decided upon a rating from one to seven for each of the evaluated dimensions. They then prepared a final report for each candidate based on lengthy discussion. The overall report provides participants with a record of how they performed and serves as a guide for future developmental action and plans. Typically, candidates are encouraged to meet personally with assessment center administrators to discuss findings in detail.

EVALUATING
MANAGEMENT SELECTION-DEVELOPMENT PREFERENCES

Perhaps one of the most revealing indicators of program performance can be found in the comparisons of the assessment center process with other more traditional modes of selection and development. In order to obtain these ratings, both assessors and assessees were asked to compare the assessment center against boss appraisal, written tests, oral interviews, experience ratings, and oral tests on seven factors. The results clearly indicate that on all points, and in every instance, the assessment center is rated superior to the other selection-development techniques mentioned. Furthermore, scores demonstrate a significant preference for the assessment center method. A more detailed picture of participant ratings can be obtained by reviewing Tables 2-1 and 2-2.

These findings do not demonstrate the inadequacy of other more traditional selection-development mechanisms, but a preference by a small number of managers for a technique which is viewed as being objectively suited to the needs of today's public executive. Interestingly, the perceived value of the assessment approach is not unidimensional. Overall acceptance spans a total range of personnel functions

Table 2.1: MEAN-ASSESSEE RATINGS ACROSS VARIOUS SELECTION-DEVELOPMENT METHODOLOGIES

	Boss Appraisal	Written Tests	Oral Interview	Oral Tests	Experience Ratings	Assessment Center
a. As a selection or promotion device	2.31	2.93	2.62	2.81	2.93	1.50
b. As an assessment of the participant's strengths or weaknesses	2.37	3.73	3.37	3.33	3.40	1.60
c. As an aid for the individual in recognizing his own strengths or weaknesses	2.81	3.78	3.50	3.80	3.66	1.40
d. As an accurate measure of the way an individual would perform in his organization	2.31	3.85	3.18	3.46	3.12	2.20
e. As a method for helping the participant establish a program for self-development and improvement	2.73	3.92	3.66	4.14	3.78	1.46
f. As a training vehicle	3.21	3.83	3.28	3.61	3.50	1.85
g. As a predictor of future managerial performance	2.37	3.57	3.12	3.06	3.12	1.81
Mean Scores Across Factors	2.58	3.65	3.24	3.45	3.35	1.68

NOTE: Based on a 1 to 5 scale with 1 for very good, 2 for good, 3 for average, 4 for poor, and 5 for very poor.

Table 2.2: MEAN-ASSESSOR RATINGS ACROSS VARIOUS SELECTION-DEVELOPMENT METHODOLOGIES

	Boss Appraisal	Written Tests	Oral Interview	Oral Tests	Experience Ratings	Assessment Center
a. As a selection or promotion device	2.44	3.56	3.89	2.78	3.22	1.56
b. As an assessment of the participant's strengths or weaknesses	2.44	3.89	3.57	3.57	3.89	1.44
c. As an aid for the individual in recognizing his own strengths or weaknesses	3.11	4.00	3.78	4.00	3.90	1.62
d. As an accurate measure of the way an individual would perform in his organization	2.56	4.40	3.78	3.78	3.44	2.33
e. As a method for helping the participant establish a program for self-development and improvement	2.89	4.22	3.56	3.89	3.67	1.78
f. As a training vehicle	3.11	3.78	3.33	3.89	4.00	1.67
g. As a predictor of future managerial performance	2.50	4.12	3.62	3.50	3.50	2.00
Mean Scores Across Factors	2.72	3.99	3.50	3.63	3.66	1.77

NOTE: Based on a 1 to 5 scale with 1 for very good, 2 for good, 3 for average, 4 for poor, and 5 for very poor.

including: promotion and selection, development, training, and performance prediction. Such wide acceptance of this nontraditional approach is even more surprising when one closely analyzes participant
compositions. For example, nine out of ten assessor-administrators
were senior personnel people either in agencies or associated within civil
service, while eight of seventeen assessees held similar government
positions. In addition, it should come as no great shock to anyone
familiar with the field that participants gave the poorest overall acceptance rating to written tests. It is no wonder, since many of these
examinations have been successfully challenged through the courts, and
they consistently have been found lacking in job-relatedness. More
unexpected, however, is the finding that the two most highly rated
methods—assessment centers and boss appraisal—are precisely those
two mechanisms that neither the state of New York nor its localities
incorporate into their civil service or selection and development system.

These findings alone, although admittedly on a limited scale, should
trigger a reevaluation of the policies and procedures of personnel
systems that judiciously avoid methods of selection and development
perceived by managers to be most acceptable. Such results should not
be easily dismissed, especially when it is taken into account that these
comparative ratings were not based upon hearsay exposure to the other
listed selection-development methodologies, but, as shown in Table 2-3,
were based upon personal experience with and knowledge of other
techniques.

Upon further analysis of the data, it was discovered that of the
responding participants, 88 percent felt the assessment center should be
included in the existing selection-promotion-development system, while
only 4 percent said it should not be, with 8 percent having no opinion.
Moreover, most assessees (62.5 percent) agreed that if the assessment
techniques were officially adopted, future advancement should be
dependent on 50 percent job performance and previous experience and
50 percent assessment results. Several assessees (25 percent) thought
advancement should be dependent on 80 percent job-performance
results, while others (12.5 percent) wanted to see the ratio pegged at 20
percent performance and experience and 80 percent assessment results.

More specifically, a review of questionnaire results indicates that
assessors, for the most part, were quite satisfied with the assessment
process. When asked if they felt the assessment center was a useful
management tool, 70 percent said it was to a very great or great extent,
and 30 percent said it was to some extent. It also appears as if assessors
place much emphasis on the assessment center as a means for making
promotional decisions, as 90 percent feel a great deal of weight should

Table 2.3: EXPOSURE TO SELECTION AND DEVELOPMENT MODALITIES

	Boss Appraisal	Written Tests	Oral Interview	Oral Tests	Experience Ratings	Assessment Center
Assessors, in percentages	100	100	100	90	70	100
Assessees, in percentages	94	100	67	77	67	100

be placed on the results when considering candidates for promotion (10 percent were missing). Similar results were found when assessors were asked how much reliance a participant should place on assessment of center results when making developmental plans.

Analysis of findings also reveals underlying confidence in the system's ability to objectively measure a candidate's capacity for management, with 80 percent having a great deal of confidence, 10 percent having some confidence, and one response missing. Similarly, assessors indicated trust in the accuracy of overall judgments made by other assessors.

Obtaining indications of manager or client support for the assessment techniques is the obligatory first step in the long, arduous development process. Without general acceptance and perceived credibility, no personnel system or policy could be successfully implemented. Likewise, existing mechanisms that do not generate such support will continually meet derisive rejection, causing the expenditure of time and energy to support a selection-development system that often just does not work. Continued apathy to management preferences and constant resistance to change and innovation will inevitably lead to increased dissatisfaction with the civil service structure. Such actions can only become aggravated because of the already restricted public employment picture. Managers are seeking a selection-development device that will engender confidence and trust, or one that will objectively measure their capabilities and performance. The best game in town, as it appears now, is the assessment center. Consequently, serious consideration should be given to its utilization at the state and local levels.

SO YOU WANT TO START AN ASSESSMENT CENTER

A basic criticism of the assessment center, and probably the main drawback to the implementation of the process, focuses on its expense in terms of time and money. This complaint is legitimate if you take into account both developmental and operating costs in traditional assessment center approaches. As in the case of any product, the cost of the center will vary depending upon the amount of tailoring desired, the sophistication required, the numbers to be processed, and the level of the candidate pool. A prepackaged "off-the-shelf" center will cost approximately $4,000, with the more customized versions running well over $100,000—both exclusive of operational expenses. For example, approximately $100,000 was expended by the state of Wisconsin for the development of a fully functional assessment center which is linked to entry into their senior civil service. This amount does not include such costs as staffing, equipment, and the rental of space in a converted school. In addition, Wisconsin uses paid assessors at certain times and contracts for assessor training. Expensive, yes. Is it worth it to the state of Wisconsin? Apparently it was.[4]

In times of budgetary stringency, it is most difficult to implement new, experimental programs, even if the benefits far outweigh costs. Hence, full-scale implementation of the assessment method, in the state of New York, at least, would be dependent on reducing the costs to a point where it becomes competitive with existing testing procedures, such as development and administration of written tests and convening of oral boards. A pilot public-sector senior assessment center was developed at an organizational expense of approximately $27,000, a fraction of the amount expended by Wisconsin. Even more interesting is the fact that this amount does not represent a cash transfer of funds, but represents overhead costs in terms of staff time to develop and administer the center. Similarly, it is not necessary to expend great sums of money in terms of program operation.

Assessors could be recruited from senior public manager ranks. Technically, this task involves a book transfer of funds in terms of off-site management time. However, the benefits accrued to the assessors probably outweigh costs, because one of the primary beneficiaries of the assessment center is the assessor who gains knowledge and skills in observation, counseling, management, and administrative techniques. The center administrator could also function on a rotating basis, being drawn from various agencies for a specified period of time, as AT & T does. Hence, with full utilization of internal resources, the new operational outflow of cash could be held to a minimum.

There is also no doubt that the participant-processing time is a potential drawback. In traditional centers, approximately five days is needed to train assessors and two and one-half days for the assessment itself, with two more days allotted for final evaluations to be completed on-site. Consequently, to assess twenty-four individuals, twelve assessors and two administrators must devote approximately 198 man days (including preparation of final reports by administrators). However, through a careful revision of the existing traditional process, there can be great time and money savings; for example, the number of dimensions can be reduced. In the pilot center, fifteen dimensions were used. Nevertheless, a new center is presently under development that will incorporate only ten dimensions at no expected loss in center validity or reliability. The advantages of it are: (1) The number of exercises to which assessees are exposed can be curtailed. (2) Assessor training time would be cut because center procedures and the number of variables to be measured would be minimized. (3) Final assessment procedures would be shortened for the same reason. (4) The assessor to assessee ratio can be increased from 1:2 to 1:3 at an additional saving in time, manpower, and money. These suggestions should do no permanent or radical damage to the assessment concept.

The technology for successfully operating and conducting assessment centers already exists. With administrative manuals and guidelines readily available, exercises can be purchased by the abundance. However, there are certain suggestions and caveats that should be internalized by all potential assessment center operators prior to any substantial investment in the concept. First, assessor training is probably the most crucial factor in the assessment center process. Well-trained assessors will not necessarily guarantee assessment validity, but poorly trained ones will surely lead to program failure. The assessors are the stars of the assessment center, with all other processes dependent upon their good judgment. While the simulations, scoring procedures, and instructions are highly formulated, the training process hinges on the skills, experience, and knowledge of the training consultants. Unfortunately, there is limited documentation on how to train assessors, yet the process must rely upon people who have intimate knowledge of the assessment system. It is this primary ingredient that assessment-consulting firms necessarily withhold from public purchase.

Second, it is crucial that exercises and simulations be designed to bring out clearly the behavioral dimensions under consideration. In order to accomplish this, a series of mixed exercises should be developed. In typical manager assessment situations, the in-basket is the kingpin around which other exercises revolve. The exercises and simulations used can be likened to a launching pad from which all observations are made and results tabulated. All exercises should undergo considerable pretesting prior to their inclusion into the assessment center. Additionally, in order to ensure good candidate response to the initial exercise, sufficient warm-up time and orientation should be allowed before thrusting participants into the first experience. It might be worthwhile to conduct mock exercises to calm jittery nerves and thereby give assessors the chance to get clean observations the first time around.

Third, the dimensions selected should represent a cross section of the activities or functions performed by the managers being evaluated. Dimensions are usually selected on the basis of detailed job analysis or through researched management functions common to the executive pool which is being assessed. A review of other senior management assessment centers shows a dimension norm from twelve to eighteen, with this particular pilot project incorporating fifteen. Ease and accuracy of dimension measurement and observation appear to be dependent on these characteristics: (a) concrete and intuitively reasonable definitions; (b) ample opportunity to observe dimensional behavior, (c) high degree of definitional separation among dimensions being measured; (d) adequacy of training; (e) ability of individual assessors. If any one of these characteristics is grossly deficient or absent, assessors will have great difficulty in accomplishing their tasks of dimension measurement.

Fourth, be prepared to evaluate and compare program impact. It is not easy, but it is essential. Prior to its adoption at AT & T, a long-term blind longitudinal study was conducted providing researchers with initial indications of the program's validity and worth. Since then other research designs and replications have been completed, giving a pretty good overview of the assessment center's strengths and weaknesses. Nevertheless, this situation does not negate the necessity for every governmental jurisdiction to recertify the validity of the assessment approach for its own particular operations.[5]

ASSESSMENT CENTER–A VALUABLE ADDITION

It should be pointed out that the assessment center is not being proffered as a cure for all the shortcomings of an ailing personnel system, but as a tool which has definite uses within the existing framework. For instance, in New York, it was not designed nor intended to replace the myriad of civil service tests given at all levels. Rather, it was to be economically employed under certain circumstances: first, as a replacement for a series of exams in certain job areas to establish a qualifying pool of eligible applicants who do not have to be retested for other positions in the covered category; second, for senior or sensitive management positions where careful selection is crucial; and third, as a method for determining entry into the senior civil service ranks. If these factors are taken into consideration and suggested revisions made, the assessment center probably would be economically competitive with the existing selection mechanism for middle and upper managers in the human services.

The assessment center cannot lightly be dismissed as a mere fad that will eventually disappear from the scene. It is already a fact of organizational life in hundreds of private institutions. However, the realization of its full potential as a means to evaluate individual management competency for selection or development will probably not occur until the assessment center is incorporated within the state and local context. We have the technology to reduce costs of both time and money to the point where it becomes economically feasible for the human services to consider adopting this approach for application to management development and selection. Not only does the assessment approach meet these system constraints, but it is also the preferred mode of selection and development, as discovered in New York's pilot effort.[6] It should be emphasized, however, that the assessment center is only part of an integrated whole and is not meant to dissolve the existing personnel system. Promotion or development decisions should not be based solely on center results. Findings should be used to complete a composite picture of a candidate: on-the-job performance, educational background, general intelligence, peer comments, supervisory reviews, and so forth. Assessment centers provide valuable additional information that can be incorporated into the management and personnel decision process.

The implementation of a valid selection mechanism will help break through the "staleness" which exists in human service management today. If human service managers realize that performance counts, then they will bring new vitality to a system that has been staggering under the weight of its own poor promotional and selection decisions. Productivity is not a state of mind, but a behavior. If productive behavior is wanted, then the organization must be able to recognize and reward performance, and that is what assessment centers are all about.

CONCLUSION

So we see that the first of the three-pronged approach toward improving human service organizational effectiveness must begin with the very basic selection process. Strong and weak points of the current civil service selection system have been presented. The lottery and assessment center were discussed in detail as two necessary additional techniques for the public personnel system to ensure selection and placement of the most qualified individuals in managerial positions.

Chapter 3 continues in the effectiveness improvement vein by focusing on the second tine of the three-pronged approach—a review of current and new management-development techniques. Once you have found them, you had better not let them go. Chapter 3 will outline some ways to keep personnel and allow them to grow.

NOTES

1. John S. Thomas, "So Mr. Mayor, You Want to Improve Productivity." Prepared for the National Commission on Productivity and Work Quality (1974).

2. E. S. Savas and S. G. Ginsburg, "The Civil Service: A Meritless System?" Public Interest 32 (Summer 1973), pp 70-86.

3. Douglas Bray, "The Assessment Center Method of Appraising Management Potential," in *The Personnel Job in a Changing World,* F.W. Blood, ed. (New York: American Management Assn., 1964).

4. William Byham and Carl Wettengel, "Assessment Centers for Supervisors and Managers," Public Personnel Management 3 (September-October 1974), pp. 352-364.

5. See P. Albrecht, E. Glaser, and J. Marks, "Validation of a Multiple-Assessment Procedure for Managerial Personnel," Journal of Applied Psychology 48, No. 6 (December 1964). Also C. Beech, "The Assessment Center: A Promising Approach to Evaluation," The Canadian Personnel and Industrial Relations Journal (November 1972). D. Bray and J. Moses, "Personnel Selection," Annual Review of Psychology 23 (1972). B. Cohen, S. Moses, and W. Byham, "Validity of Assessment Centers: A Literature Review," Journal of Industrial and Organizational Psychology (Summer 1973). J. Hinrichs, "Comparison of 'Real Life' Assessments of Management Potential With Situational Exercises, Paper and Pencil Ability Tests, and Personality Inventories," Journal of Applied Psychology 53, No. 5 (1969). R. Steiner, "New Use for Assessment Centers—Training Evaluation," Personnel Journal 54 (April 1975).

6. Richard Steiner, "Assessment Center—New York State Style," Public Executive Project, State University of New York at Albany (mimeographed), September 1975.

Chapter 3

DEVELOPING THE PERFORMING MANAGER

INTRODUCTION

Improving organizational management and effectiveness does not stop by merely choosing people with management potential. Attaining management positions and exhibiting quality work are not as automatic as getting on an "up" escalator, but are a step-by-step climb. This climb cannot reach the top without some kind of guiding handhold. Chapter 3 is about the handrail—management-development programs. These programs give the organization and the individual something to go by while the search is on for good human service managers.

The discussion in Chapter 3 opens with an explanation of why human service organizations need to provide individual development opportunities. Chapter 3 also discusses: articulating management positions and responsibilities, demographic data on employees, acknowledging individual career goals, developing future organizational plans, and a promotion process based on all of the foregoing as basic necessities for a development program. The remainder of the chapter is devoted to a discussion of a manpower study of social service employees and evaluating the impact of management training and development programs.

THE NEED FOR MANAGEMENT DEVELOPMENT

Human service organizations have the ability and the responsibility to control the quality of their management resources through the selection process. Indeed, much of an organization's performance is dependent on its success in identifying and recruiting individuals with high-managerial potential. Nevertheless, productive organizations do not rely on the selection process alone, but also recognize the importance of ongoing management-development efforts. The basic management-development problem faced by human service organizations today is the same one articulated by Ryan[1] in 1963—that is, turning the specialist, or one trained in social work practice, into a generalist or one who puts management skills first and social work techniques second. In order to accomplish it, organizations must provide developmental opportunities which enable staff members who are normally hired for their professional or technical qualifications to advance into higher level positions which require supervisory and managerial skills. In organizational terms, entry skills differ markedly from skills needed in upper-management positions. For example, in filling entry-level positions, organizations usually seek individuals who have specialized technical or professional skills, with interpersonal and managerial skills having secondary importance. However, for upper-level management positions, persons are sought who have high-level managerial and interpersonal skills, with technical or professional skills having secondary importance. These relative skill requirements are illustrated in Figure 3-1.

Human service organizations, however, not only must recognize individual managerial-development needs, but also must strive to arrange organizational conditions and operational methods so they will

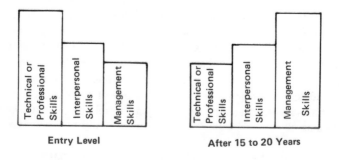

Figure 3.1: RELATIVE CAREER SKILL REQUIREMENTS

better enable personnel to optimize their own inherent potential. In other words, care must be taken to develop the work environment also. It is not enough to merely train the manager. An organizational climate must be provided that allows the manager to grow, mature, and recognize his own inherent capabilities and worth. The provision of adequate monetary incentives is not enough, since the manager must gain some degree of satisfaction from the job. Thus, employee-development programs must focus on both the individual and the job situation. Although the emphasis in this section is placed on developing individual-management capabilities, a comprehensive program of job development should include career counseling, job rotation, job enrichment, task-force assignments, and upgrading as an integral part of any overall management-development program.

While the process of management development is closely interlocked with the larger system of manpower planning and utilization, the primary functional objectives of management-development programs are threefold: first, to identify from existing cadres those with future managerial promise; second, to prepare those identified individuals to assume vacant or newly created management positions through a series of programmed tasks and experiences; and third, to improve the performance of individuals currently holding managerial titles.

Objectives such as these can contribute directly to the ultimate organizational goal of taking maximum advantage of professional and managerial skills currently available in the agency, while building a pool of qualified replacement personnel needed to fill vacancies created by normal attrition and organizational growth. Concurrently, an active management-development program tends to create an atmosphere of individual growth and development which attracts high-quality recruits, discourages transfers, and builds organizational morale.

A comprehensive management program should contain these functional elements:

—A method for identifying and cataloging managerial positions within the organization, and the specific skills and resources required for each.

—A workable and formalized performance-appraisal system that will provide easily retrievable data on the performance, skills, qualifications, experience, promotability, and development potential of all management and potential management personnel.

—A manpower plan which forecasts future management requirements in terms of the quantities and qualities of managers needed.

—A systematic plan for recruiting or promoting the numbers and types of managerial personnel needed to fill anticipated vacancies.

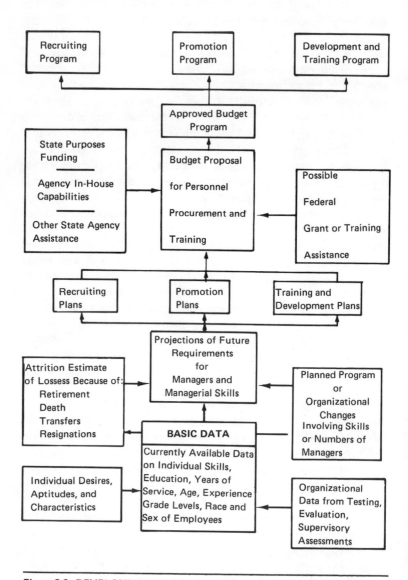

Figure 3.2: DEVELOPING MANAGERIAL-DEVELOPMENT PROGRAMS

—A coordinated program of coaching, career guidance, rotational assignments, training and educational opportunities for managers and potential managers, in order to enhance individual potential and to meet organizational needs.

—A method of selecting specific individuals to fill managerial positions through valid evaluations of the relative accomplishments and capabilities of all qualified candidates.

—An effort geared to motivate management personnel to perform at optimum levels in order to enhance their own development and continue contribution to organizational goals.

Figure 3-2 visually explains all the inputs and intricacies of putting together good management-development programs. By building from basic data on individual characteristics and desires and on who, where, and what the organization needs, plans for future managers can be made. Further inputs from outside areas—especially in funding and budget considerations—round out the process. After all is said and done, the final results should be a set of recruitment, promotion, and development and training programs that get the organization moving toward developing management people. This whole process is further delineated in the remainder of Chapter 3. The diagram can be used as a loose guideline to where discussion will go from here. First we have to know what is meant by the term "manager" and where the organization wants such people.

WHAT OR WHO IS A MANAGER?

Any program of management development must obviously start out by defining just who and what managers are within the organizational context. Unfortunately, the identification of actual managerial positions is complicated by extensive diffusions of authority and responsibility within organizations and by varying utilization of work patterns among organizations. Despite differences in terminology, there is some consensus of opinion on the definition of management and on the role managers play in organizations. Management consists of initiating and supervising the work performed by individuals and groups toward the accomplishment of organizational goals. A manager, therefore, is one whose job is to formulate, determine, and effect organizational policies. Some managers will fit this definition perfectly. Others will have mixed managerial and service functions. Nevertheless, it is up to the individual organization to determine which employees are to be cycled into the management-development program and for what specific reasons. Even so, in developing management programs, one must be aware of the various levels within this job title. In general, management positions are leveled according to these criteria:

1. Top Management. These are either the chief executive officers (commissioner, director, board president) or their principal assistants who determine policy formulation and direct policy execution. They are involved in planning, organizing, and directing one or more program areas within their agencies.

2. Middle Managers. These managers are primarily concerned with the effective administration, supervision and evaluations of units, installations, and services and programs under policies directed by higher authorities. Although they can recommend policy and program changes and initiate plans, their direct authority is generally limited to supervision and coordination, with specific responsibility for program execution and operation.

3. Supervisors. They directly supervise and control people and processes and are primarily concerned with volume and quality of work performed within policy and program structures developed at higher organizational levels. They are typically heads of subprogram units and, as such, are more concerned with individual performance than with group or program performance. Also, the supervisors' internal organization is less complex and smaller, with external contacts generally less extensive and at lower levels than the middle managers. They may supervise highly skilled technical personnel or subordinates in clerical or other routine tasks.

4. Managerial Staff. There are many professional employees who provide managerial services in planning, budgeting, management analysis, personnel, and general administration. While they provide technical or professional advice and recommendations to decision-makers, they may supervise few subordinates and have very limited responsibility for managerial functions outside of their specific fields. The degree to which such staff members should be considered to be managers must be based on the scope of their responsibilities, level of authority, and relationship to major agency programs.

For the sake of consistency, then, a social service manager can be defined as an employee who exercises direct supervisory authority and control over the employment and careers of two or more subordinates, or who performs a combination of managerial functions: planning, organizing, supervising, directing, controlling, evaluating, and negotiating.

MANAGEMENT MATERIAL IN YOUR MIDST?

The Need for Profile Data

Having once identified management positions, the next step is to develop profile data on current incumbents. Before searching the world for management potential, check your own organization. A review of data from regular organizational testing, evaluation, and supervisory assessments can very well turn up individuals ready and willing to work toward management positions. Also, good information on current employees is essential for planning future needs. In order to forecast future needs, design appropriate recruiting campaigns and develop realistic development programs, personnel managers must know the age, years and type of experience, educational levels, sex, pay grade, ethnic category, location, qualifications, and responsibilities of their managerial group. Any personnel plan or program should be based on valid information on the current situation.

Beyond these basic informational employee data, various attrition estimates are necessary to develop any kind of future need projections. Attrition rates tend to be controlled by initial recruiting patterns and changing economic conditions and retirement opportunities. Thus, retirement and attrition experience must be adjusted to the result of past recruiting programs that normally produce substantial variations in the numbers eligible for retirement each year. The same data which assist planners to forecast the requirements that establish recruiting needs also provide the basic information upon which training and development programs can be based. Training directors need to know:

—Anticipated numbers required in each category.

—Skill, experience, and educational levels of current employees.

—Individual characteristics of potential students.

—Relative needs for different skills and capabilities to meet organizational requirements.

This information is a basic requirement in the design of a development program and in the budget justification for requests to support it. Lack of such data not only inhibits the maximum utilization of available managerial potential, but also limits the validity of future needs assessments and the practical relevance of training programs. Without a sound data base, employee utilization and development tend to be haphazard and are frequently difficult to justify. In addition, those supervisors charged with the evaluation, coaching, and development of subordinates need this information in order to discharge their responsibilities.

Planning Data

Other inputs into projects of managerial requirements and skills are future plans for the organization. In projections of management needs program and organizational changes should be included if an organization does not want to be caught long on the need for managers and short on managers.

A viable management-development program should be an integral part of an agency's overall personnel plan. Based on accurate data on the existing situation, year-by-year projections of future requirements should be developed which, at least, specify, in general, the numbers, grade levels, and qualifications that will be required yearly over a period of several years. Promotion requirements and recruiting programs should be based on such a projection.

The number and type of estimated future requirements also provide a basis for a development plan which will include the courses needed not only to upgrade or refresh the skills of current incumbents, but also to prepare subordinate employees to compete for senior positions. Thus, inputs into the development plan include assessments of future knowledge or skills required, the numbers needed to have such competence, and anticipated changes in organizational structure, objectives, or policies that might require training. This development plan, which requests allocations for training and development programs, is then incorporated into the budget.

Planning and projections should not be limited to present employees. No matter how good the recruitment, selection, and training programs are, not all future needs can be met by in-house personnel. Plans should be left open enough to allow lateral entry at all points. Transfusion of new blood into an organization afflicted with tired blood, hardening of the categories, or hardening of the personalities can be very therapeutic.

People Data

Management-development programs are not based solely on straightforward data easily transferable to computer cards and projection charts. Basic data should be supplemented by information on desires, aptitudes, and characteristics of individual employees. After all, your management-development plan should be geared both to employee and organizational growth. All projections based on current status and future needs will be for naught if employees leave because they are unhappy. Information on individual goals is essential for ensuring that management development meets organizational and individual needs.

Much of the effectiveness of managerial performance depends on the motivation of individual managers. In an era of rapid change, top management should have a valid picture of the objectives, attitudes, and value systems of their subordinates. As new recruits to government bring different objectives and attitudes to their jobs, it is important for policy makers to have some specific information on the prevalence of these new attitudes and values as a basis for personnel policies and development programs.

Assumptions on how subordinates feel about their jobs can easily be off-base. Policies or programs based on these assumptions can be dysfunctional, and actually damage motivation and efficiency, rather than enhance them. Morale and motivation within an agency can be at a very low level, escaping top-policymakers' awareness. Hence, periodic assessments at different levels are needed to obtain data on prevailing managerial attitudes toward organizational objectives, policies, leadership styles, and individual goals.

Later we will see that paying attention to such attitudes and goals, and the objective factual data, will have a favorable impact on overall organizational climate and individual morale. More and more organizations are realizing that an employee's needs for self-actualization are as important as organizational goals. Incorporation of these employee needs then becomes a cornerstone in management recruitment, promotion, and development programs.

Career Guidance

Each individual is ultimately responsible for his own self-development and advancement. Modern complex organizations, however, must provide employee guidance and assistance not only to develop each employee to his greatest potential, but also to guide that development in order to fill urgent agency requirements.

Effective career guidance is based on reasonably accurate assessment of aptitudes, performance, skills, qualifications, experience, and potential. Hence, performance ratings and assessments play an integral part in a guidance and in a development system. However, such assessments which tend to rely on the subjective evaluations of superiors should be supplemented by measures to determine aptitudes, interests, attitudes, training needs, and individual goals.

Career guidance is not a one-way street. Ideally, a career plan is a culmination of discussions between counselor and employee on what the data have shown and on what an individual's career interests and goals are.

Directional information on a future career path is gained through bilateral conferences rather than through unilateral dissemination of data and an imposed plan.

Armed with such information, supervisors responsible for employee development can draw up a development program for each employee. In addition to coaching the employee on his current performance and to providing a feedback on areas of strength and weakness, such an individual program should include training courses to be taken, rotational assignments to appropriate positions, or additional education under a tuition-assistance program.

These inclusions make the plan future-oriented and provide positive direction. Training courses and additional education combine to make an action-oriented approach to a career plan. Career guidance is futile without follow-up activity.

Job enrichment and job rotation are further demonstrations of career plan implementation. Job enrichment recognizes that people rarely stay the same overtime and, individually, they vary widely in characteristics. Through enrichment, jobs are restructured according to what the worker feels comfortable with and likes to do. The job gets done, but not necessarily according to formal job descriptions. Job enrichment can also mean job enlargement. This circumstance means that an individual takes full responsibility for a total activity rather than a few of its facets. Job enrichment essentially provides opportunities for individuals to provide input into the way their jobs are done.

Another form of opportunity expansion is job rotation. Through rotation, an employee works an entirely different job. It is an opportunity to see, feel, and learn about another facet of the total work picture. Rotation can be among departments, control agencies, central and field offices, professions, or geographical areas. The important thing to remember is that the time spent in another job must be of sufficient duration to get a total feel for that position and its work environment. A week or two is not enough time.

Ratings and appraisal of the career plan should include experiences and performance in job enrichment and rotation activities. Career guidance is not a one-shot conference. People and their experiences change, and these should be duly incorporated in the career-guidance plan.

The ultimate goal of individual career guidance is to encourage each employee to take the maximum advantage of existing opportunities, to exploit his skills and interests, and to provide both the opportunities and the incentives for self-development. He should be able to complete training courses, workshops, or rotational assignments which will equip him to compete for each successively higher position in which he might be interested. Much of an agency's potential to solve its present and future problems lies in the growth potential of its employees. By using basic data and individual career-growth preferences, a career-guidance plan can produce a readable map that has strategic landmarks, helpful detours, a predetermined destination and, above all, a willing traveler.[2]

Selection for Advancement

Assuming that an agency has an effective recruiting effort which identifies and selects applicants for initial appointment, the next most important element used to develop a high-quality management team is in the system of selection for advancement. If properly fashioned, recruitment and selection programs and guidance efforts can make promotion selection easier. Of course, advancement is not a certainty because a person is identified as having management potential. Performance is a factor. Ideally, such a system would reinforce the program of career guidance and training and use the data developed by that system to identify and select the most qualified available employees for advancement, as the assessment center does.

Selection should be made from a large, competitive group and should be based on performance, experience, qualifications, estimated potential, and individual characteristics. In order to rule out individual bias, the objective judgment of several senior officials should be secured. Wherever possible, the opinions of peers and subordinates should be fed into the system in order to obtain perspectives otherwise unavailable to supervisors and superiors. After all, a person deals with others outside supervisory positions. The combined ratings from all levels, plus the previous factors mentioned, produce the best possible picture of the candidate.

The career-guidance system is important for the advancement aspect of the total management-development program. Promotion based on performance and on the career plan certainly eliminates much of the guess work in developing good management cadres. Recruitment, selection, and promotion programs, although separate, should mesh to provide natural stepping stones for management development. Of course, management-development plans do not become programs without funds to launch them off the drawing board. Financial resources and budgetary constraints should be a part of overall planning. Funding resources must be a part of planning to prevent solid management-development plans from melting under the heat of budget review.

An objective promotion system which builds on performance assessment, development programs, and the objective measurement of skills and aptitudes encourages individual improvement and therefore enhances organizational morale. It goes far toward generating an organizational growth and developmental environment to attract recruits and encourage employee efforts. Providing the opportunities for individual growth and advancement signifies organizational interest in each employee and conveys expectations of improved performance. The chances of enhancing individual performance are substantially improved by giving such expectations concrete expression in provided opportunities and selection and assignment procedures.

A major weakness in implementation strategies has been the "shotgun approach" to management development. Many human service agencies never really concerned themselves with implementing comprehensive development efforts, or for that matter, with conducting routine management evaluations. Similarly, employees who lacked any career guidance could not discern their own management needs. When managers were enrolled in training or continuing education programs, agencies tended to shuttle personnel in and out without knowing whether they needed a particular skill or knowledge. Hence, organizations found it difficult to concentrate the management-development dollar where the need was greatest. Subsequently, overall impact was reduced. Such a dilemma clearly calls for some type mechanism that would allow economical and valid identification of individual management capabilities. Once this diagnosis is completed, management-development programs can be tailored to the needs of the individual employee and the organization. The basic difference between this type approach and what is presently being done is the highly targeted and individualized nature of the development effort.

As we previously discussed, the assessment center is the best method for organizations to accomplish this individualized approach. Nevertheless, in the previous context its primary use was described as a selection device. However, it also has great value and potential as a diagnostic tool for management development. As shown here, the center focuses on three primary skill areas which are further divided into multiple management dimensions:

A. Management skills
    1. Organizing and planning
    2. Delegation and control
    3. Oral communication
    4. Written communications

B. Decision-making
    1. Perception and analytic ability
    2. Decisiveness

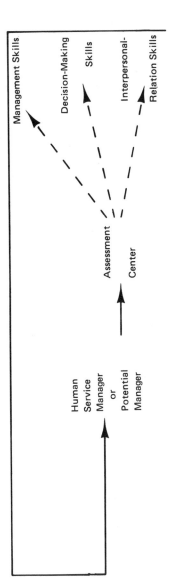

Figure 3.3: MANAGEMENT DEVELOPMENT

3. Creativity
C. Interpersonal Relations
   1. Leadership
   2. Sensitivity
   3. Stress tolerance

After analysis of the various dimensions of each individual's performance, a series of highly targeted management-development efforts and plans can be suggested. Present and future managers could then be cycled into appropriate types of courses and work experiences depending on actual need. In essence, then, what is being proposed is a highly specific system of management assessment followed by appropriate and individualized developmental strategies. It is diagrammed in Figure 3-3.

Employee Characteristics

As mentioned previously, it would be difficult, or even impossible to detail a comprehensive management plan without knowing the makeup and characteristics of the client-employee population; hence, the need for manpower planning becomes self-evident. Keeping this in mind, the School of Social Welfare at Albany, a major provider of continuing education programs in the social services, undertook a manpower survey in twenty-seven counties of northeastern New York on behalf of the New York State Department of Social Services.[3] Its basic objective was to collect and to review available data on personnel currently involved in the delivery of social service in both public and private sectors. While the data gathered did not prove startling, they were unique because they provided a profile look at the types and numbers of personnel needed to deliver a whole range of human and social services. The analysis in terms of personnel characteristics, such as age, experience, educational level, caseloads, and functional assignment, is being used to help determine the future mix of continuing education and management-development efforts.

Nevertheless, before data can be meaningfully analyzed, it is essential to understand the policy context in which these organizations operate. A number of changes in welfare programs and in policies have taken place, with circumstances causing an increase in staffing requirements and decreases in other areas; for example, new categories of aid; federal takeover of assistance to the aged, disabled, and blind; and the requirement for separation of services have had major impact on staffing patterns and management-development needs.

One can be reasonably sure that additional changes, short of a major legislative overhaul, such as federal assumption of welfare costs, will also be taking place. Increased automation of income-maintenance and medical-assistance disbursements, changes in client eligibility, and reinterpretation of services are a few. These alterations might also have significant future manpower impacts. Perhaps some caseload data would serve to demonstrate the constant shifting in priorities. In the twenty-seven counties surveyed between 1970 and 1972, total caseloads consisted of aid to dependent children, home relief, and aid to the disabled, aged, and blind. In 1972 a new assistance category was added—emergency assistance to adults. Almost simultaneously, however, three categories of aid for the disabled, aged, and blind were assumed by the federal government. As a result, there was a temporary caseload drop of 15,000. This decrease only temporarily interrupted the steady climb in caseloads experienced since 1970, especially in the area of aid to dependent children, which grew from 15,782 cases in 1970 to 24,780 in 1975 and is expected to grow by 10 percent per year by the end of the decade. Home relief cases have increased at a similarly alarming rate.

This increased workload has caused county departments of social services to increase staff at an average rate of 10 percent per year to keep up with expanding cases, and a continuous growth rate of 5 to 10 percent is not unlikely for the next five years. Add to this an attrition rate of 13 percent for administrators and supervisors, 18 percent for direct service workers, 24 percent for specialists, and 23 percent for clerical workers, and you find a vacancy rate of approximately 25 percent per year. In essence, this rate means that county social service organizations are forced to hire and train a quarter of their work force each year, which if done well, is a tremendously difficult organizational undertaking in terms of required monetary and human resources. Attrition rates will probably continue about the same as evidenced by the fact that approximately 31 percent of the employees are either uncertain about their careers or intend to make future changes in their present organizations.

Several other interesting factors were revealed with definite implications for the training and development process. For instance, it was found within the twenty-seven county region, 58 percent of the employees were concentrated in seven urbanized communities. Such vast size differences tend to increase administrative overhead in the smaller agencies because of their inability to take advantage of economies of scale, even though administrative-staffing patterns tend to be the same regardless of organizational size. As a result, administrators in smaller agencies have to be knowledgeable across program lines (i.e., Medicaid, income maintenance) because they cannot be as specialized as managers in larger, more complex organizations, yet their responsibilities remain similar. Consequently, the training problem becomes more difficult in terms of a broader-scoped effort needed to respond to the interchangeability of function and responsibilities in smaller counties. While the training and development needs are greatest here, these are just the types of organization that are unable to spare staff for any considerable time period.

The report also discovered that county social service agencies in general had a high requirement for administrative overhead, especially when compared to private social service agencies. In county organizations, for example, 13 percent of the employees could be classified as administrators or supervisors. In private organizations this category comprised only 6 percent of the total. Similarly, 44 percent of the workers could be labeled direct service workers in the county agency, compared to 71 percent of the private.

Although the training function could have some temporary impact on the problem, more permanent relief could be realized through an organizational-development effort. In fact, the surveys showed some degree of variation in organizational structure and job assignments among counties. Analysis of data revealed individuals with different educational and skill levels were employed under similar titles; also, some functions were organized differently in various counties. Perhaps some attention should be given functional job analysis to better determine appropriate job design for improved service delivery.

For the most part, evaluation of personnel educational and training levels showed that staff had at least minimum qualifications for their assigned tasks. There appeared, however, to be a substantial backlog of needed education and training, since 68 percent of the employees had less than a baccalaureate degree and over 50 percent reported not having had any job-related training. Even though private, nonprofit agencies had a higher percentage of professionals with postgraduate degrees, their organizations had even a higher percentage of members with less than a baccalaureate degree than the county public agencies did. This situation indicates the need for academic and professional preparation, along with specific job-related programs.

Examination of employee-age characteristics is clearly delineated by a bimodal curve, with 36 percent of the staff under 30 years of age and 30 percent over 51. This phenomenon appears to be caused by rapid staff expansion experienced in recent years, coupled with the departure of women from the work force during the middle of their professional careers. Such age distribution results in a substantial number of older employees occupying relatively junior positions. A smaller percentage of women than men are eligible for supervisory and management positions. Also, the uneven age distribution is partly to blame for high attrition rates because of the concentration of employees both at the more mobile end of the spectrum and at the more senior end, where sickness and retirement are prevalent. This effect becomes magnified by the fact that 75 percent of the county social service employees are female. These data provide valuable information on how to better-target management-development efforts by concentrating service resources on prospective management and supervisory populations.

The survey indicated a clear need and desire by social service employees for continued and comprehensive management-development programs. Types of efforts that could be operationalized include: in-service programs, instruction, workshops, graduate and undergraduate degree programs, graduate continuing education courses for credit, direct technical assistance, on-the-job training, and employee orientation. However, no one type or program technique can be optimally applied when matched against diverse organizational and individual needs. Consequently, implementation of comprehensive management and training programs requires a multitiered or mixed approach. There is no one training answer that is best since organizational-performance improvement is cumulative. While the survey data gathered from these twenty-seven counties might not be totally representative of the national scene, the data provide some interesting insights into the makeup of the first-line public social service agency, and its staff's needs. One thing is clear, however. Requirements for social services will continue to climb, creating a growing demand for personnel with social service competency and skills. Mounting costs will place increased pressure on the search for more productive means of delivering services. In addition to exploring organizational-performance variables, focus should also be placed on staff development, for it is the people who make an organization work.

EVALUATING MANAGEMENT-DEVELOPMENT PROGRAMS

There is no doubt that the inability of human service organizations to cope with crisis and change has spurred a renewed interest in the development and training of existing management cadres. While the provision of such services is admirable, little effort has been made to assess the impact of these rather expensive programs. Evident in the country is a native faith and simplistic trust in the power and utility of management development. In truth, however, existing training assessment techniques probably do not allow adequate measurement of ultimate results since they are often too abstract. Behavior in the organization is affected by too many other variables besides the training course. Consequently, in attempting to evaluate impact it would be more worthwhile to shorten sights, and, instead of seeking the Holy Grail of result measurement, to concentrate on locating those factors which determine participant course reaction. In other words, time would be best spent seeking an understanding of how and why management-development programs have an effect on their participants.

Recent research in evaluating management-development impact focused on attempts to isolate four participant characteristics which might interact favorably with perceptions: age, education, years with the organization, and reason for attending. In most cases, control over these attributes is in the hands of the nominating agency. Additionally, program staffing, a key attribute under the control of the provider, was studied to ascertain its place in course acceptability. Hence, this particular research effort concentrated on examining a key attribute of the program itself, as well as participant characteristics, then relating these to program successes. All too often, making sense of such findings is ignored.

Program response data were gathered on 227 middle to lower managers from the local, state, and federal government who attended one of a series of university-based management-development programs.

In evaluating how the age variable impacts program acceptability, there was a tendency for older participants to be slightly more favorable than younger ones. This circumstance was probably because to older participants such courses have increased novelty and higher impact on their knowledge because of a wider time span between formal academic training and the existing job situation. Such results counter previous findings that indicated those people over 35 tend to be less favorable to management-development programs than to those under 35.

In terms of education, no consistent impact on acceptability of management programs could be found. Again, such findings contradicted previous research, showing that increased formal participant education brought decreased course favorability. Perhaps findings could be explained by pointing to the homogeneous characteristics of this public management group who share concern, interests, experiences, and problems which overshadow any effects of differing educational levels. By concentrating on relevant job experience for the training base, rather than by using complex management jargon, it is also possible to limit differential impact caused by education. After tenure with the organization had been analyzed, it was discovered that those at the upper service spectrum (sixteen or more years with the organization) reacted more positively to courses than those with fewer years of service. Such findings counter the common assumption among trainers that it is the newer organizational member who benefits most from management-development programs. Based on these results and on feelings that they know the system well, or are getting older, one should not discount the value of management training for those with longer years of service.

The reason for attending was also found to have an impact on perceived course acceptability. In some instances, candidates were ordered to attend. Others volunteered for specific offerings. This research bears out the common sense notion that participants who volunteer for attendance in management courses will react more positively than those ordered to attend. Unfortunately, selection procedures often run counter to this fact because of failure to link the development program with the total organizational process.

Of all the variables studied, program staffing seemed to be the factor most crucial to participant satisfaction. It is very difficult to pinpoint qualities that make a good trainer—expertness, articulateness, management experience, dynamics, and reputation are a few of the many facets that might be considered. There was a direct link between satisfaction with the training and acceptability of the program, and higher staff ratings led to a more favorable course reaction. Such results would indicate that training program developers should take particular care to select and match staff with participants. In many cases, this selection is done on an arbitrary basis. Even so, it is not uncommon to find a staff member highly rated by a participant group in one program and downgraded in another course by different participants. Consequently, there is a lot to learn about selecting, identifying, and matching potential trainers with program participants.

In reality, there is a limited amount of empirical evidence on how management development works. Nevertheless, enough exists to "demyth" some of the more commonly held management-development assumptions. Organizations spending money on training efforts should realize that it is in their best interests to "professionalize" their approach in developing management potential because of its very real contribution to the improvement of social service performance and delivery.[4]

CONCLUSION

A good selection method must be matched by an equally good management-development system. The entire process of selection, promotion, and training managers requires data on what and on where and on who you have and you hope to get. Employee involvement is essential both in gathering data as well as promoting morale. Employees who feel actively involved with the agency, and who see a future in continued involvement, start development programs on a solid base. Sound data collection, assessment, and planning techniques, finding resources, and employee input are all necessary for a useful management-development program.

Management selection from those outside the agency and development of those within have been discussed as two approaches for improving individual effectiveness. The third approach encompasses the whole organization and its ability to provide a climate that promotes morale and individual effectiveness. Successful development of this type of environment also promotes organizational effectiveness.

The next two chapters form the third part of the three-pronged approach to human service effectiveness. Here, the organization itself is the unit of analysis, with particular reference being made to the organization's structural dynamics. Management-selection and -development programs are useless if they are projected into an organization that strictly adheres to and reveres its organizational chart. This type organization tends to be populated by lethargic, narrow individuals. Motivation and morale are missing, and those who have it find it quickly dissolves.

Chapters 4 and 5 review ways to develop motivation-producing and effective agencies through problem identification, organizational-development techniques, and, in particular, structural change.

NOTES

1. John Ryan, "Social Work Executive: Generalist or Specialist?" Social Work 8 (April, 1963), pp. 26-28.

2. Samuel Hays, "The Scope of Management Development," paper written for the Public Executive Project and the School of Social Welfare Continuing Education Program, University at Albany (mimeographed), 1975.

3. "Manpower Survey and Analysis," prepared by the School of Social Welfare, University at Albany (published report), 1976.

4. Richard Steiner and Frank Kelly, "A Key Factors Approach to Assessing Management Development," Personnel Journal 55 (July 1976), pp. 358-361.

Chapter 4

BUILDING EFFECTIVE ORGANIZATIONS

INTRODUCTION

We have discussed effectiveness from the individual perspective in terms of management selection and development. We now turn to an organizationwide perspective because effective, motivated employees need environments that will allow continued growth and development.

Organizational effectiveness is best attained when it stems from a willingness to admit there is always room for improvement. Chapter 4 first looks at some ways to encourage improvement by outlining effectiveness criteria. Two approaches for identifying criteria are discussed. A combination of the two is presented as a good method to use for identifying and analyzing organizational problem areas. The development of specific analytical criteria is the first step in the search for organizational problems and their solutions.

Once criteria are established as a basis for evaluation, identification and analysis of organizational problems become easier tasks. There are guidelines for focusing the search and for telling the investigator when a clue has been unearthed.

Diagnosing problem areas then leads the way for making changes to address those problems. Change in any context is not easy to introduce and rarely is met with widespread acceptance. Before dwelling on specific change techniques in Chapter 5, Chapter 4 will deal with the traumatic effects change can have on both the organization and on the individual. Some factors that set bounds on the degree of change are also mentioned.

ORGANIZATIONAL EFFECTIVENESS

Discussing organizational effectiveness is similar to talking about motherhood and patriotism—everybody is for it, but few do anything about it. If human service agencies were individually able to supply answers to two questions, they would be well on their way to fulfilling their mandate: (a) What are the characteristics of a successful or productive human service agency? (b) What are the characteristics of an unsuccessful or unproductive human service organization? On the surface, these questions appear simple; however, they require complete, searching, honest appraisals from responding organizations. Nevertheless, the evaluation process and its consequent answers might just be the key that unlocks hidden organizational-performance capacities.

EFFECTIVENESS CRITERIA

The Goal-Oriented Approach

Corrective actions can be undertaken, based on a knowledge of where effectiveness deviations occur. Unfortunately, few human service agencies are able to identify criteria for success—primarily because their organizational missions are unclear. In response, Drucker[1] puts forth the following six criteria in a discussion of requirements for program success. First, social service organizations need to answer the question, "What is our business and what should it be?" They must think through their own specific function: (a) what the organization actually does (reality); (b) what the organization is supposed to do (legal mandate); (c) what the organization should do (wants to accomplish). In essence, it is a beginning. By articulating function and mission, the agency is on the road to identification of effectiveness criteria. Many times agencies are too busy to discover what they are doing. However, such a discovery is necessary to make any kind of determination of performance.

Second, Drucker goes on to say that organizations need to derive clear goals and objectives from a definition of function and mission. Once the mission has been articulated, the foundation is laid for planning long-range goals to accomplish that mission. Organizational efforts for increased achievement should focus on effectiveness and efficiency rather than on the need for better people. Bringing competent people aboard a ship that has no navigational equipment will accomplish nothing more than having everyone sink when the ship runs aground. As mentioned in Chapter 3, competent people need a good environment, for competent people alone do not make a good organization. These people, however, must systematically do their jobs and have a result- and performance-oriented outlook if the efficiency and effectiveness focus is to work.

Third, successful organizations need to set priorities so targets can be determined and performance standards met. It does little good to spread resources and energy so thin that everything is met but the main objectives. Targets are set by defining minimum acceptable results and by setting deadlines and accountability levels. This step is also crucial to the fourth critèria—delineating performance measurements. Mission, goal, and target articulation must be followed up with a method for measuring whether performance has been met. Performance standards should directly relate to goals that are to be accomplished. Standards are absolutely necessary for evaluation; without them it is pointless to have an effective, efficient perspective. Judgments cannot be made on the success or failure of a project if there are no measurements upon which judgments can be made.

Fifth, a feedback system, thus, a self-correcting mechanism capable of assessing deviations from prescribed efforts, must be formalized. Performance judgments cannot all be left until the end of a program. Information based on performance measurements should be on a continued basis. This situation creates flexibility for building on success and provides opportunities to make adjustments in unsuccessful programs before incorrect actions are carried too far.

Sixth, establishment of organized objectives and routine audit of those objectives and results is essential. This crucial audit, again based on performance standards, determines overall success of a project. When audit and budget time comes around, it is helpful to be able to point out success stories. Evaluation determines whether the program actually met its stated objectives, or if the standards really measured objectives. Audit is the most crucial aspect of a goal-oriented approach because, with evaluation, one can determine if goals are met. To be effective, social service organizations need the continued stimulation and benefits that can be derived by being subject to performance tests and evaluations.

Drucker is the foremost proponent of the output, or goal-oriented approach, to organizational effectiveness. In fact, he is often credited as the first person to formalize a goal-auditing system called Management by Objectives (MBO), a technique used to mesh personal and organizational goals through increased communication and development of shared goal perceptions among the manager and the subordinates. The main thrust of this technique, then, is to establish a bilateral goal selection between manager and worker. In this manner, it is much like the career-guidance plan discussed in Chapter 3. Management by Objectives emphasizes particular work goals rather than career goals and has a shorter time frame. Work goals are set among the manager and employee activities and measurements for judging achievement are established. This step is followed by periodic review. The review may result in continuation of the current goal standards, or the insertion of appropriate alterations in response to the overwhelming success or failure of the original goals.

As you can see, MBO closely follows the six criteria of goal-oriented approaches to effectiveness. A basic assumption behind these approaches is the primary importance of the ratio between actual results measured against anticipated results. One can determine the degree of deviation from desired outputs by measuring organizational performance against effectiveness and efficiency variables. It is then possible to redirect the organization's people, resources, and systems toward goal achievement. In other words, organizational effectiveness emphasizes the end product itself—not how it was produced. Of course, articulating the agency's goals certainly helps to point to the product and, in turn, gives credence to the goal-oriented approach. Goals and ways to measure them are necessary for this approach to be of use. By reviewing the acceptability of the product, organizational adjustments can be made to transform unacceptable outputs into acceptable ones. This is, therefore, a working-back procedure—knowing what is wrong with the product—helps to identify malfunctioning procedures. In addition to management by objectives, goal-oriented approaches are known by such titles as managing for performance and productivity improvement. They all tend to focus on outputs when defining organizational performance and effectiveness.

The Process-Oriented Approach

There is another major approach to the problem of organizational performance—the process or organic model. This school of thought is perhaps best represented by Likert[2] and his organizational-effectiveness classification scheme. His basic premise asserts that all organizations operate on a management continuum. This continuum is composed of four subunits: System I, exploitive authoritative; System II, benevolent authoritative; System III, consultative; System IV, participative. In general, Likert concludes that organizations managed under Style IV modalities are more productive and effective, have lower operating

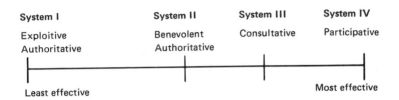

Figure 4.1: THE EFFECTIVENESS CONTINUUM

costs, and are more conducive to develope favorable organizational attitudes than those leaning toward the authoritarian end of the spectrum.

In order to get a better idea of what Likert means by an effective organization, it might prove worthwhile to quickly review varying operating characteristics. Remember, according to Likert, the effectiveness continuum moves from left to right as shown in Figure 4-1.

Exploitive, Authoritative Management

Exploitive, authoritative (System I) organizations use physical, economic incentives and status as motivating forces. They are enforced by fear, threats, punishment, and occasional rewards. In this type situation, employee attitudes are hostile to organizational goals. First-line managers often feel little responsibility for helping achieve organizational outcomes. These managers sometimes even welcome opportunities to behave in ways counter to goal achievement.

Authoritative organizations are characterized by distorted communications. In general, communication is initiated at the top and flows downward in the form of directives. Communications received from the top are viewed with suspicion. Employees feel no great need for initiating upward communication, and when doing so, they tamper with information to deceive superiors. System I organizations produce no appreciable teamwork because superiors are separated from subordinates. Employees see no way they can influence organizational activities and goals except through informal organization or unionization.

The decision-making process is characterized by partial, often inaccurate, information. In addition, decision-makers are only partially aware of problems at lower organizational levels. Control mechanisms are initiated at the top. In general, they are overtly accepted, but covertly resisted. Feedback is often distorted, and strong forces exist to falsify control measurements, as review procedures are concentrated at higher organizational levels.

Benevolent Authoritative Management

The System II organization, enforced through use of rewards and punishment, is typified by the use of economic- and ego-motivating forces. Employee attitudes are sometimes hostile or favorable to organizational goals. Managerial personnel usually feel responsibility for achieving goals, while rank-and-file employees feel little such responsibility. Often a subservient attitude toward superiors and competition for status results in hostility toward peers and condescending attitudes toward subordinates. There is little satisfaction associated with membership in the organization, supervision, and personal achievements. Communication is primarily initiated at the top. Information received by subordinates may be viewed with suspicion, while information to superiors is somewhat distorted and filtered. Such organizations produce virtually no cooperative teamwork efforts. Little influence is exerted by employees on organizational goals, methods, and activities. The decision-making process is characterized by top-level policy formulation, and lower level decisions are made within a prescribed framework. Information on decisions is moderately accurate—decision-makers are aware of some problems and not aware of others. Organizational control is largely directed from the top, with goals overtly accepted but sometimes covertly resisted. Fairly strong forces exist to distort and falsify feedback messages.

Consultative Management

To ensure proper motivating forces, the System III model of organizational management is characterized by economic incentives, ego incentives, and other major incentives. High-motivation levels are maintained through use of reward, occasional punishment, and some employee involvement. Subordinate attitudes toward the organization are sometimes hostile but, more often, are favorable and support organizational goals. Interpersonal relationships are usually cooperative, and reasonably favorable attitudes exist toward others in the organization. There may be some competition among peers, which results in hostility and some condescending attitudes toward subordinates. Satisfaction is moderately high with regard to organization membership, supervision, and personal achievements. There is some upward communication, and quite a lot of interaction aimed at achieving organizational objectives. Subordinates feel a moderate degree of responsibility for the initiation of accurate upward communication. Direction of communication is upward and downward. Some forces are at work to distort communication. Positive communication is generally accurate, but other information can fall short of total accuracy. A moderate amount of teamwork is exhibited and subordinates exercise moderate influence over goals, methods, and activities. The decision-making process in the consulting model is characterized by top levels making general decisions and lower levels making specific decisions. The information used is reasonably accurate, and decision-makers are moderately aware of organization problems. After decision-makers discuss problems with subordinates and plan actions, they set goals and issue orders. These goals are overtly accepted, but, at times, can meet some covert resistance. Control emanates primarily from the top, with some emphasis placed on the need to protect themselves and colleagues, which results in distortion of information. Information in the system, then, is only moderately complete and contains some inaccuracies.

Participative Management

Organizations which utilize the System IV participative style of management sustain motivation levels by fully using major incentives, such as money and ego. Economic rewards are based on a compensation system developed through group participation and involvement. Organizational attitudes are generally strongly favorable. Personnel feel responsible for attaining organizational goals and are motivated to achieve them. Attitudes toward others in the organization, based on mutual trust and confidence, are favorable and cooperative. Satisfaction with organization membership, supervision, and personal achievement is high. There is a great deal of interpersonal interaction. Communication is downward, upward, highly open, among peers, and initiated at all levels. Information communicated is generally accepted, with room for candid questions. There are virtually no forces present to communicate inaccurately. Teamwork and cooperation are high throughout the organization, and employees have ample opportunity to influence goals, methods, and activities. Decision-making is widely dispersed throughout the organization, but is well-integrated through a linking process provided by overlapping groups. The information decision-makers use is relatively complete and accurate, and all levels of the organization are well aware of problems. Goals usually established by group participation are overtly and covertly accepted. Control responsibility is spread throughout the organization, and strong pressures are present to obtain accurate, complete feedback.

Likert does point out that since System IV produces the most effective organization, it is appreciably more complex than the other systems. Although it requires greater learning and higher levels of managerial and organizational skills, once it is instituted, it consistently and impressively yields better organizational effectiveness. System IV must be oversimplified to make the typology work. Likert has focused on several organizational variables and on how they operate within the organization to determine its effectiveness. The variables include motivation forces, motivation-maintenance mechanisms, employee attitudes toward the organization, interpersonal relationships, organizational-satisfaction levels, communication direction and distortion, teamwork, decision-making process and source-information accuracy, goal setting and at what level, emanation of organizational control, and others. In so doing, Likert has identified those characteristics and behaviors needed to produce effective organization.

Cohen and Collins,[3] by using an action research format to test the relationship between effectiveness indicators and effectiveness characteristics, found support for the organic approach to organizational performance. The researchers adopted a social and rehabilitation service field office as their analysis unit and identified various organizational-effectiveness variables which warranted special consideration. First, widespread participation in agency decision-making was clearly shown, as a characteristic of an effective office. Second, the employers' satisfaction with the work that was being done was an important correlate of performance. Third, organizational flexibility and adaptiveness were highly related to a productive organization. Fourth, a rational, trusting environment where employees knew the rules and had confidence in their objective execution added to organizational effectiveness. Fifth, external cooperation for the organization was seen as an important factor. Finally, data showed that satisfaction with co-workers, team collaboration, and a climate for creativity are important indicators of organizational success.

The organic approach to organizational effectiveness assumes that acceptable outputs will result if the processes (systems, interrelationships, individual capabilities) are functioning at high capacity. The starting point for the organic approach is to view the organization as a whole with all its consequent and interrelated elements. On the other hand, those people stressing output or a product assume that the processes used to achieve the end results are irrelevant when the output meets quality-control standards.

The Best of Both Approaches

A better picture can be developed by looking at a combination of these two approaches. Organizational effectiveness is dependent on a range of criteria, including knowledge of what must be done, goals, how to achieve the goals, and whether the effort is worth it. This approach must be linked up with a well-developed system for instituting joint goals, plans, and decisions. These, by necessity, call for the utilization of all available human resources and skills within the organization. In addition, there should be insurance that employee group norms and attitudes reinforce organizational missions and tasks. This step is accomplished by maintaining high levels of intergroup teamwork. Achieving such teamwork is dependent on a free flow of ideas and communications within organizations, a high degree of employee motivation, a supportive management system, a forward-looking leadership style, and an opportunity to exhibit individual competence.

Hence, efforts at improving organizational productivity should concentrate on two areas. First, determine whether performance objectives were reached; if not, locate the deviations and their causes. (A methodology for accomplishing this will be described in Chapter 9.) Second, examine all management and administrative processes to determine the extent that human and physical resources are being utilized. Some areas to look out for include bottlenecks, duplication, lack of coordination, overcontrol, undercontrol, limited communications, interpersonal and interagency conflicts, and lack of commitment and motivation—all of which can reduce organizational performance.

Effectiveness, therefore, cannot be determined by focusing solely on goals or on processes. This kind of tunnel vision results in distorted perceptions of an organization's ability to be effective. Boring in on goals tends to neglect the impact of physical and human resources on productivity. At the same time, preoccupation with processes can produce a pronouncement of successful efficiency and effectiveness without determining whether objectives are accomplished. While this dual emphasis approach is more complex, it is necessary. (It does take two correctly ground lenses to yield 20-20 vision.)

ORGANIZATIONAL PROBLEMS

A more formal investigation of organizational effectiveness would focus on four major organizational categories: structure, interpersonal relationships, individual competence, and process. Typical problems which might arise in the management of a social service organization might include the following list:

I.   Structural problems are dysfunctions emanating from organizational design inefficiencies that can lead to:
   a.   Overlap of responsibility
   b.   Task ambiguity
   c.   Communication breakdown
   d.   Distorted authority networks
   e.   Program duplication
   f.   Inadequate control mechanisms
   g.   Power centralization
   h.   Dislocated decision-making systems
   i.   Excessive loss of time between problen identification and solution
   j.   Increased emphasis on collateral coordinating activity
   k.   Staff/line ratio inequities
   l.   Excessive administrative overhead
   m.   Underdeveloped linking mechanisms

II. Interpersonal problems are dysfunctions emanating from management style deficiencies and lead to:
   a.   Excessive interpersonal conflict
   b.   Overabundant interprogram or intergroup competition
   c.   Inadequate conflict resolution mechanisms
   d.   Weak employee commitment to organizational goals
   e.   Low level employee morale
   f.   Job and task dissatisfaction
   g.   Lack of supportive program mechanisms
   h.   Excessive defensiveness and resistance
   i.   Turf or jurisdictional disputes
   j.   Inadequate opportunities for achievement, growth, and development
   k.   High absenteeism and turnover rates
   l.   Constant complaints and grievances in regard to working conditions, assignments, and duties
   m.   Insufficient efforts at teambuilding
   n.   Lack of mutual trust and respect

III. Process problems are dysfunctions emanating from poorly designed and implemented procedures and lead to:
   a.   Excessive paperwork
   b.   Duplication, red tape, and overlap across program lines
   c.   Pushing decisions higher into organizational hierarchy than needed
   d.   Constant questioning on worthwhileness and use of data-collection and management-information systems

    e. Massive, rather than selective, dissemination and retrieval of information

    f. Distorted and inaccurate data

    g. Dissatisfied clientele because of excessive procedural requirements

    h. Wasted monetary, human, and time resources because of duplicate procedures

    i. Scheduling difficulties

    j. Overly complex procedures for resultant value

    k. Unnecessary extra steps

    l. System maintenance overemphasized in relationship to program output

    m. Overroutinization of workload, causing job dissatisfaction

IV. Individual competency problems emanate from inadequate selection and development mechanisms and lead to:

    a. Inadequate individual knowledge-base

    b. Inconsistent management behavior

    c. Lack of management skills

    d. Low motivation levels

    e. Underdeveloped, supporting attitude structures

    f. Inability to perceive importance of individual function in relation to output produced

    g. Limited interest in personal advancement and betterment

    h. Inadequate technical competency

    i. Reluctance to take risks

    j. Lack of creativity

    k. Poor external relationships and perceptions

    l. Stagnant positions that close promotional opportunities to those in lower levels

DIAGNOSING ORGANIZATIONAL PROBLEMS

The preceding list was merely a sampling of the types of problems that can cause organizational inefficiencies. Obviously, many more can be recounted. Nevertheless, the difficulties outlined are to some degree correctable. No one expects an organizational Valhalla devoid of all problems and conflicts. By working out problems, new and exciting solutions to complex social issues arise. Changes can be made in organizational structure, management systems, personnel policies, task assignments, supervision patterns, and other areas. The principal difficulty, however, lies not in the ability to put new people in different organizational boxes, but in accurately diagnosing organizational problems. Oftentimes changes do not respond to overriding organizational problems. They only serve the ego needs of senior staff. Cosmetic change strictly for show, and unrelated to identified organizational problems, not only is doomed to failure but also is likely to further impede performance. Take, for example, the case of federal expenditures for Aid to Families with Dependent Children (AFDC). Between 1970 and 1973 funding increased some threefold from 6.25 million to 1.9 billion dollars per year. Nevertheless, the question remained whether such expenditures had their intended impact. The Government Accounting Office (GAO)[4] wanted to know if the goal of getting people off welfare was being achieved.

In a rather elaborate study, GAO set out to evaluate the social services provided to AFDC recipients in order to determine whether: (a) such services effectively help recipients achieve self-support or reduce dependency, and (b) this goal, with its present nature of services and determination, could be realistically achieved.

GAO defined social services as developmental services, or those services that could directly assist recipients to achieve self-support or reduced dependency. These services included counseling or referrals to job-training programs, job training, or job placement, and provision of maintenance services that could help recipients sustain or strengthen family life—day care, for example.

The results, although negative, were not unexpected. The evaluation showed that social services had only a minor impact in directly helping recipients develop and use skills necessary to achieve reduced dependency or gain self-support. In a review of closed cases, the evaluation showed that in only 4.5 percent of the cases employment services had some direct impact with 2 percent showing decreased dependency.

The GAO report did acknowledge the existence of barriers to self-support not directly influenced by the provision of social services. Such barriers included limited employment and training opportunities and child-care facilities. Although such conditions did mitigate program impact, the report stated that program administration would have to be improved if goals were to be achieved.

Four major delivery weaknesses were highlighted in the report. First, that local welfare departments do not have adequate systems to assess a recipient's self-support potential; hence, they cannot ensure that service resources are allocated for maximum benefit. Agencies were criticized for leaving service decisions to the subjective judgments of caseworkers who are less able to objectively assess recipient potential. Second, caseworkers have not fully understood program goals or their roles, and their ability to effectively interact with recipients has decreased. Also, there is an insufficient number of caseworkers as caseloads increase.

Third, federal leadership has not been aggressive enough. Fourth, program accountability has not been emphasized.

In this instance, GAO has provided an in-depth diagnosis of social service organizational-delivery programs. Unfortunately, many organizations are reluctant to accept the notion that anything could possibly be wrong with their operations. If agencies behave in this manner, then it is a rather safe bet they are on the lower end of the performance spectrum. Agencies receiving this treatment, or a similar type of external critique, should initiate an in-depth analysis of findings in order to generate corrective recommendations.

The first issue to be faced is whether program goals are realistically set. If not, then measures should be taken to change them. If it is determined that the objectives not only are realistic, but also have social significance, then it is incumbent upon the operating agency to improve and develop the delivery mechanism so it is able to achieve these designated outcomes.

In the difficult, but often fruitful, search for corrective actions, it should first be ascertained if the organization is structurally able to handle the delivery process. For example, as the GAO report points out, such agencies as the Department of Labor and the local contract organizations are involved in delivering services. Here it is important to ensure that linking and coordinating mechanisms are well-developed and in place. Similarly, internal links should be formalized, especially in social service organizations where service delivery is oftentimes fragmented by program area.

In terms of potential or actual problems, efforts should be made to determine whether program results are hampered by low-motivation and job-interest levels, excessive intergroup conflict, or the like. There should be concern whether organizational procedures are designed to enhance goal achievement—as is the case when supportive client and community resource data, formalized needs assessment systems, and feedback information are used to determine whether adequate services were delivered. Also, attempts should be made to improve individual functioning by examining knowledge and competence in the area of AFDC. When weaknesses are found, training efforts should be designed to mediate these effects.

Organizational problems are amenable to solution if the commitment is made to systematically diagnosis, critically analyze, and implement recommendations for improvement. Problems remain problems when there is no effort made to uncover the reasons behind them or their solutions. Many times the activities needed for a Holmesian investigation into organizational problems entail more money, time, and energy than organizations are willing to expend. It is much easier to complain about how poorly things are being done than to discover why they are done poorly. Many times people fear that organizational Sherlocks will pinpoint their department, job, or even them as the villain responsible for problems. Investigations are difficult to conduct without the cooperation of the organization. Change, or the threat of change, can have far-reaching impacts on an organization and on the people in it.

MEETING THE DEMAND FOR ORGANIZATIONAL CHANGE

As our human service organizations rapidly approach the post-Orwellian date of the year 2000, we can expect to encounter significant forces for change from within and outside the system. The increasing complexity of operationalizing existing delivery mechanisms and constant growth in service eligible populations either will serve to cause the system to collapse or will signal major and drastic change in the delivery process. Since the "future" is actually here today, social service managers must learn to cope with, adjust to, accept, and utilize their creative instincts to bring about organizational innovation and change. In order to accomplish this feat and to adapt existing organization to future trends, the manager must be adept at identifying forces for change presently at work within and outside organizational systems.

In general, everyday organizational growth and development indicates that an organization is continually changing. It is rare for an organization to go years, or even months, without change. The kind of change we are addressing here is intentional change. Intentional change requires diagnosis, analysis, implementation, and follow-up evaluation. It is this kind of change that human service agencies need in order to answer their critics with any kind of clarity or determined action. Intentional change brings a method to the madness of random organizational growth and development.

Organizational Diagnosis

The decision to make changes in an orderly manner requires an assessment of the present situation and a desire to get from the present to a future goal. Change then becomes harnessed and directed, rather than something which just happens. Runaway innovation for its own sake is hardly conducive to establishing organizational effectiveness. Just as management selection and development programs require planning, so do overall organizational-effectiveness designs.

Problem investigation actually starts the change process. By stopping to look and to ask questions about itself, an organization is headed toward intentional innovation. It is through investigation and diagnosis that an organization becomes aware of problem areas, thus pinpointing places to begin change. Those who embark on the diagnosis become catalysts in developing a systematic view and procedure toward change. By asking pertinent questions, those people charged with the diagnosis from inside the organization or those hired as consultants start the organization's thinking in terms of unaccustomed perspectives. Verbalization of feelings and of situational circumstances and awareness of different perceptions within the organization opens up many eyes and initiates a commitment to change—a commitment at least at the diagnostic phase. It also serves to arouse curiosity and to stimulate interest in the whole process of change. People begin to think of new ways to do things and begin to approach their feelings for the organization in a different manner.

Organizational diagnosis is best accomplished when it views the organization as a system. A system implies interrelationships and dependencies among parts. The basic components of an interacting system (as outlined in Chapter 1) are inputs, thruputs (processes), and outputs. Inputs and outputs are the foundations for realizing that every system is but a subsystem of even larger systems and subsystems. Also, in a system view, there is recognition that an agency influences and is influenced by the environment (politics, economics, client demands) outside its immediate boundaries.

Once this systemwide perspective is established, such areas as structures, types of tasks, technologies, and environments, people, leadership style, and motivation all come under the range of organizational analysis and change, and the study becomes more comprehensive and demanding. Hopefully, it lessens inclinations toward developing and imposing one best way of structure and change technique for all agencies. Basically, the system perspective of diagnosis and change gives an organizational consultant a broader range of contingent factors to acknowledge, investigate, and consider as influential in the makeup of an agency's character or climate. It also helps the consultant remain aware of the differences within and among organizational climates.

As mentioned before, correct diagnosis of the problem areas is probably the most crucial phase in organizational change.[5] The tone and commitment to change are essentially established in the diagnostic period. Most of the burden for setting this tone rests on those who conduct the diagnosis—the consultants. Organizational consultants can be from inside or outside the organizational system. It cannot be stressed strongly enough how important it is for those participating in organizational-change efforts to create an atmosphere of trust. After all, we tend to shy away from medical diagnosticians we do not trust. The same holds true for organizational consultants. The most accurate information and pertinent symptoms are obtained from those who have confidence in the people who are asking the questions.

Probably the most crucial point in organizational diagnosis (besides deciding what to do with the information collected) is to enter into an agreement with the organization. That agreement and willingness to undertake a change effort should be based on trust and faith that information will be held in confidence. Building trust between consultant and the client system is absolutely necessary for a change effort.

To a large degree, impressions made in the initial contact set the tone and path of the entire process. The relationship between the client organization and the change consultants is established at this point. An atmosphere of trust or mistrust and, consequently, the quality of information gathered and the accuracy of problem diagnosis often hinges on the first impressions made by the consultants.

Focus of the diagnosis for change should be on the entire organization, not just the top. Without viewing the organization as the client of the study, commitment and support dwindle, perspectives become distorted, and chances for system-wide change and perspective substantially decrease. The consultant should always remain aware that the client is the system. The consultant and client are better-able to discover the most effective-change technique once the diagnostic focus has become the system and an attempt is made to examine structure, process, and human relations perspectives. Nothing serves better to ensure an appropriate renewal of organizational change than a comprehensive analysis. Essential to building a trusting relationship and gathering accurate data is stress on the confidentiality of gathered information from individuals. Also essential is the consultant's projected image of assisting the total agency system. Whatever method is used to gather information (interviews, questionnaires, or other means) requires that a foundation of trust be established before anything solid is built from the resources at the disposal of the consultants and the organization. Interview and questionnaire diagnoses will crumble if their framework is not built on mutual confidence and understanding of what the process is. Both the consultant and agency must, from the start, agree on why and how the process will be conducted. People who neither trust the questioner, nor understand why the questions are being asked, feel no great commitment to divulge accurate information, and chances are they will feel no commitment to resultant change efforts.

Overall, diagnosis is best done when it is based on group perceptions of the activity's value and utilizes systemwide perspective to gather its data. This approach to determining organizational effectiveness, based on goal and process, has systemwide parameters. Structure, process, interpersonal relationships, individual competency, and other human relationships will all be effected by change and should therefore be a part of organizational-diagnosis technique and perspective.

Organizational Analysis

Upon completion of the diagnostic phase, the next step is analysis of the collected information. A good entry and trust-producing diagnostic phase will generate a great deal of wide-ranging information. Perceptions and perspectives from every area of the organization can present an awesome, even confusing, picture of the organization. One might begin to wonder whether even a meaningful collage could be developed from such a collection of organizational snapshots. By using a variety of focuses, angles, and lenses, however, the developed picture takes on a three-dimensional character. The detail and accuracy of such a picture far surpasses that of a single photo taken from one perspective.

Information obtained from a systems approach ensures the possibility of a more encompassing analysis than that which can be derived from solely looking at the agency. A systems diagnostic framework gathers information on the agency, its environment, the structure, the process, and the people-based problems. Analysis is made based on those parts. At this point, the consultant must step back and piece together all that the organization has told about itself. Out of facts and impressions will emerge patterns and areas of concern that are consistently delineated by organization members. These patterns will begin to narrow problem sources. An objective-analytical eye should be able to pick up these recurring themes and the more pertinent problem areas.

Impressions of possible problem areas begin to form even during early diagnostic activities. A tour through the organization can provide a wealth of information on the structure, the tasks, the processes, the interpersonal relationships, and the general organizational atmosphere. From then on, the data gathered confirm, refute, and build on these first impressions.

Analysis is both a looking backward and forward process. A review of notes made during interviews and compilation of questionnaire data puts the present organizational atmosphere into focus. In other words, analysis is the point where all that was gathered during diagnosis is put into perspective. In this sense, it looks backward. Good diagnosis and analysis will include a history of the organization so that one can achieve an understanding of why the organization exists as it does.

Organizational analysis also begins to look forward to the actual change process. An idea of where the organization is now opens the way to where it can be in the future. Methods, strategies, and change result from a developed sense of where the organization is and where it wishes to go. Understanding the present and the future hopes of the organization triggers the consultant to think in terms of change strategies that will help the organization coherently bridge the two time orientations with minimum difficulty and maximum benefit.

By the time the search for information is completed, problem areas are somewhat outlined in the consultant's mind. The opportunity to organize and add detail to the outline comes with analysis of the organization as it is presented to the consultant. From this outline, an encompassing organizational narrative can be written complete with setting, characters, action, plots, and subplots. Just as an author must be able to analyze the possibilities for an interesting storyline from these parts, so must a consultant be able to assess the possibilities to develop an effective organization from the given diagnostic information.

The consultant, however, should not be the sole author of this organizational-change narrative. The organization itself must be the co-author in order for the story to be complete and win critical acceptance. The analysis and plans for change will face their toughest critics in the organization itself. From the start, therefore, the best method for ensuring acceptance of change is to include the organization in designing plans. The organization is the most important source of the information on problem areas; equally, it is an important source of information on solutions within the organization's boundaries.

Analysis is not totally in the hands of the consultants. As mentioned before, just by beginning diagnosis, people start to acquire a different type of thinking about their organization. This circumstance very often triggers new awareness and perceptions. Although they may not always recognize it as such, the agency people are analyzing their work environment as they gain a wider perspective of all that makes up the organization.

In order for change strategies to be accepted, therefore, the implementation plan must include suggestions on areas of change in which agency people appear most excited and committed. Analysis consultants must take into account that by coming to help the organization and asking thought-provoking organizational questions, they have opened new vistas for the agency people. These new horizons create a vested interest by agency people in the change process. To forget them in analysis or in a change of plans will virtually doom the intentional-change effort to failure.

Once the analysis of the client system is made, a formal change process begins. The agency has already undergone some informal changes (seeing itself from a different viewpoint) by the mere presence of the consultant. The remaining task is to channel the change effort so that it most benefits the organization, those in it, and those connected with it.

ORGANIZATIONAL-CHANGE IMPLEMENTATION

Intentional or managed change can be handled in a number of ways. To carry out change, diagnosis and analysis are not necessary in some cases. However, for the best effort the consultant or catalytic agent of change should have an in-depth knowledge of the organizational values and norms. Some form of diagnosis should, therefore, precede a change effort. As we have stressed, a systemwide diagnosis is best by virtue of its broad scope.[6]

The actual plan for directed organizational change grows out of the diagnostic and analysis process. By this time, the consultants have become aware of the organization's problems and have an idea how to deal with them; however, the choice of a change strategy can make or break the entire effort. Introduction of any wide-ranging change is a delicate operation. A comprehensive diagnosis, but the wrong prescription for a cure, can make the patient worse.

An organizational patient actually has a lot more to say to determine the cure than the medical patient. From the beginning, the agency and the consultant have been partners. The agency's understanding of the helping effort by consultants and the importance of the agency's own insights have built a mutual trust that allows a partnership to exist and, thus, develop a remedy for the agency's ailments. Agency input is important for every phase of the change effort. To discover solutions to its problems and to institute change, the actual change strategy should therefore rely on the organization itself. This type of change is known as intervention theory. Argyris is its foremost proponent.[7]

A brief explanation of intervention theory is in order. An interventionist is a consultant. Intervention is to enter an ongoing system with the purpose of assisting it. The implicit assumption behind intervention is the independence of the consultant and the client system. This situation allows the client system the opportunity to make its own decisions rather than having to rely on the consultant to make decisions.

The consultant has these tasks:

1. Help the client system generate valid information about itself as a total system.
2. Give the client system free choice among alternatives so that decision-making is placed on the client and not on the consultant.
3. Develop a feeling of ownership (thus, commitment in the client system) about the choice made.

Accomplishment of these three tasks results in a powerful commitment to change by the client system. Discovery of their own strong and weak points, and decision on actions to deal with them, creates a vested interest and commitment to see them implemented. Like any architect, after developing the change blueprints, the agency has an interest and obligation to oversee onsite construction.

The role of the consultant, then, is that of a facilitator. Consultant expertise is used to help the system develop its own information. The questions posed during diagnosis ask nothing of the agency that it does not already know. What they do is encourage verbalization and communication on problem areas and put everyday knowledge in a new light.

With the client system involved in every step of the change effort, the risk of defensiveness toward change is greatly lessened; therefore, when the consultant leaves, commitment toward change does not. An ongoing internal change process has developed which is backed by the client and not imposed by the consultant. The result can lead to greater organization health and capabilities for change adaptation.

Diagnosis of its own problems does not mean that the client system will not benefit from a consultant diagnosis. The consultant's job is not to impose analysis of the system on the organization, but to use his expertise to help the system arrive at its own diagnosis. The consultant must also be able to step back and not interfere when the client's analysis and change procedure differs from what might be best. The client's ownership of the data, knowledge, and problem-solving is the key to successful implementation of organizational change.

In effective organizational change, the organization is an integral part of the whole change process. Therefore, good consulting is more than entering the organization, conducting a diagnosis, analyzing data, and presenting a report. In fact, the biggest mistake an organizational consultant can make is to conduct a unilateral study and hand down a traditional consulting report. These kinds of sterile reports recommend consultant-generated changes and expect the organization to accept them with open arms and to implement change without question. In reality, this type report usually ends up stacked with all the other consultant reports on a forgotten shelf in the record room. When the agency feels apart from the consultant study, there is no reason to believe it will accept the recommendations coming out of that study. Criticism in any form is difficult to accept gracefully under the best of circumstances, but it certainly is more palatable, and even enlightening, when the recipient of constructive criticism is also the chief critic.

Gouldner[8] has outlined the differences between the consulting model that presents a rational report and assumes the organization to follow through, and the model that assists and uses the client system as a partner in the change process. He has also outlined the different perspectives of report-oriented consulting, and/or partnership-consulting. These differences are basically those that have been outlined in Chapter 4.

The strategy used by the consultant to guide the agency in identifying problem areas is also crucial. Improper guidance at this point can negate the entire effort. A good organizational consultant is not tied to one method. Those who use only one technique are most likely to introduce an unsuitable, or even harmful, change strategy. Diagnosis, analysis, and partnership with the agency are futile when organizations and their problems are treated alike through standard change practices. Utilization of a strategy because it worked before does not mean it will work in all situations.

The best consultants operate from the viewpoint that there is no best way to structure an organization, nor is there an all-purpose change technique. Ideally, the models of organizational diagnosis and change a consultant uses should be encompassing enough to prevent the consultants being locked into a narrow analytical perspective or into a single-change technique. This framework also requires a great deal of organization input to obtain an understanding of the organization's particular climate and character. Wider consultant perspective, more comprehensive diagnosis, and more opportunity for organizational input present more available options to institute change and gain greater organizational effectiveness.

The Trauma of Change

Beyond the decision to innovate, the process of change itself can be traumatic both at individual and organizational levels. Think, for instance, how hard it is to part with an old, favorite piece of clothing.

You become used to something familiar, its ease of use and easy fit. Old organizations are like old sweaters—they become comfortable. Change can be threatening, traumatic, and confusing, if poorly executed. Consequently, it is important for the manager not only to know what to change, but how to bring about the change. Many good ideas have died because they could not be integrated into the organizational setting. Change-process facilitation is a high-price skill—one which few social service managers currently possess. As we have seen before, effective change facilitators must have extensive knowledge and expertise both in organization and in human relations skills.

Before initiating organizational change, one should be aware of potential areas of concern. The following statements outline some of these possible trouble spots. Shifting responsibilities or tasks are inherent in organizational change. This situation can be threatening to the status of certain individuals. Some of the biggest arguments and roadblocks to change occur over job titles on the organization chart. In addition, during the alteration process, there is constant employee fear that jobs will be cut, and that his will be among them.

Also, confusion can arise over new roles, authority, missions, and relationships. When individuals are physically moved into new work environments, there is initial unfamiliarity with colleagues and work behavior which necessitates creation of new interpersonal relationships. Similarly, such alterations mean employees have to develop not only new working relationships, but also new friendships. Breaking someone away from a long-time lunch or coffee-break partner can have serious performance consequences if the employee is not helped to develop new informal relationships or contacts.

Change also has the tendency to disrupt both formal and informal coordinating linkages, especially if movement is outside a program area. Such movements can cause loss of employee commitment to, or identification with, the new organizational unit. In the same manner, there is general unfamiliarity with standard operating procedures which often causes a loss of self-esteem when performance does not immediately meet previously held personal standards. Likewise, there is always the problem of individual misassignment or placing employees in job situations where they are plainly not able to properly function.

In conjunction with shifting people, it is crucial to ensure that resources and equipment are likewise reallocated if the innovation is to be successful. Therefore, if potentially disruptive problems are to be minimized, just as much attention should be paid to planning as is paid to the actual implementation of change.

Limiting Factors of Change

Consequently, managers must be aware of certain inherent organizational limitations to change and innovation. First, most employees will feel threatened and insecure at the slightest hint of suggested change. Since employees have a proprietary interest in their current work environments, they should be concerned, as their jobs can be dislocated in a change situation.

Second, individual organization units and programs become highly defensive and overly critical of change, especially if they have had free access to substantial resources and, thus, have substantial influence. Change in this instance can be viewed as a power play by the "under-privileged" to steal resources and personnel. In this case, change becomes one more danger signal which calls for revamping of the circumstances to prevent the loss of resources, personnel, and power.

Third, reorganization basically tends to deal with tangible and visible elements; thus, it does not take into account the crucial role of the informal communication links that allowed the old organization to perform. Similarly, functional work teams can become dislodged if great care is not taken to maintain them. This situation is why many organizations which are involved in major overhaul immediately experience significant drops in productivity. Such reduced levels of performance will continue until the informal lines of communication, coordination, and functional work teams are reestablished.

Finally, when change is mandated from senior-management levels without participative decision-making, many of the informal procedures and relationships that assisted in accomplishing work and making the job bearable are overlooked and disrupted.

Most, if not all, of these traumatic and limiting-change factors can be avoided when the total organization is involved in the effort from the beginning. Change for greater organizational effectiveness is a difficult and complex process. Systemwide and participative diagnosis, analysis, and change implementation, however, tend to avoid the pitfalls of intentional innovation and result in longer lasting, effective change.

NOTES

1. Peter F. Drucker, "Managing the Public Service Institution," Public Interest 33 (Fall 1973), pp. 43-60.

2. Rensis Likert, *The Human Organization* (New York: McGraw-Hill, 1967).

3. Michael Cohen and John Collins, "Some Correlates of Organizational Effectiveness", Public Personnel Management 3 (November-December 1974), pp. 493-499.

4. U.S. General Accounting Office, *Comptroller General's Report to the Congress, Social Services: Do They Help Welfare Recipients Achieve Self-Support or Reduced Dependence?* (June 27 1973), pp. 1-6.

5. Harry Levinson, *Organizational Diagnosis* (Cambridge, Mass., Harvard University Press 1972), pp. 3-52.

6. Edgar F. Huse, *Organizational Development and Change* (St. Paul, Minn: West Publishing 1975), pp. 30-61.

7. Huse, ibid., pp. 92-95.

8. Alvin Gouldner, "Theoretical Requirements of the Applied Social Sciences," American Sociological Review 22 (February 1957), pp. 92-102.

Chapter 5

ORGANIZING FOR SERVICE DELIVERY

INTRODUCTION

The discussion on organizational diagnosis, analysis, and change implementation in Chapter 4, although it was not labeled as such, was a general description of organizational development (OD). It emphasized effectiveness from an organizationwide perspective. To round out the discussion on the three-pronged approach to organization performance, Chapter 5 continues the organizationwide perspective. Emphasis here is on OD as a change process. Organizational development is first presented graphically, and Chapter 5 is punctuated by examples of the process in the human service setting. Previous chapters have shown that there are many potential change areas in an organization. Special attention in Chapter 5 is placed on structural reorganization as a selected organizational modification designed to alleviate an identified problem area. Four types of possible organizational structure for the human services are delineated. Reorganization is not always the answer (though it often is prescribed as a cure-all) for solving organizational problems. However, there are times when it is appropriate. Reorganization is used here as an example of a systematic change effort because it is the type innovation that easily lends itself to visual impacts and example, and, therefore, must concern itself with almost every other aspect of the organization.

CHANGE THROUGH ORGANIZATIONAL DEVELOPMENT

The techniques for improving organizational effectiveness through systematic implementation of change have become formalized through a process called organizational development (OD). Beckhard[1] defines organizational development as an organizationwide effort managed from the top, designed to increase organizational effectiveness and health through planned interventions in the organization's processes by using behavioral-science knowledge. The goal of this procedure then is to improve an organization's performance characteristics.

In order to fully understand Beckhard's definition of OD, it is essential to understand what he means by organizational effectiveness. He describes it in this manner:

1. Work is managed toward goal achievement.

2. Form or structure follows function or tasks to be accomplished.

3. Decisions are made near the sources of information, regardless of relative position in the organization.

4. Personnel are rewarded or punished for performance or lack thereof.

5. Communication is undistorted in all directions.

6. Win/lose situations and conflict are held to a minimum.

7. Conflict is focused on ideas, not interpersonal difficulties.

8. Organization is an interactive "open system."

9. There are feedback mechanisms.

10. A management strategy exists to support the effective organization.

Beckhard also cites certain conditions that call for OD efforts, such as the need to improve or change: (1) managerial strategies; (2) organizational climate and attitudes; (3) cultural norms; (4) structure and roles; (5) intergroup relationships; (6) communication patterns; (7) planning processes; (8) work-force motivation; (9) organizational adaptability to new situations and environment.

In general, the OD effort can be envisioned as a five-stage process diagrammed in Figure 5-1. The remainder of discussion will elaborate on and provide examples for a better understanding of these five stages of organizational development.

The Need for Change

The first requirement for change is an awareness of the need for it. While change is both inevitable and continuous, it need not imply

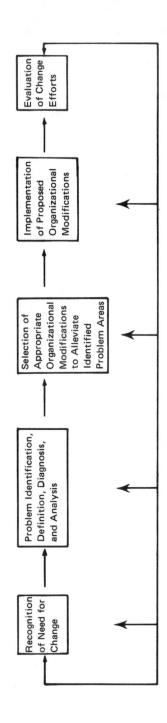

Figure 5.1: STAGES OF ORGANIZATIONAL DEVELOPMENT

105

constant organizational upheaval. In fact, change strategies that cause major dislocation are introduced over a relatively short time span and are doomed to eventual failure. The louder the pronouncements of immediate success are, then the more likely it is to be a flash-in-the-pan operation. One of the most prevalent forms of organizational change is reorganization.

As Hays[2] indicates, while reorganization is no panacea for low effectiveness or efficiency, there are times when it can be useful and even essential. For example, reorganization might be indicated when: (1) organizations change their mission and focus, which necessitates new structural and personal relationships; (2) there are severe budgetary cutbacks calling for consolidation and retrenchment; (3) new technologies have been developed that are not compatible with existing structural limitations; (4) there are significant personnel and philosophy changes in senior management positions; (5) the organization has grown too large and in such a helter-skelter fashion that existing management systems are unable to cope with the random growth; (6) there is a sense that, although the mission is being carried out in an acceptable but mediocre fashion, the organization has a hidden capacity to make additional, significant impacts.

If an organization fits any of these categories, then maybe the need for reorganization does exist. Nevertheless, in a truly adaptive structure, reorganization comes about through evolution—not revolution. There are, of course, instances when drastic actions must be taken.

The inevitable panic, confusion, falling morale, and lowered performance that typically accompany reorganization can be avoided if change is gradually introduced with the employees' full knowledge and consent over a long time frame. The most long-lasting and effective efforts at reorganization are those that are unnoticeable to the casual viewer. There will be more about this later.

Problem Identification

For the purpose of example, let us assume there is an organizationwide feeling that all is not well and that something should be done. The next step is to formalize this "feeling" and begin to identify problems that would be amenable to change and reorganization. Assume further that the organization discussed is a local district office or a county social service department responsible for delivering a whole range of services and maintenance programs. For example, local offices are directed to provide services which work toward these national goals:

1. Achieve or maintain economic self-support, or prevent, reduce, or eliminate dependency.

2. Achieve or maintain self-sufficiency.

3. Prevent or remedy neglect, abuse, or exploitation of children and adults who are unable to protect their own interests and preserve, rehabilitate, or reunite families.

4. Prevent or reduce inappropriate institutional care by providing for community-based care, home-based care, or other forms of less intensive care.

5. Secure referral or admission for institutional care when other forms are not appropriate, or provide services to individuals in institutions.

Policy Problems

In order to carry out such mandates, local offices must offer a variety of services that include: adoption; day care; adult and child protective services; social welfare education; family planning; social group services to senior citizens, transportation, information, and referral; homemaker, housekeeper, health-related information; foster care for children and adults; and employment services while immense in monetary terms constitute only a small fraction of county agency budgets. In the state of New York, for instance, services account for approximately 8 percent of local budgets, with the bulk of money spent on income maintenance (27 percent) and medical assistance (32 percent).[3]

Management Problems

While providing services to eligible individuals is of strategic managerial importance, it palls in relationship to the management problems faced in implementing mandated medical and income-maintenance programs. For example, in December of 1974, 1,396,271 people in the state of New York were receiving public assistance at an annual cost of over $1.5 billion. Audit- and quality-control data showed overpayments registered in 29.7 percent of AFDC cases. In the state of New York local districts are responsible for verification of client assertions during application and recertification for public assistance. Additionally, districts are given the added chores of administering: work programs, such as the Work Incentive Program (WIN); food stamps; supplemental aid for aged, blind, and disabled; emergency assistance; interim assistance during Social Security determination, and others. Add to this over $2 billion spent on Medicaid and the Child Health Assurance Program and you have an administrative nightmare at the point where all these services and programs are provided—the local districts.

The basic identifiable problem with such an obvious plethora of mandated services and programs is deciding how to organize in order to provide for their most efficient and effective delivery. Such demands for social services have sent local welfare costs spiraling to the point where the ability to pay no longer exists. In fact, Senator William Smith, chairman of the New York Senate Social Services Committee, states, "Somewhere along the line we must balance our social efforts against the ability of our people to pay for them. We must weigh adequacy against equity. By blindly attempting to be all things to a people we may spend ourselves into bankruptcy."

Smith goes on to point out that New York's AFDC benefit is 55 percent above the $7742 national average value of welfare benefits for a family of four (including food stamps and medical assistance). It is interesting to note for comparative purposes that the official HEW poverty level for a nonfarm family of 4 is $5038, some $2704 below what an average family receives on welfare.[4] He also goes on to note that in Great Britain, where free medical services are available to all, the per-capita expenditure for such services is $131. In the state of New York, where free medical services are available only to a limited population, the per-capita cost is $102 for a comparable year.[5]

Senator Smith is raising two important questions. First, a policy question—how many public dollars should be spent for those in need of assistance, and at what relative affluence level should they be maintained? Second, a management question—how can the state of New York better-organize and administer the delivery of services and assistance to cut waste and prevent payments to those without legitimate entitlement and, at the same time, provide an adequate level of assistance to those in need?

The first question involves policy matters that require legislative and executive attention. However, local districts should have input into policy areas, although they legally cannot make independent assistance and service-level determinations. In the area of administrative efficiency and capacity, on the other hand, significant local district improvement can be made.

The steady increase in demand for social services is caused by a combination of factors: the breakdown of the nuclear family, liberalized federally regulated eligibility standards, welfare benefits which exceed wages earned in low-paying jobs, a passing of the traditional stigma to view welfare as charity for society's outcasts, and a declining economic base in local districts which produced administrative and fiscal chaos.

Separation of Services and Paraprofessionals for Effectiveness

In an effort to respond to these trends, social service organizations, spurred by federal and state mandates, have attempted reorganization to promote more efficient service delivery. The overload of clients and cases had put such a heavy administrative burden on professional social workers that traditional services and consultation could not be provided. Consequently, in the late 1960s, attempts were made to separate the functions of service provision and income maintenance. After this innovation, known as separation of services, another major reordering followed—acceptance of paraprofessionals as members of the social service delivery structure.

In theory, the paraprofessional would be trained for the specific duties of welfare- or income-maintenance examiner to handle intake certifications and recertifications. This situation would free the professional social worker to engage in activities related to the social well-being of clients.

Perhaps the idea was sound, but it faltered in application. Some of the reasons for failure of this approach are: (1) inability to develop sufficient backup data and computer systems; (2) inadequate income-maintenance examiner training: (3) lack of acceptance and understanding by professional social workers who strongly resisted bifurcation efforts because they felt threatened by the new class of workers and were strongly tied to traditional client-professional relationships; (4) inadequate planning before instituting such a drastic delivery innovation.

THE SEARCH FOR A PROPER STRUCTURE

Application of objective program-performance measures, such as those used that the GAO report previously cited (Chapter 4, ref. 4), indicated that while separation of services did bring some order to a chaotic administrative situation, it did not meet primary service goals. As a result, the search is on for another structural system that can meet the dual demands of improved service delivery and administrative coherence. There is, however, no standard organizational model complete with available options that can be used to deal with specific strengths and weaknesses caused by the addressed problem area.

The truth is that any organization, no matter how ineptly designed, will function well if the employees so wish. The trick to making organizations effective is to shift energy away from making the system work to enabling individuals to perform.

If the existing structure requires constant tampering to hold it together, then maybe it is a candidate for organizational renewal. In any attempt to make an organization function better, emphasis should be placed not on making the structure more complex and difficult to manage, but on simplifying procedures, relationships, and formats. There is elegance in simplicity, while chaos follows complexity.

It is no mean feat to design an organization with crossed, dotted, and splayed lines of authority. The skilled organizational practitioner knows that even though a concrete, concise, and complete design takes more time and effort, it pays off in easier implementation. Before a line is changed on an organization chart, it must first be determined what the problems are and what their subsequent consequences for the agency are that reorganization will solve.

Organizational analysis and diagnosis can provide new organizational structure and processes. If the diagnosis is faulty, then proposed solutions will follow suit. Prior to structural change, it is imperative that a clear understanding and agreement be made on the mission, scope, goals, and objectives of the organization, both now and in the future. Consequently, a review of program structures, delivery strategies, procedures, systems, functions, and activities must be undertaken to determine possible shortcomings and potential improvements in each area. Accomplishing this task necessitates compiling an inventory of objectives, major tasks, and functional activities, in addition to identifying areas which need improved coordination, communication, and cooperation.

Once these activities are accomplished, then and only then should the task of reorganization be undertaken. When one designs a new structure, or modifies an old one, special attention must be paid to developing a structure that will simplify coordination and communication, consolidate functional activities where possible, reduce overlap and duplication, fix responsibility to program action, minimize ambiguity, and provide for adequate supervision and control.

After agreement on structural changes has been reached, the proposed design should be compared with current structure, available staff, program requirements, and physical space. This step helps to define: (a) changes in type and quantity of staff relationships needed to make the new structure work; (b) changes, upgrades, or abandonment of physical facilities; (c) short- and long-term costs in implementing the new organizational strategy; and (d) problems that might be directly related to the newly imposed organizational structure.

To a manager on the firing line, all these words of wisdom and caution might ring hollow. If organizational restructuring has a potential-performance benefit, more must be done than merely telling others how to do it. The true test of concept and theory is in application. It might be helpful to demonstrate practical reorganization strategies by carrying through to conclusion the previous example of problems in administration of local social service districts.

Lack of Program Integration: An Example of Reorganization Strategy

As mentioned earlier, the concept of service separation facilitated organizational performance in some areas (client processing), but caused agency dislocations in others. Copeland[6] cites lack of a managerial concept of program integration as the major social service delivery problem.

Typically, local social service agencies administer a group of programs that nearly always include: Aid to Dependent Children, Medicaid, food stamps, and general assistance and services. As proof of integration shortcomings, Copeland points to the separate eligibility systems used for each program. For instance, each uses different client questionnaires and forms, separate calculation logics, different eligibility criteria, federal-audit standards, quality-control systems, and different training methods. Although he indicates that system integration could be achieved through the legislative process, this situation does not seem likely. Nevertheless, integration could be carried out at the local level where agencies have control of their own physical organizational and fiscal program elements.

In order to accomplish this, four subsystems should be fully developed—eligibility, fiscal, service, planning and management. The first subsystem to be improved under Copeland's plan would be the eligibility subsystem. Integration would call for a single point of entry, a single processing stream, and a single management of eligibility for all means-tested cases. An integrated eligibility system is expected to result in lower administrative costs because processing duplication is reduced, thus the number of clients workers can handle is increased. In addition, ancillary costs, such as training, supervision, and the number of payment errors, should decline.

Mistakes in Organizational-Structural Design

According to Drucker, there is no such thing as a perfect organization; at best, an organization structure should not cause trouble. He goes on to outline common mistakes made in designing organizational structures. First, the most prevalent, serious mistake is maintaining a multitude of management levels. In other words, keep organizations as "flat" as possible in order to shorten the chain of command. Every additional organizational level makes it more difficult to attain a focus on objectives and direction, increases communication "noise," creates stress, acts as sources of inertia and friction, increases the time span to move managers up the hierarchy, and promotes overspecialization. Second, organizational structures should gear employee attention toward major organizational decisions, key activities, and performance rather than etiquette, procedure, proper behavior, and jurisdictional conflicts.

Third, a well-designed organization does not have to rely on an overabundance of coordinators and assistants in order to function. Such an abundance indicates that jobs have been too narrowly defined or organized according to skill and not results. When this happens, work becomes fragmented and requires coordinators to pull the various pieces together. This situation can cause friction, oversensitivity to feelings, and neglect of performance. Fourth, a reorganization has failed when common organizational problems recur, albeit in new forms or guise. This circumstance is indicative of unthinking application of organizational principles that treat the organization mechanically in attempts to solve deeply rooted performance problems simply. Fifth, if the new structure fosters continual meetings, it is a sign of organization failure. Drucker feels meetings are needed to help operating managers think through priorities, needs, and opportunities, but too many is a concession to organizational imperfection. As a rule, when managers below top levels spend more than 25 percent of their time in meetings, jobs have not been clearly defined, sufficiently structured, or made truly responsible.

Drucker goes on to say that organizational structure should not be allowed to evolve, but requires thinking, analysis, and a systematic approach. Also, managers should not start the process of designing organizational structure without first identifying and organizing the building blocks—activities that need to be included in the design. Finally, the structuring of an organization should follow a strategy. That is, the organizational structure decided upon is merely a means of attaining organizational objectives and goals. Therefore, work on structure must follow agreement that makes capable operation of key organizational activities occur. As Drucker states, "the key activities are the lead-bearing elements of a functioning structure." Drucker urges managers to focus on four questions when designing organizational building blocks:

1. What should the units of organization be?
2. What components should be joined and kept apart?

3. What size and shape pertain to different components?

4. What should their appropriate placement and arrangement be?

In addition, organizational structure must satisfy minimum requirements within these dimensions. First, a need for clarification exists so each member knows where he belongs; to whom he reports; and where he gets information, assistance, or decisions. Second, with an emphasis placed on performance—not on organizational upkeep—structure should promote the economy of effort needed to control and supervise. Third, organizational structure should direct managerial vision toward performance to make it possible for people to work for results. Fourth, organizational structure should enable personnel to understand both their own and the organization's tasks. Fifth, decisions must be forthcoming on the right issues at the appropriate level and be converted into commitment. Sixth, in order for organizations to perform, they need a degree of stability—but this does not imply system rigidity. Relationships cannot be constantly changing. Individuals need some consistency if performance is to be maintained. Seventh, at the same time, organizations must be self-renewing and flexible enough to adapt to new situations, demands, conditions, and personalities.[7]

The Informal Structure

The formal structure of an organization has a significant impact on its performance. Nevertheless, structural implications can be substantially modified by the managerial style and methods employed and the informal network of individual contacts and coordination that can supplement, or even bypass, the formal structure.

Nevertheless, sound organizational formats are essential elements in an overall design for organizational performance. A well-defined structural organization in detail spells out: relationships among individuals and departments, lines of authority, communication networks and channels, task responsibility and accountability, and job activities and functions. An organizational chart should not be used as a weapon to put "unruly" individuals and departments in their place, or as a means of justifying status and salary differentials. Rather, its primary use is to give those inside and outside the organization a notion of what the organization does and how things get accomplished. It is only a reference point, not a divine accounting, of the way the organization works.

Informal networks are to be encouraged, and not treated as subversive means for dissident employees to gain control and power. It is, after all, the informal organizational elements that bring life to the lines and dots on an organization chart. Attempts at overstructuralization will no doubt lead to organizational failure because it is impossible to take into account all potential manifestations of the informal structure.

Intervening Factors in Designing a Structure

Any organizational redesign effort should focus on general crucial intervening factors. For example, is the structure to promote centralized or decentralized decision-making and operations? Conceptually, most organizational specialists support decentralized decision-making. Such an approach implies that decisions be pushed down the hierarchy to bring them closer to the individuals with operational responsibility. Theoretically, this approach should improve service delivery because decisions can be made more quickly by utilizing locally generated data and information and making them more relevant to the client population. Decentralized decision-making promotes program diversity because many units are given autonomy and responsibility to conduct their businesses.

A word of caution—however—decentralization is not for the squeamish or for managers who must know every detail of every project. Managers who work in this type system must be able to tolerate, and even foster, the individuals' rights to make mistakes, but once recognized as mistakes, they are to be corrected. Benefits of a decentralized approach can be overshadowed unless line managers are highly competent, fully trained, and regularly evaluated.

Centralized decision systems, on the other hand, can be used when application of uniform implementation standards and quality control are required. Similarly, this type approach is applicable when multiple programs and territories must be integrated, promoting the need for common policy determination and centralized information and planning systems. In such organizations, decisions by design or tradition tend to end up at upper management levels, but as uniformity prospers, both timeliness and relevance suffer.

Organizations should take care to analyze specific duties to be performed in the new organizational setting. Management must determine relationships or support among tasks and functions, and tasks requiring similar data base, skills, or equipment. The geographical distribution of tasks and the permanent/temporary nature of functions should also be considered.

In addition, the structure should support the agency's management style. Consequently, consideration should be given to management factors, such as: the amount of desired flexibility; the expected degree of subordinate participation in decision-making; the amount of delegated authority and responsibility; the openness, direction, and speed of the communication system; the type supervision and control exercised by the supervisor; the legal contraints on where decisions can be made and by whom; and the number of people supervised (known as the span of management).

Similarly, the proposed functional interrelationships, coordination mechanisms, and accountability procedures must be taken into account. For example, an assessment must be made to determine the degree of close, continuous, or periodic coordination required by different functions, and the need for sharing resources. Likewise, determination must be made about the proper mix between line and staff, and the level of appropriate autonomy for specific tasks and functions.

Expected level of employee satisfaction with the system should also be considered. Organizational structures should provide for individual growth, development, and advancement, while avoiding individual loss in status, rank, or position. Also structures determine how many old work groups break up and form new groups as a result of dislocation. In addition, structure should take maximum advantage of individual skills, aptitudes, and experience, and provide large, interesting tasks to facilitate job satisfaction.

Additional concerns should focus on statutory or practical requirements for review boards, commissions, appeal procedures, and external relationships to be maintained for maximum performance. Consideration should also be given to the volume, type, and quantity of expected workload in an effort to avoid bottlenecks and unwieldy coordinating, control mechanisms. Provisions for easy access to public and client opinions, assistance, and information also must be made.

SELECTING ORGANIZATIONAL DESIGN

Once all these varied factors have been considered and appropriate determinations made, selection of an organizational design can be made in order to optimize chances of successfully accomplishing performance outcome. Although many organizational typologies exist with a multitude of possible variations, discussion here will center on three commonly used formats; functional (traditional line and staff), regional (decentralized), and matrix (team).

Functional

Most agencies which deliver social services at the local district level are organized by function, as described in Figure 5-2. This method is by

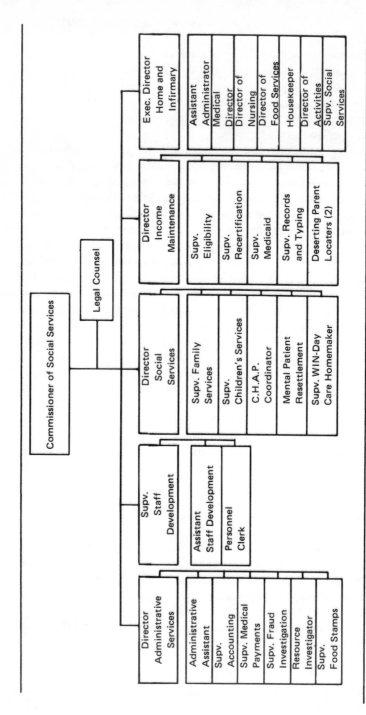

Figure 5.2: FUNCTIONAL ORGANIZATION

far the best to provide services. Generally, each service has a place at the top of the organizational hierarchy and is headed by a program director. Subunits, or individuals with direct function area input, are typically displayed in descending order according to size, status, or importance. In larger organizations, subunits are further divided.

Strengths of this organizational format center on its capacity to specify and order relationships among individuals and departments. Everyone knows his or her place, and lines of communication (who you may or may not talk to) are highly formalized. There is limited confusion in supervision since everyone has a boss. Supervision is forced downward because, in the centralized nature of control structure, there is uniformity in the command structure. In addition, this structure encourages specialization and differentiation of skills and tasks. Only senior managers have broad-scope knowledge or responsibility. This situation tends to lessen training requirements because knowledge is highly content specific. Since most of our social service organizations use some variant of this functional design, the method is familiar to most and requires the least effort and adaptation to make it work.

While the approach has structural strengths, there are some inherent weaknesses in it. For instance, because of its highly specialized nature, few individuals outside the top levels can see the overall picture or know where each function fits into the final mission of the agency. This narrowness promotes destructive competition for resources, recognition, and personnel among functional areas. Coordination occurs only at the program-director level, and limited provisions are made for horizontal communication among subunits. Coordination problems result. Limited opportunity exists to move information up the hierarchy since most communication is directed downward. This circumstance stifles attempts at participative decision-making. Similarly, there is limited opportunity to share resources, people, or ideas, because each functional area becomes its own entity, complete with organizational headhunters. Because the flow of communication and authority is downward, there is little delegation or responsibility. Therefore, jobs are limited in scope and fail to respond to employees' growth and motivational needs. The very shape of the organization, narrow at the top and wide at the bottom, appears to push decision-making away from operational centers to higher organizational levels. Thus, decisions are long in coming and often lack direct relevance to the current problem.

Separation of services commonly used at the local district level mandates that some type functional format be implemented. Even though suited to the implementation of service separation, functional organization aggravates other kinds of organizational problems. For example, this structure is not able to adequately cope with a poorly developed concept of program integration. Consequently, the search for a more effective organizational format necessarily requires a focus on the remaining two structural types.

Regional

The next approach is the regionalized structure, shown in Figure 5-3. This format is best adapted to program administration in large geographical areas, where organizations are substantial in size and handle large numbers of clients.

A geographically oriented structure has several inherent organizational advantages. First, it lowers organizational and responsibility levels and properly places the decision-making burden at the operating level. Second, it allows anu encourages client-agency interaction because it is physically close, less imposing, and facilitates feedback. Third, it is a more responsive system since it can more readily adapt to local conditions. Fourth, because of its localized nature, planning can be specific and based on a more accurate reading of existing and potential conditions. Fifth, there is opportunity for employee growth not only by moving within the regionalized structure and up to more senior coordinating levels, but also by attaining positions with greater responsibility and scope in area offices. Sixth, since areas are smaller and concise, employees have an opportunity to see the total scope and impact of the operation. This situation should reduce some destructive competition. Seventh, such a structure allows for local community recruitment and personnel-placement efforts.

There are some problems associated with this system. Basically, the approach calls for duplicate structures in each area. Efficiency suffers because of an inability to take advantage of the economies of scale. Also, it is difficult to adapt staffing requirements to seasonal- or client-population changes because a full range of programs must be provided in each area, despite relative differences in client size. In addition, the coordination problem is magnified because communication links among areas are established only at senior levels. Despite the advantage of adaptability, uniformity of application might suffer because of varied interpretations of rules and regulations. Finally, training or recruitment of area office administrators could prove to be difficult, since administrators must be familiar with many highly complex program procedures and processes. This step requires a technocrat-generalist of the highest order. Hence, the regional approach has

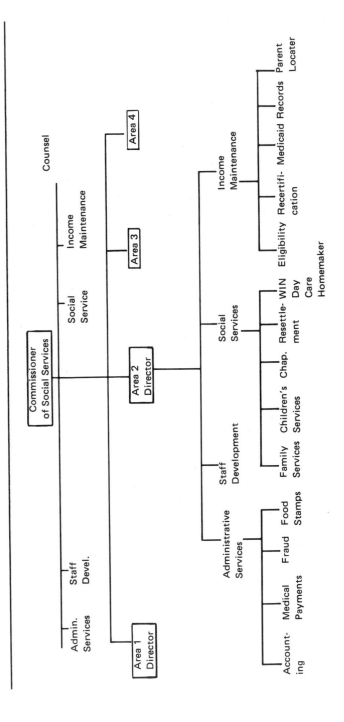

Figure 5.3: REGIONAL ORGANIZATION

119

key advantages, but it does little to solve the primary problem of program-managment integration.

The organizational format most able to cope with local district delivery and integration requirements is probably a matrix structure, or its variant.

Matrix

In order to be consistent and follow the format, a matrix organization which uses existing structural components could be depicted in the manner shown in Figure 5-4. Nevertheless, with some changes, the matrix format could provide the type structural integrity needed to integrate both programs and program administration. This feat could be accomplished by creating an organization designed in Figure 5-5.

The matrix organization provides process continuity and technical competence. This method is accomplished through a dual authority/responsibility network of relationships that produce a gridlike structure. A well-managed vertical flow allows for functional or program integrity. Each programmatic area is staffed by a specialist who can assure consistent, uniform administration of procedures and regulations across team boundaries. Horizontal relationships, on the other hand, provide program and client continuity with each individual's being treated by a team concept and no longer shunted from department to department or program to program.

The team is staffed by a combination of specialists, generalists, professionals, and support personnel. They are organized into service or program groupings and are headed by a team leader. The leader, along with all members, is responsible and accountable for team performance and client outcomes. Although team members have specific assignments, their main obligation is to enhance team functioning. Such an approach demands task flexibility of its members. Its antithesis is a "not my job" attitude. In this format, it is imperative that each and every member not be familiar with details but know the major activities of all the various areas within each jurisdiction. Additionally, since outcomes are stressed, not procedure, the team has ample opportunity to attempt innovative, creative approaches to service delivery and program objectives.

Similarly, this approach is conducive to applying MBO or productivity measurements that reward performance and allow flexible administration. Also, with the team approach, comparative evaluations can be made across team lines, provided healthy competition focuses on performance rather than resources and prestige disputes.

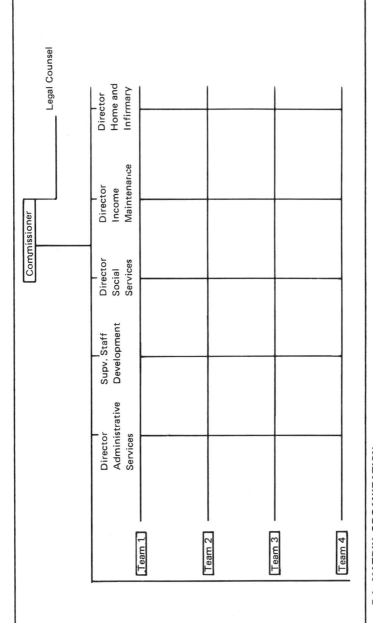

Figure 5.4: MATRIX ORGANIZATION

121

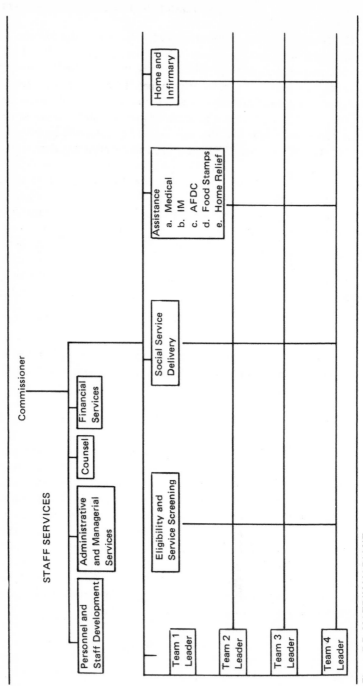

Figure 5.5: MATRIX VARIANT

The proposed matrix organization might function in this manner. A client comes to a district agency and requests assistance. Based on random, alphabetical, or geographical criteria, this individual is assigned to an agency team. The client then hopefully becomes the responsibility of the team from the initial determination until the eventual case closing. The next step is to make a rather detailed assessment of client needs and eligibility. This feat should be performed by integrating the eligibility unit across program lines. Initial eligibility determinations for various income- and medical-assistance programs are made and can be adequately handled by nonprofessional employees. Following these steps, a qualified professional makes a service assessment which details an action plan ready for implementation. The individual who makes the assessment would be responsible for ensuring that recommended services are adequately delivered and for helping the client achieve the previously determined treatment goals. In cooperation with various program and service areas, the plan is then implemented with assessment, eligibility, service, and assistance people who have regular meetings to discuss client progress and determine future needs and directions in specific cases.

Unfortunately, such drastic changes do not come inexpensively. There are some problems to be overcome. For example, a basic flaw in this approach is its ambiguity. This format demands the kind of individual who functions well in unstructured, open situations. It demands high tolerance for processing relationships and places a premium on intergroup cooperation and team accomplishment. There are no rules or procedures that can be recited to make these relationships clear because of the free-flowing pattern of service and assistance delivery. Hence, the team leader has to pay constant attention in order to maintain team functioning and viability. Although these individuals are responsible for overall team performance, they do not have control over functional areas. Team members provide and receive information, supervision, and direction from programmatic units and, at the same time, receive information, supervision, and facilitation from team leaders. It takes a very special type employee to be able to live and function in this environment. However, this employee is one which we must find or train, since matrix organizations and the team approach are the waves of the future.

IMPLEMENTING THE STRUCTURE

The next stage, perhaps the most crucial, difficult stage in the reorganization, is implementation. Regardless of the thoroughness of design, the expertness of manipulations, and the beauty of the new organizational chart, they will never be used unless there is active acceptance by the agency staff. It is possible to mandate acceptance. This approach achieves surface agreement, but does violent damage to the reorganization purpose itself—a search for integration, coordination, and cooperation.

The new structure cannot be expected to become fully operational in a short time period. Rather, it takes considerable time to break-in large innovative measures. Most massive structural changes do not meet their full increased performance potential for three years. Reorganization is neither an easy nor a short-term modification effort. Nevertheless, there are actions that can be taken that will at least assure greater chance for organizationwide acceptance of the new format. First, initial reorganization planning should be thorough by giving in-depth consideration to implementation and acceptance strategies.

Second, if planning is done properly, the reorganization announcement should be a surprise to no one. In fact, at all stages of the planning process, employees from every level of the organization should have ample opportunity for participation and feedback. This situation reduces potential confusion, apprehension about the future, and improves overall commitment. Consequently, there should be early, thorough dissemination of approved modifications and scheduled changes. Third, a new structure should not be thrust on an existing organization with a demand to immediately conform. Rather, it is advisable to have a gradual, coordinated phasing-in of reorganization in order to maintain organizational integrity and operational capability during the changeover period.

Fourth, in developing organizational modifications, it is essential to build in as many possible growth, challenge, reward, and advantage potentialities for employees. This step will aid them to develop trust rather than fear perceptions. Remember that employees, regardless of their dissatisfaction with the existing structure, fear the unknown more. Along the same line, keep reductions in grade, authority, and responsibility to a minimum. Attempt to qualify long-time employees for new jobs through training programs as much as possible, and attempt to absorb organizational reductions in force through attrition. Also, strong efforts should be made to transfer complete units and operational teams wherever practical.

Fifth, develop a mechanism for mutual coordination and exchange of facilities, supplies, equipment, and other resources among old and new organizational components. Sixth, in addition to phasing-in the new organizational format, it would be advisable to phase-in new people through gradual transfer of functional responsibility and authority. Nothing can have a more disconcerting impact on staff than to have their supervisor summarily wrenched from the unit and replaced by an unknown quantity of "dubious reputation," and with perceived evil intent.

Finally, since reorganization emphasizes structural changes, equal attention and effort should be paid to the process dimensions so important to successful implementation of organizational modifications. There are a host of behavioral and system techniques available to the modern manager who is concerned not only with building acceptance of organizational change, but also with ensuring its successful continuance. Some available formats are: team building, operational training, management development, retreats, workshops, managerial grid training, sensitivity training, organizational and self-analysis, instrumentation and intergroup-development exercises, management by objectives, System 4 management, job enrichment, and productivity-improvement methodologies.

EVALUATING THE STRUCTURE

The final stage, as in most change situations, is evaluation of the entire effort. Too many organizations abide by the assumption that if the modification is planned and implemented, then it must be successful. Nothing could be further from the truth. An attempt must be made to measure the performance of the organization under the new structural format against initial expectations and goals. In most cases, if the reorganization is handled properly, only minor adjustment will be needed to keep it accurately targeted on problem areas. Nevertheless, efforts should be taken to determine if production schedules are met, communications are processed smoothly, clients and staff are satisfied, and efficiencies are realized. After all, the reorganization process was not undertaken to exercise organizational imagination, but to improve the organizational functioning in relation to mandated missions, goals, and objectives.

Organizational missions are constantly changing, and attempts to have the organizational structure keep pace are folly. Rather, once satisfied with the basic type of organizational format, efforts at massive alterations should be discouraged. It is possible to keep the structure current and flexible by focusing on small procedures that leave the format basically intact, while fine-tuning the structure to meet new demands and situations.

The essential ingredient in organizational development and change is a willingness to admit that performance can always be improved. Such improvement is predicated on an open, complete, and participative dialogue among all levels of management and staff. Organization development functions by and through a cooperative spirit. Mandates or demands from any single individual are just not effective.

CONCLUSION

We see now that by using a three-pronged comprehensive program approach, methods are available to increase efficiency and effectiveness in human service organizations. From the individual perspective, the lottery and assessment center were offered in Chapter 2 as selection, placement, and promotion techniques to be used in addition to the much-maligned civil service system. Beyond initial selection and placement techniques, management-development programs present an ongoing effort to recognize potential managers among existing employees, prepare their advancement, and improve present manager performance. We discussed in Chapter 3 management-development programs as the second of the three comprehensive program approaches. Moving from individual to organizational emphasis, Chapter 4 dealt with organizational diagnosis, analysis, and change implementation. Chapter 5 continued in this organizational vein by expanding on the organizational-development change technique and using structural change examples. Discussion of examples and reactions to pilot projects on the preceding techniques demonstrates their potential to improve the human service delivery system.

NOTES

1. Richard Beckhard, *Organization Development: Strategies and Models* (Reading, Mass.: Addison-Wesley, 1969), pp. 9-20.

2. Samuel Hays, "Reorganizing For Fun and Profit," School of Social Welfare and the Public Executive Project, New York: State University at Albany (mimeographed), 1975.

3. New York State Department of Social Services, *Annual Report*, 1974.

4. Office of the Secretary U.S. Department of Health Education and Welfare, *Poverty Study Task Force* (September 1976).

5. "Yes! Smith's Welfare Cuts Are Defensible," *Empire State Report* 2 (June 1976), p. 206.

6. William C. Copeland, "Laboratory For Public Welfare Administrative Systems Development" (mimeographed), April 1976.

7. Peter Drucker, *Management: Tasks, Responsibilities, Practices* (New York: Harper & Row, 1974), pp. 518-599.

Chapter 6

GENERATING PRODUCTION—NOT CONFLICT

INTRODUCTION

The constant change and need to respond to outside influences presented in previous chapters creates an almost continual atmosphere of conflict in human service organizations. However, contrary to popular perceptions, not all organizational conflict is necessarily bad or destructive. Chapter 6 examines the good and bad consequences of conflict and external and internal conflict situations.

Chapter 6 opens with a discussion of the human service organization as a system and the necessity for a feedback mechanism to deal with change. Conflict is then presented as a continuum with degrees of functional and dysfunctional characteristics. A general theory of conflict, a method for classifying conflict, and conflict as a process are all delineated for a general understanding of conflict in organizations. Development of methods to control, identify, and resolve organizational tension follows. Some general types of human service organizational conflict situations are presented with relevant examples. Finally, three methods of conflict resolution are presented as ways to help keep conflict functional and promote organizational achievement.

During recent decades, organizations have witnessed, and its members have been exposed to, an inordinate amount of conflict. There are several explanations for this increase in organizational tension. First, organizations—particularly in the human services—are attempting to cope with and to understand the modern worker.

Today's employee is a new breed with different values, needs, and motivations. The typical human service worker is more highly educated than those preceding him or her by even a few years. As a product of the knowledge explosion, the employee has developed greater political, social, and economic awareness. Workers not only want the organization to do more for them, but also want fuller participation in the management process itself. Second, the organization itself has found the employees to be less easily managed by traditional controls and motivators. Managing the new worker has become an ever more-complex, tension-ridden task as organizations seek techniques and knowledge to aid their search for increased organizational productivity. Third, organization mission and technology are in a constant state of flux. This perpetual change tends to cause dislocations as interest groups form various approaches to set up situations ripe for potentially destructive competition over control of delivery mechanisms and resources.

Because of its important, ubiquitous nature, conflict has become a major focus of organizational concern. Conflict can be described as both a characteristic and fundamental organizational process. Although many view organizational conflict negatively, it should not be thought of solely as a manifestation of irrationality, since a certain amount of "creative tension" is always needed. It is through the give-and-take of ideas and philosophies that organizations regenerate to gain vitality for tackling new, more demanding missions. Conflict is also healthy because it serves to clarify positions and delineate actions, and makes future resolution and conciliations possible.

THE ORGANIZATION AS A SYSTEM

In order to understand how conflict works within the organizational context, it is essential that the organization be viewed as a system of interacting parts rather than elements in isolation. Knowledge of how the organization as a system reacts to tension will better enable the manager to minimize the system's destructive tendencies and increase its potential value.

System Behavior and Structural Responses

All organizations, because of their individualized natures and missions, exhibit particular structures, behaviors, and states. Human service organizations, which on the surface appear to have much in common, behave differently because they are responding to different sets of stimuli and environmental constraints. In other words, before performance potential can be adequately predicted, there must be a detailed definition of organizational inputs and a detailed definition of what makes the organization react and expend those resources. Structure, on the other hand, is the arrangement of interrelationships among organizational elements. As demonstrated earlier, organizational behavior and structure are closely related to organizations which exhibit deterministic or random behavior. When organizations exhibit deterministic behavior patterns, they respond predictably and sequentially to stimuli; for example, this action allows several organizations to respond to outside mandates in a uniform and orderly fashion. This step is essential if decentralized organizations are to survive. At the opposite extreme are those organizations which react in a random fashion to external mandates. They handle stimuli in one way the first time and in a different manner the next.

In addition to behavioral patterns, there are two basic types of structural relationships. First, hierarchical organizations are structured so that changes in one unit or department will have definite rebound impacts on other units within the organization. Hence, the addition, deletion, or movement of one organizational element will inevitably change the formal whole configuration. It is a ripple effect: throw a small pebble into a pond and the entire body of water reacts. Similarly, change one job title or unit designation in a tightly controlled hierarchical structure and the entire network is disturbed. Second, there are those organizations, typically the matrix or team models, that are less sensitive to change at any one point in the organization. These types of structural configurations allow for change with little disturbing impact on the core structure. The traditional hierarchical organization can be likened to a machine which reacts invariably to outside stimuli unless it is otherwise programmed. In this type of organization the interrelationships are narrowly restricted, and individuals or units have limited opportunities for exhibiting differential behavior. The hierarchical structure tends to be rigid, but constant, over a period of time. The matrix organization is organic in nature and allows for movement, change, flexibility, and adaptability. Relationships in this organization are more dependent on communication than mandated spatial arrangements, such as the hierarchical organization.

System Growth or Decay Changes

As with most living systems, organizations change and grow. Organizational changes take one of two forms: decay or maturity. Organizational decay can occur for many reasons. The most prevalent reason is a continued pathological conflict which destroys its very fiber. In this case, one finds that the organization is no longer able to work as a team toward common objectives—elements and systems no longer fit together or operate smoothly. There is steady degeneration toward a state of organizational chaos. On the other hand, there are organizations that, through the nurturing of creative dialectics and tension, are capable of utilizing energy generated by conflicts. These agencies are the ones most likely to mature into successful institutions. Hence, units grow to become more complex and differentiated in response to increasing performance demands. Systems and subsystems mesh in an effort to achieve common organizational goals. It is this crucial point, the purposeful nature of organizations, that separates it from other types of more casual human groupings.

System Feedback Mechanism

Organizations are, or should be, teleological in nature; that is, designed to accomplish a goal. In order to accomplish this step effectively, organizations must have highly integrated feedback or homeostatic mechanisms. The concept of feedback is critical to any discussion of organizations. Simply put, organizational feedback tells where the organization is going in relation to where it should be headed. It is a measure of how close the organization is to achieving desired objectives, and while organizational feedback loops provide data on what is happening, the homeostatic mechanism is designed to interpret this information in order to take actions to keep the organization on course. An example of this step might be the highly complex navigational aids used on commercial airplanes. In traveling from city to city, planes are kept on course either by radio waves or by on-board radar systems. These are the feedback mechanisms that take constant readings of where the airliner is in time and space in order to compare the readings against programmed knowledge of where the airplane should be. If a discrepancy is detected, this information is fed to the pilot, who then takes corrective action to return the plane to a proper heading. In other words, the pilot is the homeostatic mechanism.

Effective organizations function in much the same manner. Instead of using radio beams or radar, performance-oriented organizations have highly developed data-gathering and evaluative mechanisms which constantly take readings and provide information on where the agency is in comparison to a projected target. If the organization or its various programs are found to deviate substantially from expectations, this finding is an indication of malaise or misdirection. The manager—much like an aircraft pilot—must use the feedback data to determine what actions are necessary. The manager then exerts his role as a control mechanism by trying to reduce the mismatch between performance and goal achievement so that organizational actions are initiated to decrease the degree of discrepancy.

Nevertheless, there must be the realization that no human system, human service organizations not excluded, can ever be totally teleological or self-directed and correcting. Such honors are left to mechanical systems, such as complex computers and the common thermostat. At worst, human service organizations attempt to achieve goals haphazardly with no plan in mind. At best, these organizations are able to correct mistakes through a process of adaptive behavior before they become institutionalized, and are able to maintain goal direction. Such organizations can have higher performance levels than many previously believed possible. The one element that has prevented human service organizations from reaching such exalted heights is conflict.

THE CONFLICT CONTINUUM

In discussing conflict, it is obvious that organizations do not exist in a state of complete conflict or peace, but range over a lengthy continuum. The manner in which organizations behave depends on a mixture of external and internal stimuli and system structure. As we stated earlier, organizations can be deterministic to random in behavior. Consequently, over a period of time, the organizational conflict system can be characterized as either completely determined or irrational. The conflict continuum can be depicted diagrammatically in Figure 6-1.

Dysfunctional Conflict

The representation of the conflict continuum is based on a model operationalized by Ackoff.[1] If organizational conflict tends toward the random pole, it probably means these conditions hold: First, organizational conflict has become endemic and pathological. Second, regulating mechanisms within the organization have become debilitated. Third, while managers recognize that alternative courses of action are available, they are unable to embark on a corrective course because individuals are too splintered. This circumstance minimizes the possibility of coalitions and cooperative action among organizational members. It occurs because management is unable to demonstrate the clear benefit of proposed alternatives to individuals or groups. If this situation happens, organizational conflict tends to be random, aimless, and continuous, with little hope of resolution. In this situation, the conflict itself becomes the generating organizational force. It can be compared to a sniper's randomly killing people just because he likes to shoot a

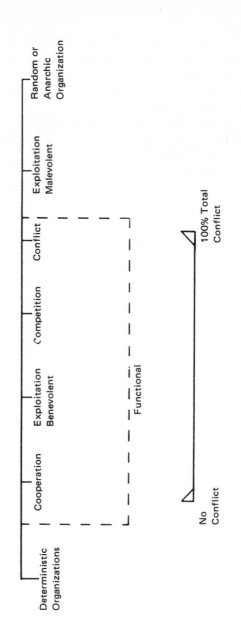

Figure 6.1: THE CONFLICT CONTINUUM

gun. The conflict mechanism is not being used to solve organizational problems; rather, in the minds of the organization and its members, the conflict becomes the sole reason for being. Such aimless conflict is pointless, useless, and, more than likely, causes organizational disintegration.

At the other extreme you have conflict that is of a determined nature, or zero conflict. It is organizationally dysfunctional since, with no conflict, change and adaptiveness is held to a minimum. Think of it, with a steady diet of no conflict. General Motors might now be producing horse-drawn coaches and buggy whips. When an organization has all of its potential actions determined outside its boundaries, the manager not only loses total control over the organization, but also becomes a useless appendage. If our technology develops to the point where an automatic pilot can do the same things as its human counterpart, then one of them will be without a job. Consequently, if we could develop a "social service machine" that could determine eligibility, assess client needs, and write checks and deliver services, then we could abolish the human organization, negating the possibility of conflict. Nevertheless, for the sake of this discussion, it is necessary to assume that nonpathological conflict is functional. Any factor which reduces conflict to the point where it no longer can exist, or is no longer tolerated, is, therefore, organizationally dysfunctional. Hence, managers who attempt to prevent legitimate concerns and needs from being discussed, or who force work cadres into narrowly constricted boundaries, are doing irreparable damage to the organization by stifling its effort to adapt to constant environmental constraints and changes.

Functional Conflict

One step up the conflict continuum is the condition called cooperation. Cooperation can be viewed as the opposite of conflict since it represents a state where individuals have entered into organized, mutual, and orderly attempts to solve problems. Obviously, cooperation is functional to the organization in its efforts to achieve specified goals. Benevolent exploitation, although an unequal cooperation, is likewise considered functional, since it is a form of cooperation. In its benevolent form, there is cooperation on particular tasks by the parties, departments, and agencies, but one will receive greater benefit or value than the others. The notion that all organizations or individuals have to share equally in the fruits of their labor is complete fiction. Some are always called upon to make sacrifices for others. Nevertheless, it does not mean that one agency, unit, or person should be the constant winner at someone else's expense, but the situation calls for an equitable distribution of the spoils. Competition, the third form of functional conflict, is really a form of regulated conflict. The purpose of this regulation is to keep conflict within a functional framework. A good manager knows how to use competition for organizational advantage. You see positive aspects of competition in blood and fund drives or when people are given awards for achieving predetermined objectives. The next point on the scale is conflict. Organizational conflict is considered to be functional so long as the resolution mechanism is allowed unobstructed operation. If the resolution process falters or breaks down, conflict can become dysfunctional. Malevolent exploitation, however, is considered dysfunctional since it represents a collapse in the orderly conflict-resolution process, leads to consistent and inherently unequal payoffs for participants, and consequently carries organizationally debilitating results.

Organizational disputes, tension, and conflict are normal outgrowths of man's attempts to manage the complex human service system. Conflict, although not necessarily bad, is one of those activities that can have long-lasting and debilitating impact on an organization if techniques are not developed and implemented to keep it within acceptable limits. The remainder of Chapter 6 will therefore be devoted to the specification of what conflict is; why it occurs; and how it can be controlled, ameliorated, and channeled into creative organizational energies.

CONFLICT THEORIES

In his landmark work *Conflict and Defense,* Kenneth Boulding contends there is a general theory of conflict.[2] His approach to conflict is: First, for a conflict situation to exist, at least two parties must be involved. Conflict parties consist of individuals who are capable of assuming different positions and at the same time, retaining a common identity. It is then possible to define three levels of conflict by the nature of parties involved. There is simple conflict which consists of individuals acting on their own behalf and not in a representative capacity. In organizations this form is interpersonal conflict. Next, there are conflicts among such structured groups as departments, agencies, unions, and professional societies. Finally, in what Boulding terms the ill-defined middle ground, conflict exists among informally organized subgroupings, such as professionals, secretaries, supervisors, blue-collar workers, and the like.

It Takes Two to Tangle

Conflict is a situation in which there is competition between parties who are aware of the incompatibility of potential positions that each wishes to occupy. Awareness of some incompatibility of positions becomes the key element in this definition. Consequently, if two parties are totally unaware of each other and one another's situation, conflict may not occur if there is no strong desire on the part of one to contest the issue. In other words, each may not be happy with what is going on, but it is not important enough to be turned into a major bone of contention.

Nevertheless, individual personality characteristics of organizational members are at the base of interpersonal conflict within the organization. Boulding finds that the constantly frustrated individual tends to develop reactions among himself and others in the organization which cause tension and subsequent boundary breakdowns. In general terms, the individual party in conflict possesses such traits as hostility, aggressiveness, touchiness, and dominance that cause him to develop ideas which are consistently and sufficiently different from others within the organization and, thus, cause conflict. Group conflict, on the other hand, is vague and less well-defined than conflicts among individuals or organizations. Group conflict frequently exists without formal organizations and is often complicated by cross memberships. This case can be exemplified by the "we" vs. "they" attitude often found in organizations where lower echelon employees treat management as enemies rather than as members of the same team. There is no formal organization of operational workers. There is only the feeling that as a group they are being "put-upon" by someone at the top. Such situations often make life miserable for first-line supervisors, since allegiances are split among the workers from where they came and among mangement from which they receive the sanction to supervise.

Boulding finds that group conflict tends to easily pass into organizational conflict. This tendency toward more formalized conflict within organizations has probably been spurred on by the growth of bureaucracy and its consequent departmentalization and specialization. Before conflict can exist among organizational subunits, three prior conditions must be fulfilled. First, the other unit or department must be present in the image of the responsible decision-maker—in other words, he has to know that it exists. Second, some activity or decision within the organization must have a potential impact on two or more subunits. Third, the reactions of the managers in each unit must affect the other in an unfavorable manner. Thus, if one subunit is not aware of another's potential for negative impact. or if the decision is not felt to be unfavorable, conflict will not occur. Nevertheless, conflict becomes almost inevitable when departments attempt to expand into a field of activity in which others have ownership.

Unsnarling the Tangle—Conflict Resolution

According to Boulding's conceptualization, conflict never really comes to an end; it is continually being created. Each particular conflict has a life cycle. It begins, peaks, and diminishes, then certain inherent processes bring it to an end. This resolution process can take several forms. The first, most common method for ending conflict is through avoidance. Here, parties in the conflict simply remove themselves from the dispute until contact is lost; for example, some types of organizational conflict—especially those fostered by too much proximity or intimacy among units—can be ameliorated by putting physical or social distances among the feuding units. Another, perhaps less-desirable, mechanism for ending conflict is through forcible removal, in which case, one party is clearly victorious, thus causing the removal or displacement of the other party from the field. This situation occurs when certain organizational units absorb the functions of others they might previously have been competing with for resources.

If parties are unable to conquer or successfully avoid each other, more formalized resolution tactics become likely. Boulding distinguished among three types of procedural conflict resolution. First, there is reconciliation. This circumstance occurs when parties to the conflict perceive mutual benefit or adopt the others' position. For instance, almost everyone agrees that no one should go hungry in this nation; there is no conflict here, but conflict does flourish when debating the methods for achieving this goal. The second form is compromise. Here, value systems are different, and parties have varying perspectives on what the final result should be. Rather than continue the conflict, each party is willing to settle for less than total success on all points. Compromise is reached through a bargaining process. Finally, the third form of procedural conflict resolution is award. It occurs when an outside, or third party, is called in to arbitrate a dispute. A settlement is reached when the arbitrator awards a decision that determines the outcome. The parties in conflict agree beforehand to accept the decision of the arbitrator.

Classifying Conflict

Rapoport, as did Boulding, attempted to bring order to the complex system of interactions inherent in conflict situations.[3] He provides an exhaustive, if not detailed, conflict-classification scheme. Rapoport identifies three basic types of conflict: fight, game, and debate. The opponent's role provides one of the key differentiating factors among the preceding three conflict situations. Such classifications apply across the board to individuals, groups, entire organizations and subunits.

In a fight, the opponent is mainly a nuisance. The other party should not be there, but somehow is. The object here is to eliminate the opponent and make the opposition disappear or cut down his importance. The object of a fight is to harm, destroy, subdue, or drive the opponent away. In a game, however, the opponent is essential. Take, for instance, a budget conference. In essence, this situation is a game with its own rules and sets of behavioral expectations. The budget officer anticipates inflated requests, so, in his own mind, he discounts it by a set percentage. The agency director, knowing this fact, attempts to beat the budget office by inflating the budget by a factor of two. When budget people pick this up, they will deflate it by a like amount, which is neither more nor less than grown men playing a game called the "budget-go-round." Opponents in a game cooperate. They cooperate by following, without reservation, the rules of the game and by presenting each other with the greatest possible challenge, thereby they make the game both interesting and worthwhile. The debate, however, presents a situation where opponents direct arguments instead of physical moves. The object here is to convince the other party to see things your way, rather than to harm or outwit him. One of the most usual techniques is persuasion—to convince others of the worthiness of your position.

The Conflict Process

Ackoff, in particular, has developed an operational model of the conflict process which is simple in execution, but detailed enough to allow for the mapping of significant interrelationships.[4] Although Ackoff does not display a conflict model, it can be visualized. See Figure 6-2.

The schematic, as depicted, displays the basic component of an organizationally applicable conflict system. It consists of eight basic component parts. The first two general components are "Purposeful Entity A" and "Purposeful Entity B." It is only through the interaction of two such purposeful entities as organizational members that conflict or cooperation can occur. The conflict system is triggered when the following situations occur: (a) two different organizational members place a specific value on the attainment of a particular outcome; (b) the action of either member affects the value that is placed on the outcome or negatively leaves no impact on the chances of achieving this desired

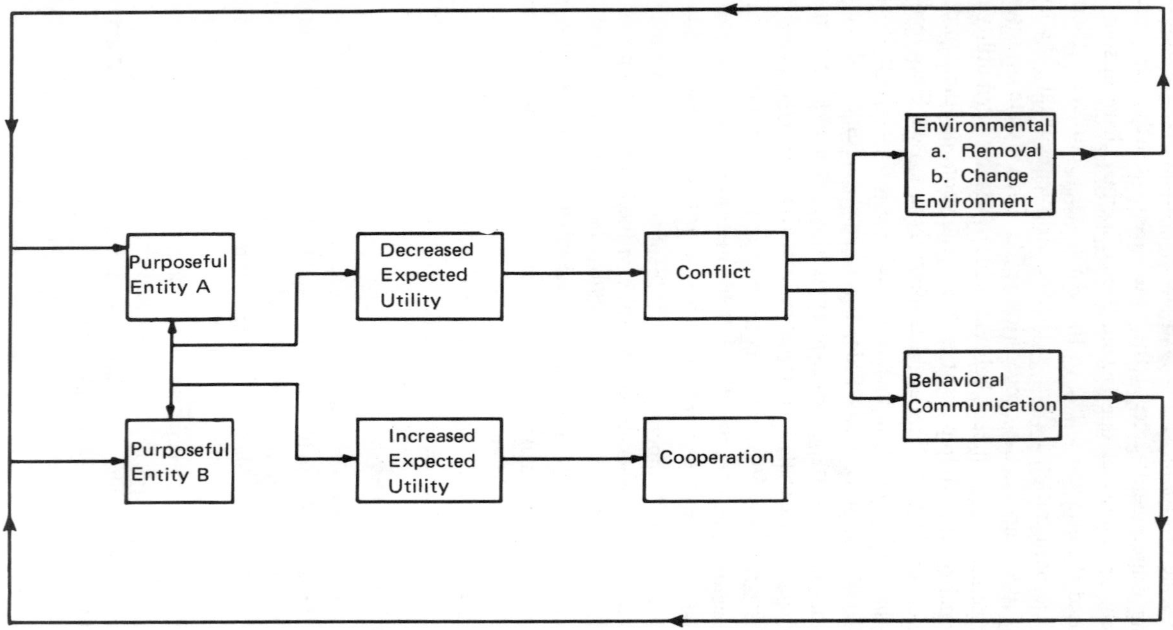

Figure 6.2: CONFLICT PROCESS

138

outcome. In other words, two potentially conflicting parties must exist in the same environment and, in some measurable way, must alter an existing achievement state of the other. Consequently, the presence, decision, or actions of one organizational member have in some way decreased the effected utility of the other, and a conflict situation has, therefore been initiated. This part is the third component. The fourth part of this model is the cooperation mode. Such a state occurs when one organizational member's behavior adds to the expected utility of an individual or of a group present in the organization. In other words, the happiness quotient of the parties is mutually increased. Since feedback loops do not continue the interactive network once a cooperative state is achieved, the process is considered complete according to this model. As indicated in the diagrammatic exposition, once conflict is entered into there are basically two modes which affect its outcome—components five and six.

Behavioral conflict resolution occurs either when there is a change in the action alternatives selected or in the utilities placed on the outcomes. For example, two units are at disagreement over how a set sum of money is to be allocated between day-care services for children and nutritional programming for the elderly. One method to resolve this conflict would be to have one unit switch its position and select another alternative or to have it withdraw from the field of conflict. This circumstance often occurs during final assessment, when people agree that the issue is not worth all the effort because there are more important things to be concerned about. Additionally, a compromise could be reached on procedural matters. For example, in the first year, programs for the elderly will receive the lion's share and, in the second year, funding emphasis will be on day care. At any rate, behavioral-conflict resolution is normally accomplished through some type of communication.

Next, there is component six, the mechanism utilized to physically alter a conflict situation. Also known as the environmental mode, resolution is achieved by removing parties from the environment or by changing the physical surroundings. A common example of this circumstance is the "firing" of an employee who, in a manifest or latent manner, constantly opposes established organizational norms and procedures. Another approach to physical conflict resolution might be to isolate, "in a job sense," individuals who have great difficulty in handling interpersonal relationships. Take them out of the "line of fire" and have them work in areas where personal contact either is minimized or is not crucial to job fulfillment.

Consequently, once conflict is joined, entities can attempt to alter the existing situation by selecting a behavioral—or an environmental-resolution procedure. Once the choice is made, the process starts anew with decisions and actions based on input factors derived from the two types of conflict alteration. If the new inputs lead to increased expected utility or add to the happiness quotient of both parties, then the situation changes from one of conflict to one of cooperation. If, however, both parties are still not satisfied with suggested modifications, the process is slanted back toward the conflict side and repeats itself in this manner until either resolution or conflict becomes unsolvable, indeterminate, random, or pathological. Similarly, the arrows joining the environmental and behavioral modes indicate that these two strategies are interchangeable and that decision-makers have freedom to move from one to the other.

CONTROLLING CONFLICT

As indicated previously, organizational conflict and tension are not necessarily bad or destructive. Rather, organizational conflicts are man's attempts to manage and harness the energies and potentialities of our complex human service delivery mechanism. Within this context, it is the job of the manager and the organization alike to develop formal or informal procedures, processes, and techniques to prevent conflict from becoming dysfunctional.

Swiftly running water cannot produce electricity until it is linked and channeled by mechanical or natural means into a series of dams and hydroelectric generators. An ecological, economic, esthetic price must be paid to accomplish the task of controlling and organizing waterways so they will have a payoff of energy production which is convertible to man's needs. If the payoff in terms of energy produced is greater than the price paid, it could be said that the effort was worthwhile, depending, of course, on your value system. The same thing applies to controlling man's natural energies within the organizational setting. We all pay a human price for the privilege of living, working, and benefiting from organizations. On the one hand, you pay real costs in terms of freedom of action, individuality of expression, and sublimation of personal drives for the good of the whole. On the other hand, individuals benefit because work becomes a meaningfully directed joint effort that has a potential for good which far exceeds any individual efforts, not to mention the economic benefits which the individuals receive for providing services. Organizations, in other words, take this natural resource called human potentiality, channel it, develop it, and guide it for the benefit of the individual and the society. How successful an organization is at managing these resources determines how productive the organization will be.

Just as in the case of building electricity-producing dams, the inevitable result of harnessing and controlling individuals is the production not only of a product or service, but also of conflict. While man is a social animal, it does not mean that he is social in all situations and environments. Through the organization's structural integration, management team, mission and goals, technology, and interpersonal linkages, it must be capable of creating among its members a dynamic force which will generate maximum productivity and minimum waste. In energy transmission, especially when it is sent over long distances, some of the electrical power is dissipated as heat loss. Organizations experience the same phenomena, for if they are not managed properly, much of the effort becomes just wheel-spinning and lost energy. Consequently, the main thrust of the delivery of human services becomes secondary in importance or is sidetracked when simple activity replaces productive action and then becomes and end product itself. A good deal of this lost energy and excess activity is devoted to starting, maintaining, and feeding organizational conflict. Unfortunately, in all too many organizations, the conflict cycle consumes, like a ravenous organism, the human, physical, and monetary resources. Put simply, the greater the degree of conflict present in an organization, then the greater are the amounts of resources needed to produce a constant output.

Thus, organizations which tolerate inordinate amounts of tension and conflict are, by definition, inefficient. The sad part is that suffering is limited not only to organizational members, but also to its clientele. First, entitled or needed client services are not delivered. Second, people who are unhappy with their organizations make poor spokesmen for the cause and thereby limit future resource acquisition. Third, client relationships deteriorate because of internal feuding and dissatisfaction which become highly visible in client interactions.

CONFLICT IDENTIFICATION AND RESOLUTION

Nevertheless, prior to developing effective conflict-control mechanisms, it is necessary that one identify potential conflict areas and thereby limit the likelihood of their uncontrolled growth. Thus, the two greatest problems of organization conflict-control systems are conflict-signal detection and resolution implementation; in other words, knowing when something has to be done and knowing what to do about it. The basic problem becomes one of conflict-monitoring and detection for the amelioration and prevention of organizationally destructive situations.

Attempts to alleviate activities that wear down the fiber of organization support and performance have concentrated on two obvious, but difficult, approaches. First, there is the modification of the person to fit organizational constraints. Second, there is the adaptation of organizations to fit to the person's needs. Modification processes, as they relate to organizational members, are usually behavioral in nature. Such programs are typically initiated through concerted management efforts, including job enrichment or enlargement, employee motivation, participant-decision structures, management objectives and development, and others. Such programs basically seek to help the individual cope with, survive, and grow within the organizational setting when the organization provides opportunities for advancement, responsibility, job satisfaction, and task accomplishment. Here, the sources of potential conflict, which are rooted in the individual's need to be part of a meaningful process, are confronted by the organization's providing the wherewithal for successful achievement.

The next major approach in designing organizations that allow achievers and managers to function is another method aimed at conflict reduction. What is the sense of having good managers if the human welfare organization does not provide the resources, structure, and support essential to healthy functioning? Why bother teaching managers to be flexible and creative if the organization, through its procedures and structure, is rigid? Consequently, through structural and system modifications, the organization must be prepared to deal with areas of potential and continuous conflict. Hence, sources of organizational conflict must be identified and categorized. With this identification importance in mind, the next section identifies some types of organizational conflict in human service agencies.

HUMAN SERVICE CONFLICT SITUATIONS

Ideological Conflict

The following general types of conflict situations can be found in human service organizations. First, there is the ideological conflict generated when a wide variation exists between what an organization says it will do and what it actually does. The most visible manifestation of this conflict occurs when organizational members and clients perceive a wide gap between policy and deed. Many individuals working in the human services do not commit themselves to the necessity of organizational functioning, but to the principles on which the organization was founded or to the missions it was designed to pursue. While both ideological and ethical involvement are welcomed and encouraged, under certain conditions, they can prove to be a constant source of organizational tension. An overabundance of those people who are interested in ethics, philosophy, and service will almost guarantee conflict, especially when matched against the grittier necessities of making the organization work within the framework of an imperfect world. It is, after all, the astute administrator who can square the realities of organizational life with the most abstract and doctrinaire policies within which such organizations operate.

Very few, for example, in the abstract would argue against providing medical services to the elderly; but, turning this ideology into programs is both expensive and conflict-inducing from a social and individual standpoint. Should those over 60 or 65 be included in such programs? Should all the elderly or only the poor be included? Should those without alternate health insurance or those presently enrolled be included? What about the permanently disabled of any age? To develop equitable solutions to problems within the fiscal constraints is a wrenching process. Add some practical considerations to the social considerations, such as how these services are to be delivered and organized. Such programming is fraught with management pitfalls. Should the commitment to medical services for the elderly be diminished because the mechanism for the delivery is neither well-established nor well-developed? The answer is maybe, and this area is where conflict between the idea and the practicality is most acute.

Such ideological conflict can also assume individual dimensions. Think of an organizational member, a staunch antiabortionist, who works for an organization that either performs abortion procedures, such as a hospital, or approves of and provides payment for abortions, such as social service agencies. Another common form of conflict that occurs when social service organizations fall into the operational category is the tension among organizational and professional value structures and ethics, as was somewhat elucidated in Chapter 1. Because of the basis in differing ideological norms, these types of general conflict situations tend to be long-lasting and acute, once they surface as major organizational difficulties.

Structural Conflict

The second general conflict category is of a structural variety. Structural conflict has its roots in the nature of organizational functioning. Every organization, if it is to be productive, must provide structured and formalized mechanisms for the control of workers and work. Consequently, conflict arises among the organization's requirements for consistency, conformity, and orderliness, and the individual's desire for freedom of movement, selective interrelationships, choice of facts, and control over personal environment. In fact, organizations evolved for the specific purpose of structuring relationships among people, differentiating roles, and dividing labor. Because most of today's human service agencies maintain a hierarchal framework, material-conflict situations are generated because of power, status, and position differentials among organizational membership. Similarly, because work is highly routinized and specialized in these types of structures, job satisfaction and task accomplishment are neither promoted nor rewarded. In productive organizations, individuals channel energies into task definition and completion, with a constant search for new challenging work. When such activities become sedentary, an energy vacuum is created. No longer does an avenue exist for the expenditure of creative energy. Since such organizations are not typically outcome-oriented because of structural exigencies, worker resources become sidetracked into less-productive avenues. For example, workers have intensified interpersonal and intergroup conflict, or withdraw from the necessities of organizational reality. Consequently, how an organization is structured can somewhat determine the type and nature of the conflict which occurs.

Functional Conflict

In addition to conflict generated by an organizational need to control and structure roles and relationships, there is the kind of conflict which is an outgrowth of functional differentiation among various units within the organizational framework. This is the third major area of concern, called functional conflict. While it is true that organizations are supposed to be composed of interrelated units which are designed to achieve a common objective, it is not often the case. Since many units need the support and cooperation of no other units, many organizational subunits view themselves either as independent power centers or as the cutting edge of organizational operations. Unfortunately, if you carry this logic to its natural extreme, the only thing left is a conglomeration of self-contained units that, upon first glance, would not appear to be working.

Often, the only thing that binds organizational subsystems is a paycheck from a common source. This fortresslike mentality occurs for the following reasons. First, there are differing sets of norms and values sometimes caused by the professional mix in the work unit or by the nature of the job itself. Take, for example, a budget department staffed by individuals who, by virtue of their education and experience, have a different set of expectations about the function of a social service agency compared to service staff. Budget departments are typically concerned with minimizing and controlling expenditures, while service units are more interested in delivering assistance—sometimes with and without regard to cost. This attitude leads to an environment which is conducive to boundary conflict. While these units are theoretically part of the same system, they have totally different individual perspectives. Second, there is a natural tendency on the part of management to treat service agencies as a specialty grouping, with each unit having its area of expertise staffed by technicians. Because of their training, few people in this type management atmosphere are capable of integrating the sum of the parts into the whole. Also, it is easier for management to grasp and to deal with the organization if it is composed of smaller, separate entities. An organization that spends over $100 million at a local level becomes an almost overwhelming vision to management, but when units are viewed as individualized contributors to this massive spending, the spending becomes more acceptable.

Jurisidictional Conflict

Turf Disputes. The fourth form of conflict which is common to most social service organizations is jurisdictional. Such conflict situations typically take one of three forms: conflict over (a) turf, (b) clients, and (c) resources. Jurisdictional conflict, most of all, tends to be highly developed and ritualized and, at the same time, is amenable to long-range solution. Take, for example, turf conflict, which occurs when organizations or units push their boundaries too far into a real or imaginary environment and cross lines that other significant parties believe to be within their territory. There is constant turf conflict among state and local departments of social services. Local departments are fighting a never-ending battle over what they term illegal mandates to provide services their constituents neither want nor have money to pay for.

States often are not willing to take regional differences into consideration. They risk the wrath of growing resistance movements that seek redress through political and judicial means. The cause of such conflict is easy to diagnose. State or control agencies have the administrative necessity to provide uniform services and care over large geographical areas. Local districts, on the other hand, have particular needs which might or might not conform to the state's requirements of all categories of programming and service. Hence, there is an attempt through decree and control to maintain not only uniform implementation procedures, but also quality- and audit-control mechanisms. Neither state nor local departments relish their positions. They both realize they are creatures of confusing and often contradictory legislation and policy mandates. The departments have not been able to arrive at a compromise to help them find more meaningful, less cumbersome ways to deliver services and programs at local levels.

Turf conflict is also found in interorganizational situations. For example, should line or staff departments be allowed to make personnel, budget, and planning decisions? By going either way, the answer to simple, yet critical, questions could drastically change how a department operates.

Client Conflict. Client conflict is in two forms—for clients and between client and agency. Contrary to popular slogans, human service agencies do not want to put themselves out of business, since survival is a basic organizational instinct. One of the most important tasks of a service organization, then, is to identify and capture a clientele through the provision of specialized programming, highly developed expertise, or monopoly control. Many human service organizations, especially those in the child-care business, exist based upon contractual reimbursements for provided services. A day-care center, for instance, might be paid $60 a week per child by a county agency. If there are 100 children, the center receives $6,000 in revenue every week. The day-care program then hires staff, provides material, resources, and physical facilities, based upon a yearly budget of some $312,000. In other words, they incur this amount in financial obligations. In this type situation, it would not be in the best interests of the child-care agency to reduce enrollments. Consequently, in order to maintain its financial integrity, the agency needs every available seat filled by a child, whether that child needs this type care in terms of quality, time, and duration. Hence social service laws themselves create organizational dependency to the point where agencies become permanently bound to a reimbursement system which requires them to keep clients rather than rehabilitate and release them. In such situations, the end result becomes the client, not the need to deliver services. Agencies become "junkies" who need ever-increasing doses of financial assistance, for just as the human body builds a tolerance to narcotics, so do agencies develop ever-larger appetites for funds. Rather than rewarding agencies for reducing dependency and rehabilitating clients, we pay them to keep clients and increase admissions. Agencies find themselves in the position of having to constantly add the right type of client to their registers, particularly the type who is eligible for some kind of reimbursement through the local social service agency. Just as in hospitals where there are usually more beds than patients, service agencies must be on the lookout for clients who can be easily converted into financial support.

Conflict between client and agency, on the other hand, focuses not on the competition for bodies, but on the relationships between service-provider and service-user. A more detailed discussion of this phenomenon can be found in Chapter 7, which contains an in-depth discussion of how clients and agencies interface.

Battle for Resources. The third variety of jurisdictional conflict—or the battle over resources—is simple to comprehend and is, perhaps, the most obvious conflict mode. Resources, in this instance, can be broadly defined as physical, monetary, and human. An agency's ability to gain resources is dependent on power, influence, prestige, service available to clientele, product, and others. In its purest form, resource conflict is readily ameliorated when available resources are greater than the cost of meeting anticipated agency needs. Nevertheless, even when agencies have adequate resources, conflict can still be sparked by perceptions of relative deprivation. Here, it is not the total amount of allocated resources which is disputed, but the fact that one unit or agency has more resources than others feel are deserved—the "I want what you've got" syndrome.

These four general conflict groupings—ideological and ethical, structural, functional, and jurisdictional (turf, client, and resource)—compose not all of the potential organizational conflict situations, but they are a fairly representative sampling of the types of conflict, and their concurrent causes, that human service agencies might anticipate. One major category, which has been almost totally ignored, is interpersonal conflict. This omission is not one of neglect, but one of intention because of time and place. Interpersonal conflict will be fully covered in a follow-up text in this series that highlights the individual's contribution to organizational productivity.

CONFLICT RESOLUTION

Problem-Solving

One of the most productive mechanisms for solving conflict, both from an individual and organizational perspective, is through a decision- and problem-solving mode. Here, conflict is handled as inevitable but solvable. The machinery of the organization, its systems and managers, approach the conflict situation as they would any problem, by using both logic and expertise to arrive at acceptable responses to issues

created by the dispute. In other words, there is an attempt to proce-
duralize the solution process without having to develop extra-organiza-
tional mechanisms for dealing with serious, but perhaps routine,
organizational problems. For example, assume there has been a reduction in financial assistance to a local agency. Technically, a conflict
situation is created between the agency and its funding source. The
decision mode for resolution would dictate, however, that steps be
taken (1) to ascertain why the cut was sustained, and (2) if it could be
restored to original levels. Once it is ascertained that financial reductions are, in fact, nonreviewable, it is incumbent upon the agency to
seek ways to minimize the potential impacts of the reduction. This step
perhaps would be best accomplished by reviewing current programs,
forming a task force, and arriving at a range of acceptable alternatives
for action from which a final outcome would be selected. The focus in
the decision-resolution mode is not to continue the conflict once it was
determined that the possibility of gain has been eliminated, but to seek
ways of lessening organizational impacts directly traceable to the conflict
situation.

Negotiation

The second method for dealing with conflict is by negotiation. In
this instance, resolution attempts are geared to mutually acceptable
compromises. This act can be accomplished through informal means,
such as private discussions between parties where nothing is recorded,
except if, and when, a formal agreement is reached. Next, there is the
highly formalized and ritualized process called arbitration, where a
third party acts as an impartial hearing officer who tenders a binding or
voluntary decision based upon the presentation of facts and evidence.
In this case, records of the dispute are maintained. Employee-grievance
machinery is a perfect example of a formalized negotiation-resolution
mode. Looking back to the original example of the agency's sustaining
budget cuts, once the agency received notification of its budget
reduction, it could suggest that an informal session be held to see if
some acceptable compromise could be reached. If still dissatisfied, the
agency would probably have the option of appealing the decision to
another governmental body in a more formalized manner. This step
could take the format of an official complaint or charge against the
parent agency for such reasons as malfeasance or favoritism, with
charges filed administratively or through the court system. The end
result is perhaps a long delay in reaching a final decision that could
cause programmatic confusion and a funding hiatus. Any time conflict
enters the formal or ritualized resolution area, greater polarization

tends to settle in, and conflict becomes more intensified because parties are forced to drag up all previous disagreements, even though they have long been solved or forgotten. Hence, negotiation, while it appears to be a highly equitable way for solving conflict, does have some negative side effects.

Contention

The final resolution mechanism available is the contention mode. This process is entered into either by organizations that are in the enviable position of having overwhelming power and influence, or that have exhausted the other two modes and are still not satisfied with the outcomes. Here, there is an effort to force the other party to submit to imposed solutions through the use of threat, force, and influence. Typically, threat only works when there is the ability to carry it through. Implicit in the threat itself is the willingness to cause the suggested damage. Returning to the original scenario, the agency that receives its allocation decrease could threaten political ramifications. Think of the potential power of a local agency if the congressman from that district happened to be a senior member of a congressional committee that might, in some way, have control over the funding agency's appropriations. Such factors greatly increase the viability and potential fatality of a threatening alternative. Unfortunately, in most conflict situations where contention is used, there is no clear-cut superiority of one party over another. There are several implications for the use of a contention strategy. When contention is selected, basically a potentially long-lasting and destructive conflict process is entered into, which ends only when all concerned have exhausted their physical and human resources.

The type resolution procedure used in a particular tension-producing situation is dependent upon a host of factors: the nature of the parties involved; the importance of the conflict relative to organizational survival; the potential impact on service provision; the environment in which the conflict is conducted, and others. Remember, just as the best part of a fight between husband and wife is in the kissing and making up, the most beneficial aspect of conflict is in its resolution. Organizational conflict will add to productivity when it is kept within limits of what can be termed bounded rationality. This step means that sincere efforts are made to play by the rules of the game and to resolve the conflict not in favor of individual needs, but to further organizational achievement.

NOTES

1. Russel Ackoff, "Structural Conflicts Within Organizationss," *Operations Research and the Social Sciences,* J.R. Lawrence, ed. (New York: Tavistock Publications, 1966), pp. 427-438.

2. Kenneth Boulding, *Conflict and Defense: A General Theory* (New York: Harper Torch Books, 1962).

3. Anatol Rapoport, *Fights, Games, and Debates.* (Ann Arbor: University of Michigan Press, 1960).

4. Ackoff, ibid., pp. 427-438.

Chapter 7

SURVIVING TO ACHIEVE: THE ROLE OF

PUBLIC RELATIONS

INTRODUCTION

Public relations in human service agencies is the subject of Chapter 7. A valley has developed among resource-providers, service recipients, the public, and human service agencies. Poor communication takes the blame for most organizational problems but, in fact, is a symptom of larger malfunctions. Public relations as a specific form of organizational communication, responsibility for developing it, its function, purpose, and errors in implementation are presented in Chapter 7.

Most of the public relations problems are seen as the result of three organizational shortcomings: expectation/reality gap, nature of bureaucracy, and failure to recognize responsiveness and accountability to the public. These shortcomings are discussed, and an analysis of research findings is presented to further demonstrate lack of organizational responsiveness.

Suggestions on how to overcome these organizational shortcomings and develop positive public relations and ultimate organizational survival close the chapter.

HUMAN SERVICE AGENCIES AND THEIR STOCKHOLDERS

All public human service agencies, and many private agencies, because of the nature of their funding sources, are legitimized through public ownership. This condition makes every citizen a stockholder. The public, therefore, has a right or obligation to use these resources, or to question their existence and validity. Similarly, these same organizations exist in a constant state of competition among themselves and programs outside the service spectrum. In our governmental system, program survival is not automatic. Financial sustenance at public or private levels is neither guaranteed nor endless, but it is a renewable resource that varies from year to year. The critical operating assumption elucidated in Chapter 7 is that an organization must first exist before social services can be delivered. Hence, a manager's paramount obligation and task is to ensure the organization's capability of delivering services. In order to properly perform the delivery function, the agency must be able to survive without major disruptions or dislocations for a continued time period. It is through operating that organizations gain the experience needed to tackle a growing list of social problems. Fortunately or unfortunately, depending on your perspective, an organization's longevity and growth potential are determined by its hold on scarce resources—particularly money and good people. Ensuring continued funding and support for uninterrupted operation is an organizational reality that must constantly be faced.

Human service organizations exist, survive, grow, or die depending on their ability to command resources. These agencies are forced to operate in environments where determinants of survival are outside their direct control. Nevertheless, human service agencies can have great influence and input into this process which allows some agencies to grow and survive, while others shrink and disappear. There are several factors that determine the extent to which resources are distributed to human service providers: (1) the ability and strength of professional associations and interest groups to state their case to all factions of society; (2) the encouragement of favorable public opinion to provide a supportive base on which administrative and legislative bodies can justify positive funding decisions; (3) the development and instigation of client pressure for increased services and programs; (4) the provision of effective, efficient programs for the solution of social problems to create an atmosphere of continued support and confidence in launching further efforts; (5) the finesse exhibited in counteracting those opposed to increased human service expenditures; (6) the ability to shift or determine priorities so that human service programs are always at or near the top; (7) convincing the public they are well served or benefitted by massive financing of the human services; (8) not appearing greedy by allowing enough funds to flow to other types of services and programs that the public perceives to be essential to their well-being; (9) maintaining support and cooperation of the vast army of human service employees for continued programming.

The Gap in Trust

Unfortunately, there is growing distrust between social service provider and citizen. This inevitable confidence gap is a result of various forces operating in the environment. First, human service agencies and their clientele are in a state of confusion over their roles. Human service organizations and their clientele simultaneously perceive each other as both master and servant. Second, there is a continuing shift to a more highly controlled, centralized distribution system which removes service determination away from local offices. Third, the media has become more active and questions human service programs and policies. Fourth, there are countless incidents of inconsistencies between pronouncements of success and actual results. Fifth, the human service organization is dealing with a more aware, concerned, and educated public. Sixth, there has been a phenomenal growth and professionalization of public interest groups.

In most cases, the client receives requested or entitled services and treatment is fair, courteous, and quick. Nevertheless, there are all too many instances when the client is obviously mistreated. This situation can occur because of an overwrought, impolite employee or by a computer. At any rate, a dissatisfied individual, whether he is a person who failed to receive a welfare check on time or a corporate president who abhors "welfare cheats," becomes another public relations problem with which human service agencies must deal. What is even more worrisome is that mistreatment of the public by one agency often predisposes citizens to have a negative attitude toward all human service organizations. People tend to generalize their feelings, and, although the offending agency or employee may be quickly forgotten, the bad memory still lingers.

Consequently, the common assumption that human service agencies are created to meet the expressed human needs of a varied, diffuse public is seriously being questioned. In fact, lately a very real issue has been raised, the issue being who is best capable of determining needs— agency or client? This rethinking is partly caused by the new consumerism. Because of the recent emphasis placed on consumer rights, many individuals no longer see themselves as helpless and unable to influence their own destinies. There is evidence of a return to the classical economic model, where survival and growth of an organization are linked to its ability to effectively serve the consumer.

Human service managers must face the fact that there is a growing chasm between the public and the provider. Hostility is manifested not only in terms of increased verbal dissatisfaction, but also in falling budgetary allocations. Government and the public are no longer willing to tolerate vague pronouncements of "do-goodism" as substitutes for observable program impacts. They are demanding proof of accomplishments rather than continued promise of future benefits. It should be apparent that the growth and multiplicity of human service agencies and their advancing bureaucratization, specialization, and complexity have caused a split in the relationship between public and agency. What many managers fail to realize is that while the public consumes services to satisfy legitimate needs, they are also the ultimate controller over how resources are distributed to clients. The public, as clients, demand more and more, but as stockholders they want less and less expenditure. The reality is that not everyone can be pleased. Rationality of such a system might be questioned. Nevertheless, it exists and effort should be expended not to decry its hopelessness, but to find ways to overcome its failings.

COMMUNICATIONS—IS THAT THE PROBLEM?

One generalized heading that has received more than its share of blame for problems is communication. Phrases such as communication breakdown, communication barriers, poor communication, and communication gap have facilely, if not carelessly, been used to account for the clash of ideologies, the public's mistrust of the social service delivery system, failure of multibillion dollar programs, and even breakdown of the family. It does appear that too much emphasis is placed on responsibility of the communication process for our shortcomings rather than on the need to achieve a deeper understanding of causative factors. Such emphasis implies that many of the problems faced by human service agencies are basically those of communication. The contrary appears to be the case. It is more likely that poor communication, rather than a basic cause, is only one visible manifestation of a deeply rooted organizational process which has become dysfunctional.

The communication function should not be thought of as all-encompassing. It is possible that administrators too frequently allude that this thinking exists. The communication process can be identified as part of the total organizational process. When this step is done, there is a basis for identifying those areas and problems where communication, or the lack of it, significantly interacts with other organizational variables.

The organizational communication function has been defined in many ways, but it can basically be thought of as the transfer of information among decision centers within organizational subsystems and various and separate systems, including interchange with the environment. Unfortunately, while human service managers have been trained academically and experientially to deal with such typical management functions as planning, budgeting, controlling, developing, coordinating, and organizing, they are oftentimes less than competent communicators. Consequently, many managers are unable to understand, or even cope with, communication as a separate, yet integral, organizational variable.

The Variety of Communication

There are many types of communication systems within an organization. We are probably most familiar with terms such as upward, downward, and lateral communication. These have often been put forth as explaining the total flow and pattern of communications within organizations. Organizations can basically be subdivided into three distinct functional parts in terms of overall commitments: (1) technical—a set of actions and operations which fulfill the primary commitments of providing a service, producing, or manufacturing; (2) administrative—a set of operations which fulfill the commitments of planning, directing, and intergrating technical activities, and (3) institutional—a set of operations which fulfill the commitments of adapting to a higher level of societal and environmental constraints. These are different manifestations of communication content and structure within these functional areas. Thus, to describe organizational communication, we can divide it into technical, administrative, and institutional communication functional areas, all of which can be managed and organized.

Public Relations

By looking closely at the triadic nature of organizational communication systems, it becomes obvious that institutional communications can be identified more commonly as public relations. Public relations, defined in terms of management of institutional communications, seeks to optimize communication among clientele groups and contributes to the adjustment activities of the organization. Institutional communications, then, enter and leave the organization at many diverse points. It is not, as usually thought, within the sole domain of a few selected individuals; rather, all those who communicate across organizational boundaries engage in institutional communications. Unfortunately, there is a reluctance on the part of human service managers to admit they are responsible for public relations. This situation is partially caused by the administrator's basic unfamiliarity with institutional communication. In addition, management has never traditionally viewed the administrator or bureaucrat to be an integral part of the institutional communication system. Instead, management relies on a small cadre of "professionals" to advise, create, and develop public relations programs.

Public Relations—"It's Not My Job"

There are other reasons why the human service administrator, either by chance or design, shuns the role of institutional communicator. First, administrators and service workers have a low opinion of public relations and those involved in it. Many feel that public relations seeks to glorify at the expense of truth. Some see public relations as oriented solely toward advancing the careers of certain key personalities within the organization rather than advancing the interests of the total unit and recognizing the accomplishments of career personnel. The public information officer, at the same time, is viewed with suspicion and hostility. It is, in some part, because of jealousy, since the public information officer has easier access to and more contact with higher officials than do most senior administrators. Also, it is felt that the public relations people are unable to understand technical, complex problems faced by the workers because of their tendency to gloss over difficulties and to concentrate only on accomplishments. Thus, public relations as viewed by the administrator is a job of little substance and much fanfare. On the other hand, the administrator must realize that public relations is not merely smiling and shaking hands at the proper moment. Public relations is an important organizational process upon which the organization depends for its very survival.

Second, administrators have little opportunity to communicate with the public, since communication is generally reserved for selected officials. Career people write the speeches and develop the programs to be presented to the public. These programs pass through a filtering mechanism that usually consists of political appointees who must, by necessity, maintain a different survival posture. Political appointees often see the administrator as a "first-draft writer" whose acumen and opinion are not to be trusted when he deals with sensitive or political matters. This attitude leads to a self-fulfilling prophecy. Political appointees see administrators as incompetent institutional communicators. Such expectations become internalized by the administrator, who then either shies away from, or even subverts attempts at, institutional communications. This trend has become obvious in federal agencies where disgruntled career people "leak" information that normally does not flow through institutional channels. It is partially caused by a belief that those people in control of institutional communications are not telling the public the full story. Hence, more surreptitious avenues of communication develop, which bureaucrats often promote to get their viewpoint across.

Third, administrators and human service workers have all too often witnessed the misdirection of massive, expensive public relations efforts. For example, the state and federal governments are expending huge sums to advertise the availability of food stamps, and at the same time, they are seeking legislation to curtail eligibility and denounce the program's astronomical rise in costs. Similarly, efforts to find foster parents and adoptive homes for hard-to-place children through public relations efforts have not been a resounding success. Perhaps this is caused by placing too much emphasis and trust in the power of communications. With this in mind, human service managers are hesitant to enter into a process where experts with ample resources managed to fail. There is also a serious question whether public funds should be expended to launch major public relations efforts in support of legislation and proposed programs backed by politically partisan groups.

Finally, managers in the human services often lack the training and theoretical and technical knowledge needed to execute programs of institutional communication. This happens because most schools concentrate on developing the student in the areas of planning, organizing, and controlling. Little thought or time is devoted to management of organizational communications, public opinion assessment, or client relations.

The crucial point is that institutional communication should not be the private province of a few selected political appointees and public information officers. Organizational survival is everyone's concern. In the political governmental system, all parts are interlocked and dependent upon one another. In order to survive, the agency is dependent on the legislature for authorization and funds, the labor market for employees, the voter for support, the culture for values, and the continued existence of clientele to serve. The agency is often unable to fully control all or some of these means. The agency becomes dependent on actions of others and subject to environmental forces it cannot directly affect. In order to ensure continued survival and growth, an organization must successfully interact with those upon which it is dependent or with those who can withhold vital services and goods. It is the function of institutional communication to establish the legitimacy of what you are doing and proposing. In other words, the communication which goes out horizontally is one that will enable adaption to the larger society. The question has to be asked of all the organizations, groups, and clientele that exist in the environment: What factors am I so dependent upon that withdrawal of support will severely influence my survival? It is the responsibility of all organizational members who interact with clientele and of others in the environment to maintain and build an effective, efficient, institutional-communication system.

Open Up Those Channels

However, when there is failure to develop adequate lines of institutional communication, or when these lines are tightly controlled or exhibit limited-access characteristics, then the system is operating at less than optimum level. Such an organization takes on the characteristics of a closed system. Even with administrative and technical communication flowing freely, a lack of institutional communication will serve to isolate the organization from the environment. With all closed systems, when there is no interaction with the environment, disorder increases to a point where the organization ceases to operate or settles at low-performance levels. The ultimate fate of the closed organization is dependent upon conditions imposed on its boundaries. Open organizations, on the other hand, are typically those that engage in interchange with the environment.

Communication across organizational boundaries is an essential factor in an organization's viability, growth ability, and adaptability. Thus, the organization that optimizes institutional communication maintains itself in a continuous inflow and outflow of information. Because it is an open system and can readily transmit and receive institutional communication, the organization is able to react to environmental intrusion. Rather than disintegrate under environmental pressures, the open organization by elaboration and change is able to adapt to what might be otherwise a wrenching experience. Take, for example, the recent experiences of both the March of Dimes and the Tuberculosis Association. Because of their efforts, along with advanced medical technology, they managed to do what almost every helping organization claims they want to do—put themselves out of business. This situation could have meant dismantling sophisticated machinery with consequent loss of a nationwide network of volunteers. Nevertheless, a reworking of goals and objectives quickly put them back into the mainstream, which enabled these organizations to utilize their highly useful systems to combat health challenges such as pollution, lung disease, and birth defects.

Because of their highly developed sense of institutional communication, these organizations were able to respond to one of the most dramatic of challenges—a complete loss of clientele. This step was accomplished by effectively communicating a need to exist in order to combat other major problems. To combat other health dangers, the organizations developed an entirely new set of clientele to serve. The much talked about anti-poverty programs, on the other hand, basically failed in their efforts to survive because institutional communications had been severely restricted to the limited clientele group directly served. While such programs created a base of support among minorities and the poor, they were unable to gain acceptance from groups which had the political and economic power to ensure long-range continuation of such programs. Hence, by limiting institutional communications, local poverty programs managed to seal their fate by failing to satisfactorily justify their existence to those who could affect their survival capability.

Consequently, it is in the open organization where environmental intrusions, which might at first appear destructive, become structured because of the adaptive capabilities of the system. The closed organization cannot successfully adapt to changing environmental conditions. It is because of lack of transfer of information and communication with the environment that open organizations may become more orderly or negatively entropic.

Organizations that remain sensitive to the clientele served and that are continually aware of environmental changes can maintain themselves at a high level and increase orderliness and the ability to deliver services. Organizations that do not successfully communicate with the environment increase their entropy and slowly run down, as exhibited by failure to meet clientele commitments, internal conflict, and low levels of efficiency and effectiveness.

Public Relations—It's Everyone's Job

It should be obvious by now that institutional communication is the responsibility of all those who communicate across organizational boundaries. By viewing institutional communication in this context, we see that a wide range and type of personnel represent the organization. Hence, every administrator and career government official are responsible for both the continued survival and growth of the organization. Administrators given greater responsibility and credit for institutional communication will tend to build a more committed staff, a more productive organization, and a better-served clientele. Every effort should be made to transfer and distribute public relations functions throughout the organization and, especially, to those areas where there is frequent contact with other organizations and clientele. Institutional communications should not enter and leave the organization from some narrow gate controlled by a few politically sensitive individuals. Instead, any comprehensive program of institutional communications should heavily depend on the fullest use of managers and workers who are key links within and between the organization and the environment.

Public relations, therefore, should be considered both as an operating concept of management and as an organizational-survival mechanism. It does not exist in isolation from organizational mission and objectives, but provides the wherewithal to make their implementation possible. More specifically, the purpose and function of public relations in the social service setting includes:

1. Informing the public about the scope, purpose, and impact of service programs
2. Obtaining support (volunteers, money, public opinion) for continued program operation from the public, legislatures, clients, and interest groups
3. Providing data on public opinion and prevalent attitudes toward the agency, and its varied services
4. Developing formalized communication networks with opinion leaders, mass media, and potential funding sources for the purpose of influencing favorable and beneficial actions
5. Instituting a feedback mechanism allowing for community input and decision-making—especially in determining service mix
6. Gaining acceptance for the implementation of new services or the reduction and termination of ineffective ones
7. Informing the public about the types of programs and services available and eligibility requirements for participation

Reaching and Selling Your Public

One of the most prevalent mistakes in managing human service organizations is to underestimate the importance of marketing communications. Communications are necessary not only for resource gathering, but also for attracting a clientele willing to seek and accept agency services. There is nothing so disturbing as a well-funded service operation waiting with open doors for clients that never appear. A primary justification for program existence is not only that people are helped, but also that they are willing to take advantage of offered services. Just as Proctor & Gamble uses advertising to attract customers, so must human service agencies. The marketing or public relations process is then critical in terms of telling about services, attracting consumers to these services, and, consequently, attaining funds for continued service.

The first step in developing a viable organizational-public relations effort is commitment to its functional importance. This applies to managers, employees, and even clientele. In addition, the organization must have a public relations plan. Good public relations, like good management, requires an ongoing, highly coordinated, systematized approach that is guided by individuals with an understanding and competence in public relations concepts and application. Public relations should not be treated as a step-child utilized when and if needed or cut at the first sign of budgetary deficiency. Rather, it must be totally integrated into the management process. In fact, it is during times of financial stringency that public relations efforts should be increased and not abandoned. In the private sector, when demand for a particular product drops, or the economy takes a downturn, advertising and public relations efforts usually increase—not decrease. Perhaps, on this point human service organizations should be more willing to mimic the profit-making sector—after all, organizational survival and achievement are at stake.

Unfortunately, as in many cases, the road to failure is paved with many good intentions. Admitting the necessity for institutional communication is not alone a sufficient cause for success. Serious attempts must be made at overcoming some of the more commonplace operational errors. The most frequent shortcomings found are listed here. First, there is a failure to adequately analyze or identify the public relations problem. For example, is a program having limited success because clients do not know of its existence or because it is a lousy program and clients do not perceive it to be personally useful? The former is a public relations problem and can be ameliorated through the communication process; the latter is not. Second, public relations programs are often lacking because of an inability to define the important or interacting public; this omission is probably the most serious one committed by the novice public relations practitioner. "Shotgunning" a message across a vast audience is not the most efficient mechanism for achieving an expected outcome. Instead, it is more productive to specifically tailor the message for the highly identified target public because relevant audience, media, motivators, and other characteristics can be incorporated into the communication design. There is an almost infinite number of the "public" out there. Individuals have primary allegiance to some and secondary associations with others. It is important to be aware of the varying quality of message impact when one relates to specific types of groupings. Third, human service agencies have a propensity for crying wolf. How often have you heard that the county will be bankrupt unless assistance levels can be cut? Such abject cries of poverty have initial impact but lose vitality if overused, particularly when the threatened collapse does not occur. In general, it is best not to bring out your "Sunday punch" unless you really have to use it—do not kill a mosquito with a sledge hammer. There are more fruitful ways of getting the attention of the public without trying to cut them off at the knees.

Fourth, do not assume importance in the community that justifiably is not yours. It must be realized that people are becoming immunized to constant demands on their pocketbooks, time, and psyches. The unrelenting bombardment from the mass media, government, churches, and friends is forcing people to develop barriers. There is no reason for thinking that anyone out there either knows or gives a "damn" about what your organization does. The only time that you become important, or are raised to the level of individual awareness, is when you directly step on their turf or provide a service in which they want to take part. Fifth, along the same lines, do not make the supposition that because you are in the "helping people business" that everyone supports such efforts. A community is heterogeneous and individuals adhere to different frames of reference. Even if the "public" were not against the end result of human service service efforts, there is plenty of room for legitimate disagreement about means to those ends and their costs. Finally, your selling job becomes that much more difficult because you are dealing in intangibles. In addition, unless you can make a logical connection, the services offered are often perceived as having little immediate benefit for the individual who often involuntarily pays for their delivery.

As you can readily see, public relations is not an easy campaign to mount or successfully conduct. It requires a sensitive reading of where the public is, what it is willing to accept, how much personal drain it is willing to tolerate, and where it wants to be taken.

PUBLIC RELATIONS PROBLEMS—THREE ORGANIZATIONAL SHORTCOMINGS

Expectation/Reality Gap

The bulk of public relations problems in the day-to-day management of the human services is related to three organizational shortcomings: a first major area of concern is the divergence between expectation and reality; perhaps this statement needs further explanation. Earlier we stated that identification of the interacting public upon whom the organization is dependent for survival is critical to the successful implementation of institutional-communication efforts. Assume that two highly interactive types of the public have been identified—the client and the community. Next, specify current or potential trouble-spots that might be a source of concern to either party. This step can readily be accomplished by asking two questions and then by answering them. First, what does the human service agency expect from the public (client, community)? Second, what does the public (client, community) expect from the human service organization? It is the perceived distance between expectation and reality that causes a major proportion of existing public relations problems. Regardless of reality, people build up expectations of how they should be treated, the level of service to be provided, and the anticipated resolution. If individual perspectives on service shortcomings are shared by large groups, then the agency is faced with a public relations problems. Take, for instance, the question of agency expectations of clients and vice versa. The following typical responses are received from individuals working in local district public social service agencies:

Agency Expects of Client	*Client Expects of Agency*
Honesty	Services
Cooperation	Financial support
Responsibility	Honesty
Understanding	Courtesy
Initiative to help themselves	Receive what entitled to
Compliance	Confidentiality
Accepting treatment	Nonjudgmental attitude
Taking the cure	Understanding
Information	Immediacy of service
Promptness	Respect
	Sensitivity
	Care for problems

By and large, as you can see, each party has a differing set of expectations. It is only natural for the worker to try making his task easier by hoping for clients who come fully prepared with information, are cooperative, nonargumentative, willing to listen, and accept everything. The client, on the other hand, sees the agency and worker as a provider of "goodies" in terms of services and financial assistance.

From the client's perspective, it boils down to "How can I get the most while giving up the least?" From the agency and worker's perspective, it is "How can I give up the least while getting the most?" Such divergent viewpoints are bound to lead to some vigorous conflicts—to the point where the delivery of social services, especially in the public sector, is seen from a "we" vs. "they" perspective. Let us look at how community and agency expectations might differ:

Agency Expects of Community	Community Expects of Agency
Understanding	Accountability
Cooperation	Acceptance of responsibility for
Volunteers	poor, handicapped, and society's rejects
More community resources	ety's rejects
Rapport	Rehabilitation and solution to
Approval	problems
Support	Efficiency
Help and information	To be left alone
Praise	Clients kept out of their neighborhoods
	Low cost

As can be plainly seen, agency and community expectations of each other are in disagreement. The agency wants not only community support for what it is accomplishing, but also a blessing. The community, however, does not want to be bothered, but would be happiest if it could be completely isolated from the reality of social service delivery and its need for financial sustenance. Each type public examined, then, can be expected to have different sets of perceived expectations of social service benefits in their communities.

The Nature of Bureaucracy

Another primary source of public relations problems is in the very nature of the bureaucratic structure itself. Bureaucracy promotes specificity of expertness and also strictly limits areas of responsibility. In this case, the client is approached with neutrality, which leads to several common complaints. First, the human service delivery system is not "sensitive" to the needs and problems of the individual client.

It is very hard to explain to a distraught parent that national priorities Congress set did not provide for adequate medical care for her child. The worker, in effect, is forced to shield himself from the client's wrath by using a backup of social service rules and guidelines. Also, if a worker, when confronted with a less than routine case rigidly sticks to organizational norms, he usually fares better than if he tries to bend organizational norms to the client's needs or if he constantly goes up the hierarchy with problems. Second, the extreme pigeonholing of responsibility gives rise to the "It's not my job" mentality. Clients are routinely shunted from one agency to another, one office to another, or one window to another. This situation often leaves the citizen with the feeling that there must be a better way.

Third, client-contact level may be set too low in the organization. Typically, the client interacts with lower ranking personnel; his total conceptions about the agency and govenment, in general, are formed around these fleeting contacts. However, it is the employees at the lower organizational levels who have the least decision flexibility, the least experience in dealing with human relations problems, and the least-formalized education or training.

Similarly, once an employee has been identified as being able to handle client contact, he often finds it more difficult to attain promotion than those who might have prepared themselves for the next, less client-oriented stage by being more organization- than client-minded. In other words, client advocates within the administrative structure of an agency are often viewed with suspicion and hostility, as if they were challenging the organization's very existence. Thus, to be overly client-oriented and to transmit client demands upward can be a relatively unrewarding experience in many social service agencies.

Responsiveness and Accountability Take the Back Seat

Finally, public relations problems are on the upswing because too much emphasis has been placed on improving the production mechanisms, and too little thought has been given to the need for human service responsiveness and accountability. With Watergate all but a memory, there has been an apparent return to the "business as usual" behavior on the part of our human service agencies, which typically means defensiveness, obfuscation, prevarication, and secretiveness. If this attitude is indeed the case, then efforts to increase organizational productivity at the expense of improving responsiveness and accountability are solving one problem, but creating another with equally negative implications. Recent research by this author attempted to analyze unobtrusively one of the most important, if least understood, indicators of public-sector responsiveness—its communication behavior. In looking at organizational-communication behavior, two access points are readily available: First, organizational openness in accepting and processing information from outside the environment. Second, the organization's ability and willingness to transmit adequate and accurate information back into the environment. Research, in this instance, stressed the latter because it appeared that planned, coordinated programs of public response are the exception and not the rule.

Requesting Information: The Case of the Housewife and the Taxpayers' Organization

Unfortunately, most public programs which are concerned with internal consistency and performance images tend to react to requests for information as something to resist or attack. In order to evaluate patterns of communication-openness between citizen and government, two "blind" letters were sent to fifty-five state agencies in a large eastern state. These letters from (a) a typical housewife (handwritten on plain white paper) and (b) the Coalition of Concerned Citizens (typed on letterhead bond), a fictitious group of organized taxpayers, were similar in nature and content, made specific requests for information, and were mailed a week apart.

Initially, all agencies queried were evaluated on whether a response was forthcoming. However, further detailed analysis was reserved for twenty-eight matched pairs, or those responding both to the coalition and to the housewife. It was anticipated that the character and effectiveness of agency response reflects the quality of the organization's communication efforts, responsiveness, and its interest in satisfying legitimate queries for information. There were two thrusts in analyzing the data. First, to compare responses on seven key indicators of communication openness. Second, to ascertain whether significant differences appeared when comparing the housewife and coalition letters on these variables.

Such research is made possible by the emergence of information as a quantitative concept. As Deutsch points out, information can be counted and measured, and the performance of communication channels in transmitting or distorting information can be evaluated in quantitative terms. While some of these measurements might be termed inelegant, this fact does not obscure the importance of being able to measure at all.[1]

A Response Is Not Inevitable

A key indicator of communication-openness between government and citizen is an agency's willingness to respond to written requests for information. Of the fifty-five agencies queried, only twenty-eight (or 51 percent) responded to both letters. A closer look at response rate breakdown shows forty-four (or 81 percent) of the agencies responded to the housewife letters, whereas only thirty-two (or 58 percent) of the organizations answered the coalition. Such response-rate differences make us speculate why this situation occurred. One plausible explanation is that the coalition letter, which was professionally typed and written on letterhead stationary, was perceived as threatening. The coalition explained they were concerned with accountability in the use of scarce public funds and wanted to evaluate the services of the agency by asking some realistic, hard questions about service provision. Agencies, not knowing the motives behind such a request, probably tended to shrink away from the request and played it safe rather than to provide data to a potentially hostile organization. In fact, some support for this explanation can be demonstrated by the overt and covert search effort made by several organizations in an attempt to discover the nature, size, and disposition of the group which requested such information. Consequently, rather than reply forthrightly to a request for "public" data, many agencies adopted a defensive withholding posture. The housewife letter, on the other hand, was not written in such a challenging manner, but opened by saying that she was a mother of three whose husband worked hard and paid lots of taxes. This letter was handwritten on plain paper. Nevertheless, the questions were basically the same, although written in a different format. Apparently, agencies found this type letter less threatening because it represented the request of only one citizen rather than a group of unknown size, proclivity, and proportions. Being perceived as "harmless," this experimental treatment tended to get a considerably higher response rate.

Going a little further into the data, it was found that eight (or 14.5 percent) of the agencies responded to neither letter. Whether this represents a mechanical breakdown in the communication system or conscious policy is not known. However, these results take on greater significance when it is revealed that both the Governor's Office and the State Consumer Protection Board were among the eight nonrespondents. These two organizations should be particularly sensitive to the information needs of the public—the Governor because he is the state's chief elected official, and the Consumer Protection Board because they must act as role models for the businesses they regulate and from whom they demand compliance. Overall response rates can be visually demonstrated by looking at Figure 7-1.

Inelegant Data, But Useful Results

While initial response rates were tabulated for the total universe of fifty-five potential respondents, further analysis concentrated on those who responded to both the housewife and the coalition query. Hence, twenty-eight matched pairs were used to develop a comparative data base on the following variables: (1) response time; (2) number of

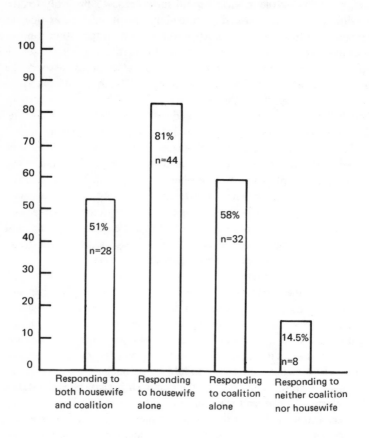

a. Fifty-five agencies were queried.

Figure 7.1: PERCENTAGE RESPONSE RATES TO HOUSEWIFE-AND
COALITION LETTER BY STATE AGENCIES[a]

questions answered; (3) status of signer; (4) supportiveness of efforts; (5) invitation to follow-up; (6) specification of cover letter; (7) and type of supporting documents.

It is important for organizations not only to acknowledge requests for information, but also to do it in a timely fashion if the act is to have positive impact and meaning. Hence, the number of days to answer queries from the housewife and coalition was seen as an important indicator of the effectiveness of in-house communication mechanisms. This dimension measure was defined as the elapsed time from the postmarked date of the inquiry letter as compared to the cover-letter date on the agency's response. Examination revealed response times ranging from a minimum of 2 days to a maximum of 69. The mean-response time to the coalition letter was 17.9 days compared to a mean-response rate of 13.5 days for the housewife letter. If one could establish 14 days as a reasonable response time, then sixteen of the twenty-eight agencies (or 57 percent) answering the coalition were within this limit, while nineteen of the twenty-eight letters to the housewife (or 68 percent) were forwarded in this time frame.

Both the housewife and coalition letters requested answers to six questions: (1) What are the goals and objectives of your organization? (2) What is your budget allocation? (3) What justification can you give in support of the budget allocation? (4) In terms of the services provided, how is the life of the average state citizen improved by the continued existence of your organization? (5) Are you providing these services in the most efficient, effective manner? (6) Are there alternative approaches that can be considered?

Two places were searched for specific responses to questions: first, the cover letter itself; second, within included supportive materials. There is a tendency for many organizations to respond to specific information requests by merely sending off-the-shelf materials, such as annual reports and pamphlets. While these might be sources of valuable information, it was felt that cover letters which deal with specific points of fact indicated a sincere attempt to meet expressed data needs of the sender. Consequently, an attempt was made to measure the specificity of the cover letter. In order to do this step, a score of one was given to each of the six questions that were specifically addressed in the cover letter. Consequently, responses were scored on a 0 to 6 scale, with a zero indicating no questions answered in the cover letter and with six showing all questions being answered. The average number of questions answered in response to the coalition letter was 3.1; the average housewife's response was 2.82. In other words, only about one-half of the questions were addressed in the cover letters.

Optimum accessibility to information is an important part of a communication mechanism. Throwing hordes of poorly organized information at a recipient is no substitute for direct, detailed responses. Surely, the step might take longer this way, but it probably pays off in terms of consumer satisfaction. Maximum use of information is attained when questions are answered in a simple, discernable manner, leaving out the "fluff" and including the substance. Failure to do so forces the recipient to flounder through piles of supportive documents searching for answers that might be elusive or just not there.

After analyzing the specificity of the cover letter, other materials included by the agencies were examined for relevance to posed questions. In searching through the supplied documents, it was found that a total 4.4 of the six questions were responded to in the housewife condition and 4.7 in the coalition treatment. The figures represent an increase of over 1.5 when compared to the cover letter alone.

In examining the questions individually, it can be clearly demonstrated that most agencies tended to disregard two specific questions: (1) Are you providing these services in the most efficient and effective manner? (2) Are there alternative approaches that can be considered? It was discovered that 45 percent of the coalition responses failed to deal with these questions at all, while 60 percent of housewife responses did not concern themselves with these issues. It appears from the data that agencies were relatively willing to share information when the inquiries focused on such nonthreatening topics as services provided, budgets, and goals. Nevertheless, when responses required self-examina-

---

    I. Chief officer (commissioner, president, executive director)

   II. Deputy level (deputy directors, administrative director, vice presidents, executive secretary)

  III. Program or unit directors

  IV. Assistant or deputy program and unit directors

   V. Staff or miscellaneous (assistant to, special assistant, secretary)

Figure 7.2: SIGNATURES BY ORGANIZATION LEVEL

tion and assessment, agencies seemed reluctant to transmit potentially damaging data.

Relative status of those signing the responses was also deemed an important measure of communication openness. The assumption here is that the level of the officer who is handling the communication is an indication of either the esteem or perception of relative power in which the organization holds the sender. Hence, it was predicted that, on the average, signers of the coalition treatment will come from higher organizational echelons than those responding to the housewife. In order to measure this prediction, a hierarchy of status levels was established, with each signer being assigned to one of five categories. See Figure 7-2 for the categories.

In comparing respondents, it was found that 61 percent (n = 17) of those signing letters to the coalition were top-agency, or Level I, officials in contrast to the housewife who received only 32 percent (nine) of her letters from the chief officer. A detailed breakdown by status of the respondents can be obtained by reviewing Table 7-1.

It is also interesting to point out that in only 10 percent of the cases were responses to the coalition letter signed by individuals who held public relations titles, while 35 percent of those answering the housewife had such positions. The prediction that the coalition letter would be handled at higher organizational levels appears to be borne out. Once again, it is probably the sensitive nature of the requests, along with the unknown size and influence of the coalition, which tended to push the response up into the organizational hierarchy. Since the coalition letter was obviously processed outside routine channels, it might account for the longer average-response time when compared to the housewife.

Additionally, agencies probably tend to develop "response attitudes," which become obvious in terms of how supportive organizations are of these searching efforts. Hence, a "supportiveness of efforts"

Table 7.1: COMPARISONS OF RESPONDENT-STATUS LEVELS

Status	Treatment			
	Housewife		Coalition	
Level I (chief officer)	32%	(9)	61%	(17)
Level II (deputy)	14%	(4)	21%	(6)
Level III (program director)	18%	(5)	7%	(2)
Level IV (assistant program director)	18%	(5)	4%	(1)
Level V (staff or miscellaneous)	11%	(3)	7%	(2)
No signature	7%	(2)	0%	(0)

measure was devised. Supportiveness of efforts was measured on a 1 to 3 scale, with a 1 indicating that the responding agency was decidedly negative in addressing itself to the inquiry. An example of this negative approach sent by one agency could be seen in a letter which went on to state, "We advise that this office cannot use tax dollars to answer all of your questions and those of others writing." A response receiving a score of 2 can be characterized as being neutral in tone, neither offering overt encouragement nor discouragement. Those letters receiving a score of 3 demonstrated high degrees of support and encouragement for the writer's efforts. An example of a nurturing approach can be seen in this letter: "I congratulate you upon the formation of your organization. A monitoring agency such as yours is a vital link in keeping government accountable to the people it serves."

The necessary point is that it costs no more in time, money, or effort to be polite, so why antagonize a "stockholder" by being overtly defensive or negative about attempts to obtain information? Yet, many organizations, whether consciously or unconsciously, manage to insult the very people that legitimize their existence. This circumstance should not be the case. Examination of the responses indicated a mean-supportiveness score of 2.14 for the coalition and 2.25 for the housewife response. While these scores represent a neutral affectation toward the inquiry, the agencies could probably be better-served if employees responsible for communication with the public made efforts to be more supportive.

Another indicator, somewhat linked to the supportiveness issue, was concerned with a desire for further contact with the sender. Such follow-ups usually took the form of encouraging continued correspondence; however, in many cases a request to meet individually with the coalition/housewife was expressed. For the most part, agencies appeared more willing to initiate further contact with the coalition than with the housewife. In fact, 60 percent of the agencies invited coalition follow-up, compared to 50 percent for the housewife. These figures indicate that only 55 percent of the agencies queried were concerned enough with the adequacy of their transmissions to request further contact. Since follow-ups demonstrate a degree of concern and openness in dissemination of information, the communication loop should be kept open by making follow-up a priority item.

Another indicator of communication responsiveness concentrated on types of additional, or supportive, materials included in the package. Materials were coded and placed into one of seven categories: pamphlets, annual reports, planning or review documents, budget documents, internal reports, legal documents, and miscellaneous.

The coalition and housewife responses differed by the types of materials received, but not necessarily in aggregate numbers. Fifty-three percent of the packages received by the housewife included one or more pamphlets, whereas in only 18 percent of the coalition responses were pamphlets enclosed. Compared to 7 percent for the housewife, however, the coalition received planning or review documents in 28.6 percent of its responses. Similarly, internal reports were part of the 10 percent of the submissions to the coalition and only made up 3.6 percent of those sent to the housewife.

These figures suggest differential treatment in the type of materials sent to either the coalition or the housewife. The coalition tended to get material of a technical nature concerned more with internal management issues. The housewife, on the other hand, received the types of literature designed for public distribution. On the average, then, only half of the agencies responded to both queries for information. The quality of responses ranged from complete to almost utterly useless. Such facts are not representative of a communication system in good working order. Public agencies, above all others, should especially be tuned to the needs of the community, not only because service programs are being attacked and resisted, but also because of the positive feedback implications inherent in a well-ordered communication mechanism.

The Public Has Recourse

The public, in this instance, is neither helpless nor unable to exert influence over the human service delivery system. Many people, in order to bring in line the delivery mechanism with existing group concepts, can attempt to modify organizational directions in several basic ways. The first is through the use of countervailing economic power. Here, an individual can legally or illegally refuse to pay taxes, withhold rent in public housing, and boycott services or programs that require fees. Because of the sanctions that can be taken against those withholding legal and just payments to government and the type allocation the government uses, this power is small in terms of its impact on large human service organizations. Second, if the consumer of a public human service possesses any significant, countervailing power, it is not economic, but political clout. There is power in one's ability to exercise a franchise to vote. Also, individuals can channel complaints to local politicians, such as party chairmen or elected legislators, in the hope that their prodding can get things moving. Third, an individual who is dissatisfied with our government has free access to the media to report apparent misdeeds on the part of errant government officials. Thus, through the media, a person can use forceful public opinion to bear down on a government agency. Fourth, the client can use established governmental mechanisms to seek redress of grievances. For example, if he believes he was not treated fairly by a local Department of Social Services, he can appeal a decision to the state or HEW. Hence, one can either file complaints one step up the ladder with regulatory or funding agencies or contact the department in which the dispute exists. Fifth, every citizen is entitled to a day in court. Through class action and other types of suits, the judicial system is increasingly becoming one of the most potent "watchdogs" against official excess. Finally, several individuals can form new coalitions around particular issues, join existing pressure or interest groups, or support and participate in the more generalized "better government" type organization, such as Common Cause. In this way, one person, through the process of mutual support, can exercise influence far in excess of his individual ability to affect governmental outcomes. It should be pointed out, however, that different types of the public are able to exercise different amounts of influence in their relations with a public organization. For example, the Welfare Rights Organization as a social welfare pressure group, although very vocal, has limited influence on determination of medical care policy when compared to the American Medical Association.

WHAT'S THE ANSWER?

The preceding discussion would indicate that unanswered expectations, poor client relationships, and lack of organizational accountability and responsiveness constitute the major portion of public relations problems faced in the management of the human services. However, to sense that this situation is, indeed, happening, or to be aware that the organization is being inundated with institutional problems as greater managerial efficiency and bureaucratization is achieved, does not mean that management has the capacity to categorize them in ways that make them amenable to solution. It explains, in part, why the somewhat vague, much-maligned term "public relations" is so widely adopted. The hope is that public relations activity might provide a conceptual and operational base from which solutions to these problems might be derived.

Public relations as a linguistic term is meaningfully defined in terms of referring to a very real, though not very well-defined, set of problems concerning stability and survival of the organization. The often-heard definition of public relations as a function which evaluates public opinion identifies the organization's policies and procedures with the "public interest" and executes a program of communication to secure "public understanding and good will." It leads logically into a blind alley. It is not clear, for instance, how the mere evaluation of public opinion will provide managment with information which is not already self-evident. Namely, management's demand for more efficiency and greater bureaucratization tends only to increase client dissatisfaction, raise the level of expectations, and reduce responsiveness. It is not clear how the mere knowledge of these problems will help management deal with inherent bureaucratic deficiencies.

Finally, one is left to wonder how management is to go about "executing" a program of communication to "secure understanding, acceptance, and goodwill." It is also not clear how much communication is necessary to solve these problems. To place the emphasis solely on communication implies that such problems are basically those of communication. In fact, the contrary appears to be the case since problems are more likely a result of bureaucratic behavior, such as depersonalization, categorization, and defensibility. Consequently, an effort to increase the tenor of communication should be directed at the reduction of those actions and reactions that constitute bureaucratic behavior. This effort, by necessity, involves more than cranking out press releases. The organization must make a commitment to change and innovation if client-relation problems are to be significantly reduced.

Open the Channels from the Outside: Bring Them In

It is impossible for any organization, private or public, to satisfy all its consumers. No one is advocating this position. However, every reasonable attempt should be made to meet client needs and, if this is not possible, then to provide alternatives. If, in fact, an organization is experiencing an inordinate amount of consumer conflict, there are various procedures that can be readily applied to help lessen its impact. One method is to develop institutionalized and formal channels of agency-client communication whereby management can regularly receive feedback and guidance from the public. The success of this approach is predicated upon an honest desire by the agency to be influenced by such contacts. The initiation of citizen boards and panels just for show or to meet government guidelines will, without doubt, lead to greater client-agency alienation.

In the same vein, decision levels should be brought down to those administrative units which have high interface with the public. This step has the effect of increasing agency flexibility when dealing with client problems and making the public feel as if they were part of the decision-making process. It is important that the public have easy access to the organization, especially at decision centers. Similarly, it is essential that some type of periodic assessment of client feelings and opinions be undertaken. Public officials should not fall into the trap of thinking because there is a citizen advisory board input that there is no longer a need to interact with the larger public. It is the rare board that represents an accurate cross section of the client public. Hence, attempts must be made to take readings on how the wider public feels about agency operations.

A word or two about the general process of co-optation might be useful. Public organizations can co-opt clients by either fictitiously or realistically bringing clients into the decision-making process. The conditions under which co-optation is real and fictitious are not firmly established. It seems that co-optation is more often applied from those in control to the clients rather than the other way around. Co-optation is often used in order to create a semblance of communication from clients to those in control without actually providing it. When co-optation is manipulative or fictitious, it not only fails to co-optate the client but blocks the expression of his needs.

A second approach is to have upper management, or those who set client-agency policy, actively in touch with the reality of client-agency conflict. The reception of client groups in one's home office or the occasional speech to the local Jaycees is not the process we refer to. Instead, administrators set aside enough time for field visits and even on-the-line client contact. In other words, visit the line troops, fill out some forms, talk to clients, punch the computer, and deal with some real-life problems. Such activities will aid in the development of new, realistic perspectives for those executives who have too long been separated from the agency's clientele. In addition, government employees should be systematically rotated on a regular basis from "back office" to contact positions. This move will help provide the needed interface between technical and actual program implementation.

Finally, employees in high-client contact positions should undergo formalized training to help deal with what appears to be an often-hostile clientele. We are all familiar with human relations. "T" groups, and sensitivity training. Although they are useful techniques, they have been found lacking in several critical areas. One new mode of employee-client interaction training that is receiving critical acclaim is transactional analysis. This approach has been successfully applied in such client-intensive organizations as banks and airlines.

Open the Channels to the Outside: Send Information Out

Such suggestions might prove useful to relieve client dissatisfaction and restore a balance between expectation and reality. Nevertheless, the question of improving responsiveness and public accountability is yet to be addressed. Hence, some guidelines are being posted as to how human service organizations can respond to public requests for information. First, an overriding communication objective should be to ensure that every request for information is honored in a timely, complete manner. More importantly, agencies must be prepared to abandon this "we" vs. "they" attitude. Second, agencies should resist the idea that an uninformed public is a pliable public. The giving or withholding of information is not used as a power ploy or a reward for political favor. Instead, all information should truly be treated as if it is in the public domain. There are very few instances where programmatic information can be classified as secret or confidential. Organizations must stop hiding behind the facade that they have always been sensitive to the needs of the public. Balderdash! The research previously discussed delineated hard data substantiating some of the more common communications abuses. The dissatisfaction of any one member of the public detracts from the welfare of all. Third, that while the most essential ingredients of public satisfaction are efficient and effective service programs, it is of utmost importance that the public be kept informed. The best way to accomplish this is to provide good program information without raising unrealistic expectations. This statement implies that communication should be truthful, informative, complete, supportive, timely, and should not overpromise. Typical public relations puffery must be avoided at all costs if a healthy communication relationship between the public and the agency is to be maintained. It should also be pointed out that the public is more concerned about program eligibility and performance than about the agencies who provide the services. Hence, by concentrating on making a name for the organization, its chief official might be self-defeating communication policy.

Finally, the essence of an effective communication-response mechanism is an integrated effort focusing on program quality control, service delivery, and public information supported by management with high-level responsibility for public affairs. This effort means that physical facilities for handling communications must be sharpened and that specific individuals be designated as communication contact points and control centers to ensure prompt and deliberate response to all requests for public information. Communication responsiveness is a management task. Attempts to legislate government openness through so-called sunshine or freedom of information laws will tend to channel and restrict communications rather than facilitate their flow and transmission. The notion of increasing communication accessibility is one that meets with much surface favor, but it suffers from undercurrents of fear of forthcoming results in terms of organizational survival. Communication openness between agency and citizen should not be a question, but a definite statement. Anything less than complete openness and responsiveness represents poor organizational management and, worse yet, disregard for the public's welfare.

NOTE

1. Karl Deutsch, *The Nerves of Government* (New York: Free Press, 1963), p. 149.

Chapter 8

COMMUNICATING WITHIN THE ORGANIZATION

INTRODUCTION

Chapter 8 continues the organizational-communications theme. It changes the focus, however, from external public relations-oriented communications discussed in Chapter 7 to internal communications within the human service organization. Lack of adequate communications, in addition to shouldering a great deal of blame for failures in interactions with the public, is also accused of being the major culprit in intra-agency failures. Communication within the human service organization is a more complex, extensive process than most managers realize.

Discussion centers around components of the communication process—the sender, the message, the channel, and the receiver. Each component has a number of factors which have impact on it that should be considered when developing internal communications. These factors are also discussed at length. A discussion on managing the communication system follows delineation of the entire communication process. Chapter 8 concludes with a number of suggestions for improving communication within the human service organization.

ORGANIZATIONAL COMMUNICATION

Communications is probably the most talked about but least-understood organizational component. Such a state of affairs is caused by the multitude of management experts either who intentionally fail to treat communications as a key dimension or who lack sufficient knowledge in the subject area to make any worthwhile comments. In actuality, communications is the glue that binds organizations together and allows them to function and achieve. After all, what is an organization but a gigantic, complex communications network. Organizational structure not only defines relationships and roles, but also channels information in a cohesive, coordinated manner among individuals and units. From a pure communications perspective, managers can be viewed as information gatekeepers whose primary task is to control, generate, evaluate, distill, and gather information from interacting units. In this sense, then, the formal structure acts as a highway system guiding both the direction of the information flow (up, down, sideways) and the distribution pattern and its terminal points.

Unfortunately, many organizations fail to fully realize the extent of communication malaise within their midst. Perhaps this failure is caused by the naive notion that improving communications is merely a matter of increasing word volume. It could not be further from the truth. Yes, all managers communicate—some better than others. Yes, all organizations act as networks—some more efficiently than others. Yes, organizational members hear and receive what is being transmitted—some with greater attentiveness than others. Nevertheless, these somewhat simplified ideas do not make up the sum and substance of administrative communications, for the transmission of information and the systems needed to propel it are the central themes undergirding organizational productivity.

The organizational-communications spectrum is both wide and diverse. Before launching into an in-depth description and analysis of administrative communications within human service organizations, it might be fruitful to spend a few moments visualizing the communication process. Researchers have traditionally broached the subject by dividing the communication system into these functional areas: source, message, channel, and recipient. In terms of organizational communications, the system consists of management which has a need to communicate something at various responsibility levels. This something is translated into a message which is transmitted through formal or informal organizational channels to an employee who is at various stages of readiness to accept the communication. Given these individual elements, the communication model can be depicted in Figure 8-1.

As an approach, Chapter 8 will focus on how each part of the entire communication process interacts with the whole organizational system. It will also detail the characteristics and dimensions needed to make organizational-communication mechanisms work. We will first look at managerial traits which impact how the manager is perceived by those receiving a communication. In addition to leadership styles,

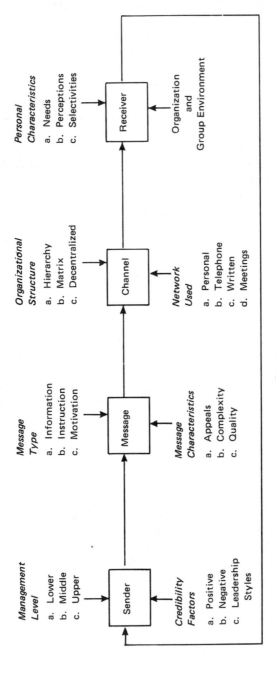

Figure 8.1: ADMINISTRATIVE COMMUNICATIONS' MODEL

181

emphasis will be placed on relevant and irrelevant source credibility factors and influence of positive and negative credibility conditions. Message variables to be considered include: type of message and appeals employed, quality, complexity, order of contents, and others. Next, the channel, or means, of communication will be investigated to determine whether particular channels have different catalytic effects on the recipient. Finally, the recipient phase will basically be analyzed in terms of individual characteristics that might affect acceptance of communication intent and the stimulation of overt behavior needed to carry it through. Once this is accomplished, emphasis will shift to identify potential communications' dysfunctions and their remedies. A serious effort will be made to describe, highlight, and pinpoint interorganizational roadblocks and facilitate factors for attaining effective communications.

THE SENDER–THE COMMUNICATOR

The communication originator, in this case, a manager, often has a naive faith in the power of the message over subordinates. Management tends to assume that its decisions are rational and objective and that proper communication through appropriate channels will transform employees into instant believers. Unfortunately, employees are not android-like in their behavior, and, counter to popular opinion, the mere sending of a communication does not propel them into a paroxysm of action. Consequently, the primary communication requirement, according to the management perspective, is to make sure that decisions, proposed actions, and changes are translated into a comprehensible format and are delivered to the recipient by some interorganizational mechanism.

Tell the employee what you want and how to accomplish it, and the communication process is finished. This kind of thinking is based on these assumptions: (1) Management's decisions are rational and in the best interests of the organization and its members. (2) Subordinates will accept and act upon communications which are sent through appropriate channels. (3) Decisions are not carried out because the messages detailing the information were either not received or misunderstood. In this instance, the fault is never with management and its formulation of the decision and the message, but with the employee who failed to attend to or understand what was being said. If this were, in fact, the case, then corrective action would be easy to initiate; that is, basically to increase the amount and flow of information in a downward direction. Nevertheless, it has been repeatedly demonstrated that organizational members do not respond to such assumptions. Instead, successful communication involves more than downward information flow and depends on a host of variables, including sender credibility, channel direction, nature of the receiver, degree of trust, type of leadership, amount of "noise," and so forth.

Management Credibility

The sender's credibility and prestige has repeatedly been found to be a key consideration in how receivers react to messages. Who says something is usually as important as what is said. In other words, how employees respond to communications is often dependent on personal perceptions of the communicator in regard to image, intentions, trustworthiness, and responsibility. Studies of what is termed "source credibility" revealed the existence of three key source dimensions: safety, dynamism, and qualifications.

Perhaps some explication is in order. Employees are always consciously or unconsciously evaluating who says what to whom and for what reasons. It is very difficult to separate interpretation of messages from the perceived motivations of the sender. In accepting and adhering to a transmitted message, one of the most important determinants of a decision to act is whether the initiating manager is considered to be a safe bet. Safety is used here not in terms of its physical aspects, but as a judgment of trustworthiness, fairness, honesty, kindness, and friendliness. If the sender is perceived as unsafe by the receiver or by the members of his work group, then the motives of the directive are usually questioned, thereby slowing up or completely stalling implementation. "I wonder why he wants us to change that procedure," or "The last time we did his bidding without question, he jumped down our throats after his boss said it was a bad idea," are typical employee thoughts from those confronted with a communication from an unsafe manager. Employees, much like the proverbial elephant, have long memories when it comes to recalling incidents of unfair treatment. It would stand to reason that messages which require action would be looked upon with a degree of skepticism when communicated by a source with a low-trust or -safety factor.

The second trait which contributes to source credibility and message acceptance is dynamism. How one portrays himself, his presence, and image, are important facets in the communication process. For instance, is the image of the manager who sends the message viewed to be aggressive or weak, emphatic or hesitant, bold or timid, active or passive, energetic or tired? President Kennedy had dynamism; it was not what he said that had impact, but how he said it—in a forceful, charismatic manner. He was an individual who demanded respect regardless of personal politics. President Nixon, on the other hand, said many similar ideas, in words at least, but portrayed an entirely different image. People, in this instance, were less likely to believe what was said because of Nixon's mode of presentation, his lack of dynamism and charisma, and his tendency to appear self-serving.

The third, and final, credibility dimension is that of qualification. Communication acceptance would be enhanced immensely if the individual who sends the message were perceived as highly qualified, expert, and trained in the discussion area. Knowledge carries with it a certain amount of inherent persuasiveness. One might not like the "person," but might respect his grasp of the subject. "He must be right, so why fight it?" could easily summarize how individuals react when, in their eyes, a highly expert manager transmits a message. Consequently, in terms of adherence by other organizational members, the potency of a message is effected by how the sending manager is perceived in terms of his safety, dynamism, and qualification.

Leadership Style

Similarly, individuals within an organized group fall into a variety of different formal and informal communication networks and develop peculiar leadership styles which then become reflected in particularized communication modes. The leadership styles adopted by management will, of course, have a great deal of influence on the climate of the organization, which, in turn, affects the degree of openness of the communication system.

By using the Nelson leadership scale, the Industrial Relations Center at the University of Chicago has identified four basic styles of leadership found in public and in other organizations. Each specific type has implications for the communication system. For example, the rule-oriented manager relies primarily on the organization's rules and policies to communicate with and control employees. When a problem arises, he might cite organizational policies and guidelines to reinforce a communication. Such communication is usually one-way, downward, with the system's operating in an authoritative manner. When rule-oriented leadership is prevalent, relationships with subordinates tend to be distant. The technologically oriented leader, on the other hand, uses knowledge and expertise to dominate the situation through the communication process. Like the rule-oriented leader, his communications are one-way, downward; he also operates in an authoritative way. Managers who practice individual-oriented leadership focus on the person and on his needs. Relationships with subordinates are generally warm and close. Communication, as opposed to the previous styles, is two-way—both upward and downward. Communication, in this instance, becomes highly personalized because friendship with subordinates is of primary importance. In fact, decisions are usually evaluated in terms of how they will affect individuals on the staff. The group-oriented leader engages in three-way communication: upward, downward, and sideways. He involves the group in problem-solving and objective-setting, with most decisions arrived at through a consensus-seeking process. Relationships with subordinates are generally close and personal, but are highlighted by a group sense of participation.[1]

THE MESSAGE—THE TYPE AND TONE OF COMMUNICATION

While the adherence to a communicated message is somewhat dependent upon source characteristics, these are not the sole determining factors; how the message itself is designed also has impact on its eventual acceptance. The message variable, for example, can be broken down into three component parts. The manager has the option of communicating messages that either inform, instruct, or motivate. It is essential that these terms be clarified because the objective to be obtained by the communicative act should correspond to the type message sent.

An informative message affects the number of available courses of action of which the individual is aware. Awareness turns available courses of action into potential courses of action. For instance, there might be ten alternative methods of solving a problem, but if the person doing the analysis knows of only one method, then he has only one potential course of action, with nine other unknown available alternatives, some of which are possibly more efficient. The act of informing converts available choices of action into potential choices of action. Informational messages can also be thought of as forming the basis of choice from among alternative courses of action. In this case, information provides a decision-maker with the necessary data to make a choice among competing alternatives. In other words, information is either a quantitative measurement (how many alternatives are available), or a qualitative factor (which alternative to choose).

Instruction, on the other hand, is communication which involves changes in the efficiency of one or more courses of action and is the equivalent of teaching more efficient performance. Efficiency must be measured in relation to an objective or outcome. In essence, efficiency is a measure of one's ability to reach an objective. Consequently, if one available course of action in a specific environment has a greater efficiency than another to achieve a specific outcome, it means the alternative with the greater efficiency will bring the decision-maker's actual position closer to the objectives desired. Therefore, any communication which increases the probability and ability of a decision-maker to reach a desired outcome thereby instructs.

The third basic component is the motivational message. A communication which affects the utility or values a decision-maker places on outcomes is a motivater. Motivational communications differ from instructional and informational messages not only because they affect values or utilities, as opposed to efficiencies and probabilities, but also because they focus on outcome rather than alternatives. Outcomes are determined by the chosen strategies and the state of the environment. Although outcomes cannot always be predicted with precision, the decision-maker usually has some desired objective in mind with which the outcome will hopefully coincide. Utility, or value, is a useful concept because it permits alternative courses of action to be compared and permits comparison of which action yields the greatest probability of obtaining the desired goal. Put more succinctly, the purpose of a motivational message is to persuade or convince an individual to value one outcome over another.[2]

The Tone, Clarity, and Quality of the Message

There can be no doubt that the effects of organizational communications are, to some degree, influenced by the character and contents of the message. Several factors should be taken into account, especially in the design of motivational messages—that is, the appeal to be used. One of the most used approaches is fear: "If welfare costs are not reduced by November 1st, the legislature will not vote any additional funds." The purpose of such a message is to spur employees to greater productivity, but, rather than casting the message in a positive tone, fear and threat are used.

The consequences of such an appeal are threefold. First, there is a tendency on the recipients' part to psychologically block out high-threat messages. In other words, the consequences appear so grave or unrealistic that nothing the recipients could do would alter the situation. Second, such communications often produce a backlash of hard feelings against what is perceived as the source of the threat—the legislature. Third, constant threats can build an immunity to such communications, thereby minimizing their potential utility when a true emergency situation exists. Strong fear appeals are most successful when the employees are specifically told what actions to take in relieving the problem or when the employees are told that the situation itself can be changed through their efforts.

Another frequent appeal is of the emotional variety. "Our job is to deliver services to children who, through no fault of their own, have been battered, abused, and neglected. By your diligent efforts, you, the social worker, can mean the difference between life and death, misery or joy." Such appeals tend to raise anxiety levels and force, through dint of their impact, some personal self-appraisal. In other words, it is attention-getting. Oftentimes, such messages deliver a "what if it were you" message or "aren't you thankful that your children are loved and cherished." As with fear appeals, overuse of emotion will jade the recipient and make him less sensitive to subsequent appeals.

By and large, the most effective type of message has a factual or rational orientation and is of high quality and moderate complexity. The basic approach here is to tell people what they need to know in a clear format so that they will understand the actions requested and the responsibilities to be assumed. High-quality messages are not one-sided, but present a well-rounded picture of the situation under discussion—both the negative and positive implications of various potential actions, and a full accounting of the facts, rationalization for the suggested approach, and substantiation of why a particular course of action should be initiated. Messages should be geared to the audience: that is, avoid jargon which might be misunderstood or misinterpreted, and utilize a comprehension level that assures understanding. All too many managers like to impress others and show off their technical skill and knowledge. In this case, overly complex messages are used as a status symbol rather than as a means of communicating. It is generally agreed that a complicated, jargon-laden message reduces effectiveness, thereby increasing the possibility that it will be ignored, partially attended to, or poorly interpreted.

In most cases, abstract messages tend not only to confuse the reader or listener, but also to lead to faulty implementation. Alfred North Whitehead is reported to have said, "It is a sage rule to apply that when a mathematical or philosophical author writes with a misty profundity he is talking nonsense."[3] It is safe to say that messages should have the characteristics listed here to ensure the fullest communication and acceptance of their contents: they should be explicit; written to the comprehension level of the recipient; geared to the value and norm structure of the receiving audience; simple and nonjargon-laden; objective; detailed with specific actions to be taken; contain specific completion dates; and hold overall length to a minimum. A well-designed communication can greatly enhance its chances of being attended to and successfully acted upon. A poorly conceived message may not enhance its impact and, in fact, might detract from message acceptance. It does not mean, of course, that communicators can create any type message with any kind of argumentation or any degree of quality and expect the message to be well-received by organization members. To the contrary, great care must be taken in order to design a message that will move individuals to appropriate action. Attention, however, must be paid to the total spectrum of intervening, interacting variables, rather than seizing any one component part.[4]

THE CHANNEL–THE FORM AND
FRAMEWORK FOR COMMUNICATING

The Network for Communicating

Another central determinant of organizational-communication effectiveness is the direction–the flow and mode of communications within a department. Essentially, there are four channels or networks for communicating with organizational members: (1) personal, one-to-one conversation, (2) the telephone, (3) meetings, and (4) written documents.

Each channel carries with it inherent advantages and disadvantages from both receiver and sender perspectives. Personal communication, for example, is a highly effective method because it shows the communicating parties that the issue is of sufficient concern to necessitate individualized contact. There is, thus, an immediate indication of topical or situational relevance. This situation can be especially enhanced if, rather than calling him "upstairs," the manager goes to the subordinate's turf.

As opposed to more highly structured formats, personal communication is often an effective delivery technique because it is more flexible and informal. Similarly, such communication is difficult to avoid; if someone catches you in the office, or if you catch him, it is difficult to put off talking. It is easy enough to put a report, "for your comments," in a hold file or at the bottom of an in-basket, but just try to do the same thing with a 200-pound employee looking you in the face as you contemplate the great unknown (reading *The New York Times* and drinking a cup of coffee).

In addition to what has already been mentioned, face-to-face communication permits greater content and scope and allows for as much or as little as is required. Also, through verbal interaction and through body language, feedback is immediate. Rewards and incentives for continued compliance can be readily transmitted, which allows for immediate expression of pleasure or displeasure to items under discussion. Personal contact itself has a persuasive power without regard to message and content. The manager is better able to convey his credibility in terms of the factors previously discussed. The one-to-one situation, which is more personal and less rigid, sets a mood when it becomes difficult to reject suggestions that might have gone unheeded had they been communicated by a different mode. Finally, this kind of communication allows for cooperative interpretation and utilization of visual aids, picture displays, and mutual computation and analysis.

The problems occurring in interpersonal communications focus on psychological characteristics—the ability of certain individuals, through rank or personality, to control or dominate a situation; and the verbal reticence of certain individuals. Additionally, without a set agenda, one-to-one communication can be easily sidetracked by either party, thus the conversation wanders into pleasant, but less organizationally related areas. Finally, many people, because they do not know how to gracefully end a conversation, continue talking far longer than necessary.

Telephonic communication is, of course, a variant of the face-to-face mode. It has the additional advantage of being rapid because no physical movement outside the work area is required. Nevertheless, telephone inquiries are shorter and more highly specific and do not allow visual or body-language feedback. Meetings, once again, are basically inter-personal situations that typically include more than two parties. Consequently, meetings allow for all types of feedback, lengthy discussion, and bring together individuals with similar concerns, which stimulate coordination and cooperation. On the other hand, meetings can become time-consuming and occupations in themselves. Meetings are sometimes difficult to control, have a tendency to be disorderly, and can become sidetracked by those with hidden agendas. They are also hard to schedule and spawn other meetings.

Written communications which might include such things as memoranda, letters, reports, decision papers, policy guidelines, and so forth, have a different set of strengths and weaknesses as communication channels. Written communication, for example, allows the sender to fully develop a topic, issue, or response, then fit these into time constraints; hence, there is a comprehensiveness factor. Along the same line, the receiver can now control when he reviews the document, for how long, for what purpose, and for what number of times. Written communications can be widely distributed and eliminate repetition that would have to take place when trying to reach multitudes through verbal communications. Documents allow for filing and retrieval, thereby, one can maintain a record, or case history, of useful actions for future decision-making. Written formats are highly recommended when a manager is interested in going on record as disagreeing with certain actions or recommending a particular course of action or for the sole purpose of leaving an audit trail.

Written communications have some disadvantages because of their highly formalized and rigid natures. Once a communication leaves your desk, it is difficult to add that additional thought or correct some early misconceptions. Also, the receiver does not have to pay attention to the document and can give it a perfunctory review. Feedback is long in coming or can be delayed. Also, when translating their knowledge to written form, managers are perhaps overly cautious, long-winded, and too wrapped up in how it is said, rather than what is said. The written document is, therefore, more time-consuming and less immediate, since it is more permanent than verbal communication.

Whichever channel you as a manager select is highly personal and situational. Remember, each mode has its advantages and disadvantages in terms of rapidity, scope, content, cost, timeliness, permanent status of receiver and sender, size of audience, and distance.

The Organizational Design for Communicating

Channel becomes an overriding communication concept and concern, especially when one considers its direction and flow. Organizations should theoretically be designed to facilitate communication flow in three patterns: vertical (one-way up or down); vertical (two-way up and down); and horizontal (sideways). Management almost universally agrees with the proposition that two-way communication is essential. After all, many of them have read books which teach you to react in a similar manner. Consequently, while many preach about the necessity for more organizational openness and two-way communication, little is accomplished in practice. The hierarchical nature of our organizations often forces our managers into a downward-looking perspective. The system was basically designed to move decisions, guidelines, and directions down from the policy centers into the lower operational domain. Management, therefore, sees communication not as a true transaction of information, but as a means of ensuring compliance. In this light, communications are viewed as operating in a closed system with little opportunity for elaboration or feedback.

In essence, the effectiveness of downward communication is dependent on whether it is complemented by upward communication. One-way downward communication has some positive assets. It is faster, more orderly, less ambiguous, and not as potentially confusing as the two-way variety. Downward communication flows are most used by organizations that insist upon total organizational uniformity in program operations and upon service delivery. Consequently, this tends to rule out creative change and adaptation. If, however, it is important that status quo be maintained or that highly technical and legal mandates be applied with a great amount of audit oversight, then one-way communication might be advantageous to the organization. Similarly, this format facilitates action in crisis, or in emergency situations, when speed and rapidity of response are essential.

It should be pointed out, however, that this downward communication pattern has severe repercussions when overly utilized. For example, it flies directly in the face of concepts which call for employee participation and upward communication. Bottling-up communications at lower organizational levels will lead to a general stifling of creativity, frustration, low morale, inadequate information data base, and decreased organizational productivity. Face it, most managers are not only more comfortable with one-way downward communication, but also are more content. Listening to what people might have to offer takes time. What is heard might be uncomplimentary and not in line with organizational thinking. If an organization wants to make decisions with inadequate information, and not take advantage of the skills and talents of its organizational members, then it wants to discourage motivated behavior, so downward communication applies here.

Many of you probably remember a childhood game called "telephone," where a message is passed from one sender to another to see how confused the message gets. Well, the same gross, often comical, distortions occur in organizations. Since one-way downward communication lacks a feedback loop, at every step in the process it is totally dependent on interpretations given to it by those immediately detailed within the communication network. Without the opportunity for elaboration and clarification, the message that goes into the communications' hopper can be quite different from what actually emerges.

Consequently, most productive organizations rely on two-way communications. Not only is it a more accurate and highly articulate approach, but also it ensures through the participation process receivers have an opportunity to respond in a meaningful way, and thereby avoid potentially costly mistakes. The chance to become an integral part of the organization and the decision-making mechanism provides a crucial, often-missing, motivational element. When people are prohibited by management or system constraints from communicating with others in the organization, there occurs a phenomenon much like the "greenhouse effect." Unable to break out from this artifically created environment, in order to communicate feelings of concern, units tend to develop high-conflict levels which become immediately translatable into reduced productivity because of poor interpersonal relationships.

The need, then, is for the addition of a feedback loop which turns the system from a closed to an open one and also introduces either extra channels or message-redundancy potential. In other words, communications travel up and down the organizational hierarchy, often simultaneously within different units. If, by chance, the message is distorted or not in the unit, the odds are good that transmission will be successfully accomplished in another. It is similar to the wartime practice of sending three couriers with the same message over different routes with the hope that at least one would get through.

Nevertheless, while most organizations—from a physical design perspective at least—are able to handle vertical communication, many are ill-equipped to deal with horizontal communications. Since coordination and communication are expected among staff and line departments, and also among operational-program units, the reality is that little is actually accomplished in any other than an informal way. There are many reasons for this situation—the primary one is that horizontal linkages were never designed into the organization. Many human service organizations realize this deficiency and attempt what can be called the "patchwork quilt approach"; that is, over each vertical relationship that has counterparts in either programmatic or staff areas is put a coordination unit or person. The net result of such efforts is that coordinators need to coordinate themselves. So much effort is expended in coordination that valuable organizational energy is channeled away from service delivery into mindless and wasteful administrative processes. This circumstance, of course, is not to say that coordination is harmful. Rather, coordination, to be effective, must be unobtrusive and a natural part, not an imposed element, of the organization's operational structure. That is why the network design is so attractive—because it ties both vertical- and horizontal-communication channels among staff and line departments into a nice, neat package.

The Informal Network—Rumor Control

In any discussion dealing with formal channels of communication, one must always be cognizant of parallel, albeit informal, networks that also tend to spring up in any organization. Often called the grapevine, these communications' networks serve a legitimate, somewhat distorted purpose. Employees within any large organization have an overriding need and desire to know what is going on. The grapevine will start humming if the formal communication links fail to provide a sufficient amount of information with a high degree of detail. Unfortunately, as with most rumor situations, there is always some truth to what is being transmitted; with truth, however, comes a great deal of distorted information.

If allowed to grow unchecked, the informal communications' networks can have serious organizational impacts. First, agencies will have to spend valuable time and effort either in corroborating and tracing or in denying sources. Second, because rumors are a more interesting, trustworthy source of information to many organizational members, they will increasingly turn to this channel as their primary source. Remember, this channel is the one over which management has least control, and instead of initiating communication, management will be forced into a position where they must always react to it. Finally, rumors—especially those perennial ones that have as their basic content agency closings, budget reduction, and firings—will disturb the organization's delicate working balance to the point where all those who believe their jobs to be in jeopardy (and that is almost everyone) will stop working until the rumor is clarified. By the way, there is always the residual impact to be considered, in that few believe everything that management says, and nagging doubts persist in the back of people's mind. Hence, they approach their jobs with an attitude, such as, "What the hell, if I'm going to be laid off, why should I bust my hump?"

There are several actions that management can take in combating rumors. First, management must develop a reputation for truth and honesty. If employees have caught you in a lie, even a white one, they will not trust either your communications or denials concerning rumors. Second, managment should develop a communication network that routinely delivers pertinent information to all organizational levels and members. Third, management should never use the withholding of information as a means of organizational control or punishment. Management oftentimes treats information as totally within their domain—to be parceled out like so much candy to those employees who demonstrate they are good little children. Consequently, in order to stimulate productivity, organizational-communication networks should be: (1) open so that two-way communications are developed; (2) perceived as highly credible and trustworthy; (3) complete and directed to all who have a personal and organizational need to know; (4) set up so that communication can be rapidly and economically disseminated;

(5) recognized as a key ingredient and factor in successful organizational performance and human service delivery.

THE RECEIVER

Finally, there is the last basic component part of the communication process—the receiver or destination. Of all the segments previously discussed, it is at the recipient end of this long chain that communication failure and breakdown are most likely to occur.

Accepting the Message

Management can cast a message in a particular format—send the message by a specific channel utilizing various media—but it has no control over how that message will be attended to and perceived at its destination. How the receiver will ultimately and behaviorally operationalize the message contained in the communication is therefore considered to be a multistep process. A message must be devised so that the possibility of its acceptance is high. In other words, it should be clear, concise, comprehensible, relevant, and helpful. This message must be transmitted or made available to the recipient. No matter how well-prepared a document is, its value is limited if the network is incapable of delivering the paper to the intended person.

Even if the channel itself functions properly and the message is delivered, it then must compete for the attention of the recipient. After all, there are demands upon the time of a manager; why should he drop everything to respond to any particular communication—unless, of course, it comes from a clearly superior office within the organization. Many organizations have attempted to devise physical signals to notify a message recipient of its importance; for example, color coding for priorities and immediacy of response. What tends to happen is that the system becomes devalued, because once employees catch on to the fact that answers are given only on top-priority items, then all communications will be sent with this coding. Other methods for physically altering messages to gain attention include size differentials and layout. With an emphasis on appearance, however, a basic law of communications is being overlooked.

The Receiver's Situation and Environment

Communication acceptance is not a physical process, but is a psychological one. Once a message is received, a recipient has several options: (1) not attend to it; (2) selectively attend to it; (3) attend to the entire message. Now, do not be under the false impression that message attendance and acceptance are one in the same. Just because a message is read—and even understood—does not mean it will become integrated into ongoing work activities. In other words, what the message says should be done, but what actually occurs can be quite different.

Each individual within an organizational hierarchy views his situation and environment in a particularized manner. From top management's perspective, it might be a simple matter to initiate a message which calls for quarterly reviews of employee performance. In this type communication, however, no consideration is given to the problems inherent in operationalizing his order. Some managers might view it as an opportunity to improve individual performance; others might see it as a way of getting rid of some undesirables; another group of managers might view it as just more administrative paperwork; and others might see it as worthless. With such a message each manager, then, has options to be either totally compliant, partially compliant, or noncompliant.

The basic question now is to determine why various levels of compliance exist. Each manager received the same message over the same network and attended to it, so why is there a difference in initiated action? The reason is simple—each manager perceives and interprets the message in his own fashion, relating it to his particular environment, experiences, needs, likings, and philosophies. If employee evaluations are one of those techniques perceived as important and needed, with potentiality of making the task more reachable, then the tendency is to accept the message and implement it in a comprehensive way. If, on the other hand, it is seen as so much extra work—useless, bureaucratic, and annoying—there is the proclivity to resist the message, distort its intent or implement it in an offhanded, ineffective manner that almost guarantees its failure.

To be accepted, the message must not only be communicated so that organizational members can readily integrate expected behaviors into their own style and the unit's working style and environment, but it must also be related to the terminology, language, and values of the recipient group. That is, when speaking to a bureaucrat, speak bureaucratically. With a professional social worker, it is best to use some clinical jargon to establish your credibility and create interest and attention in the message. A message is acted upon or accepted when it is consonant with individual and group perceptions of what must be done and is perceived as fulfilling a real organizational or individual need. Consequently, one must be always aware not only of the message itself, but also of the: (1) environment and situation in which it is being communicated and received, (2) value and philosophical structures of the intended recipient(s), (3) group in which the receiver must operationalize the communication, and (4) perceptions of how critical this particular matter is to the organization.

Remember, the communication recipient must interpret the message into the meaning which is consistent and relevant to both his individual and group identity. The receiver's ability and desire to accept the message and its contents is dependent upon various psychological, physical, social, and cultural factors. Individuals selectively receive, perceive, and attend to communications. Some only listen to certain parts of the message; some will attend to the entire message, but retain only parts—generally those parts with which they agree; others discard the entire message. It is the manager's job in this situation to help break down "noise factors," or those influences which tend to reduce message attention, comprehension, and acceptance.

Understanding the Total Process

This noise reduction can be best accomplished by having a full appreciation of the intricacies of the communication process. Consequently, before leaving this topic two caveats should be mentioned. First, in designing a communication, it is not enough to merely deal with message-based variables. Rather, one must consider such other factors as the channel by which a message is transmitted, its peculiar characteristics; the intent of the message, whether it is to inform, instruct, or motivate; audience characteristics, such as level of self-esteem or strength of existing attitude clusters; the type of appeal to be used, emotional or rational, fear or nonfear. Only by building audience and channel characteristics into a message design can a communicator hope to optimize desired effects.

Second, messages should be designed for a specific, targeted receiver, rather than peppering the same message over a wide spectrum. Instead, it is more productive to specifically tailor a message for target populations by incorporating into message design the relevant audience, media, channel, and value characteristics. In the short run, this alternative appears quite cumbersome and time-consuming, but expected long-term results of greater message acceptance can make this extra effort pay off. Hence, a message should not be communicated down to, or up to; it should be communicated to employees. It should be created for a particular purpose—for a unique audience, for a particular situation, for a certain desired effect.

MANAGING THE COMMUNICATION SYSTEM

Management-Information Systems

To command and utilize resources well, any large organization requires a formalized system for the control and flow of information. Typically, such mechanisms are called Management-Information Systems (MIS). Within the human service field such terminologies as computerized data systems, selective dissemination of information, and even MIS, are raising many blood pressures. As human service organizations attempt to bring spending and service delivery under control, they are turning increasingly to electronic manipulation of information. The end result of many such efforts has been greater emphasis on data collection and quality control—often at the expense of service delivery.

In addition, as MIS takes on added importance, agencies are forced to hire individuals trained in the use and programming of highly complex computer systems. The value systems and perceptions of organizational goals of the new cadre of human service worker often come into direct conflict with those of the professional social worker. Not only is a massive gap being created between those who collect the information and those who use it, but there is evidence of tremendous interface problems between these two groups of professionals.

As in the case of budget, personnel, planning, and evaluation systems, MIS should be considered one more tool for helping to make the organization more productive. Therefore, regardless of its power, size, or importance as a support system, it should not be allowed to dominate either how the organization sees its mission or how it is carried out. In other words, the organization should control the management-information system, and not the other way around. If this situation is to be the case, there must exist: (a) a high degree of coordination between technical computer people and service staff; (b) an attempt not to overburden operational people with a flood of paperwork, thereby hampering their performance of organizationally assigned functions; and (c) a realistic evaluation of the data's worth vs the cost in terms of time, money, and man-hours needed to collect it.

Management-information systems have a seemingly simple, but crucial, organizational function to perform; that is, at the right time, to communicate information to the right decision-makers in a usable and economic way, thereby, helping management decisions at all levels. This situation becomes particularly important in the case of the human services, since it tends to be composed of a geographically dispersed, multilevel delivery and distribution system. Consequently, a systematic approach to information collection and dissemination is need to provide a common language, bridge, and framework for joint decisions within and among human service organizations. Two-way communication and wide participation among organizational members is needed to improve planning, guidance, and control so that better decisions can be made and then implemented. A well-run MIS system can provide the mechanism and basis for coordinating different levels of the organization and assures that each level will receive and retain the particular information it needs to implement its distinctive program within the context of the human service delivery structure.

Information Typologies

In human service organizations there are basically four types of information communicated through four distinct organizational groupings, which are: (1) fiscal, (2) operational, (3) client, and (4) program. Fiscal data are typically used to alert managers to the cost of services in either units or aggregates, especially in relation to absolute spending ceilings. Operational information is concerned with how the organization functions on a day-to-day basis, providing the data which enable the agency to comply with rules, regulations, procedures, and guidelines. Client information focuses on client demographic characteristics, including absolute numbers, frequencies, and clients per program area. In addition, the more sophisticated information systems keep a running record of client progress. Program data, on the other hand, mainly deal with how the organization is functioning in relation to expectations of preset objectives. Evaluation systems fall into this category.

Communications and information-flow needs can be analyzed as they pass through various organizational levels by dividing the organization into these four distinct groups: top management, middle management, first-level supervision, and operating personnel. Top managers typically need highly distilled, meaningful information that cuts across organizational lines and boundaries. Information flows to the senior management levels, and broad administrative and organizational policies are issued from it. This level should not be interested in intricate details, but in the larger picture. If it is to function properly, top management must have accurate, reliable information that is pertinent and timely. The information reaching these levels should be synthesized and summarized from both internal and external sources and should become more highly edited and concentrated as it moves up the hierarchy.

Middle managers have the responsibility of solving problems and making decisions which are required to fulfill the goals and policies established by top management and boards. Employees at this level need more detailed information than do those in top management. It is at this level that fiscal, operational, and client data are analyzed, synthesized, and consolidated for passage up the line, and decisions for implementation in the various operational areas are made. Nevertheless, programmatic data are often directly controlled and utilized by top management, since it is from these data that large scope, integrative programmatic decisions are made. Middle managers, however, do depend a great deal on their subordinates to supply and collect data for transmission upon which decisions are made.

First-line supervisors are responsible for making sure the service provided is delivered on a timely basis within certain cost constraints and at a quality level determined by the organization. These individuals must be kept informed of what is happening in their respective fields so that they may upgrade their delivery and service skills by applying the latest, most effective methods to their jobs. This management level often supplies the bulk of statistical data, in-house reports, and documents produced by the organization.

Operating, or line, personnel, must be given the detailed data and information necessary for them to effectively carry out their job function. It might include data of procedures that must be followed, guidelines, forms to be completed, and so forth.

Information tends to percolate to top levels in many organizations. Before reaching each successive layer, however, it should be summarized, with each group's filtering out the data it needs to make decisions and control processes. After traveling this route and reaching the top, the data once again flow downward—perhaps in a different fashion. Now data are in the form of policy and guidance. Consequently, the information flow can be likened to a pyramid, wide at the bottom and narrow toward the top. As illustrated by Figure 8-2, the various data types can basically be collected and used by different levels of management for operations, control, planning, and evaluation.

Requirements for a Successful MIS

It is not enough, however, to recognize the necessity and utility of MIS. There are several important practical requirements to be considered if there is even hope of successfully designing an implementable system. First, more than most, human service organizations require joint participation in management decisions relating to MIS. These decisions include system design, goal-setting, uses, and continuing assessment and revision of the system. Second, an MIS must be tailored directly to the characteristics of the agency, taking into account the

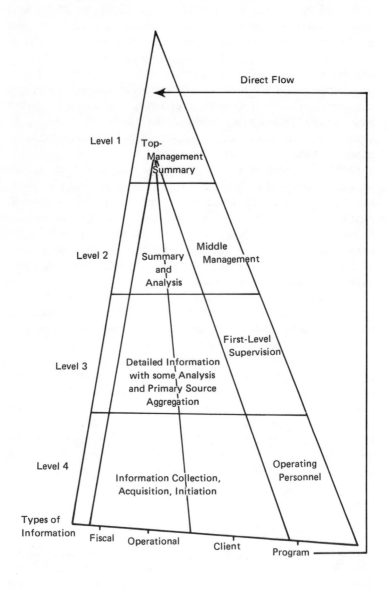

Figure 8.2: DATA UTILIZATION AND COLLECTION BY ORGANIZATION
             LEVEL

types of personnel using it, the program areas, the client populations, and others. It cannot be imposed with preconceived notions of how it should operate, but must give specific ideas on how it will operate within the organization's environment. Third, it is only after specific information needs and flows have been analyzed and cataloged that appropriate criteria for the development of an information system can be determined. Fourth, an effective MIS must serve the entire organization, not just one element. When used solely as a means for initiating funds or for meeting imposed data-collection requirements, MIS is a failure as a management system. Information will be collected that is objective, accurate, and timely only when employees benefit from the collected information in terms of utilizing the information in program management. In other words, through direct experience and through actual use of the data, key people at all levels must require the practical needs for the information to be transmitted.

Fifth, do not overcollect information. One of the most common mistakes made is that users are not able to differentiate between information vital to program operation, as opposed to information that is nice to have but which is used infrequently. Finally, keep the MIS simple. If a manual system works well for you, then keep it. All too many organizations have become overly intrigued with the computer—which can be both friend and foe. If the computer is handled improperly or used where it should not have been, it will make data collection and dissemination a nightmare. Complexity will come by itself—do not add to it. Remember, keep the system as simple as the job requires.

SUGGESTIONS FOR IMPROVING INTERORGANIZATIONAL COMMUNICATION

There are several suggestions which can be offered for the improvement of interorganizational communication. The first, and one of the most important, focuses on the improvement of organizational-feedback capability. This step can be accomplished through institutionalized methods, such as monthly employee-manager meetings, newsletters, counseling, bulletin boards; or through more informal channels, such as personal contact, after-hours socialization, shared eating facilities and lounges. The term "feedback" means the quality and the quantity of interchanges among all levels of the organization. Through the institution of highly developed feedback mechanism, an organization should experience immediate improvement in speed, accuracy, usefulness, and credibility of communications.

Second, greater emphasis should be placed on interpersonal channels of communication. Face-to-face communication allows for timely feedback, increases the message believability, and is a more familiar mode of message transmission. Third, attempt to reduce as much system "noise" as possible. Noise can be physical in the sense of a blurred photograph or a poorly reproduced memo to such psychological noise as fear, anticipation, fatique, and so forth.

Fourth, always try to establish common grounds between sender and receivers. Attempt to play down any perceived gaps between you and the position of your recipients. It is extremely difficult to send a message and have it accepted when what you convey contradicts prior expectations and predilections. Fit the message to group attitudes and beliefs by appealing to directly felt needs, then by testing the communication's acceptance through the use of feedback loops. Fifth, ideas should be presented in clear language if the receiver is to decode the message and come up with the meaning intended to be transmitted. If a lawyer is needed to translate an administrative guideline, a communication failure has occurred. From a legal standpoint, overly jargonistic technical rules and regulations might be an accepted mode, but they are lousy communications and give way to faulty implementation. Sixth, communication sources that enjoy high credibility should be utilized wherever possible.

Seventh, organizations should be structured both formally and informally to allow for free, open flow of communications downward, upward, and sideways. As a rule of thumb, the organization and communication linkages should be kept as flat as possible. Flat organizations serve to reduce the number of intercept levels and gatekeepers that serve to distort, delay, sidetrack, and misinterpret messages. Eighth, wherever possible and practical, the formalized communication lines, as outlined in the organization chart, should be followed. This ensures that managers in the hierarchy are kept informed of decisions that can operationally have impact on their units. Short-circuiting the system—that is, bypassing levels and individuals—might be faster, but creates cooperation and coordination problems if overly relied upon as a means of communication.

Finally, if information is to be of value to any member of the organization, management must ensure that, regardless of negative or positive implications for individual personalities or the organization, communications will be objectively analyzed and incorporated into the decision-making process wherever possible. Perhaps one of the key human personality weaknesses is our inability to accept criticism. Unfortunately, not all messages can carry "bravos"; there are times when communications are used to transmit data which might be indicative of organizational malfunctioning. The wise manager will use such messages to alert himself to alternate courses of action for program correction and to seek more information, rather than to suppress negative messages and, perhaps, even punish the sender.

In analyzing any organization's communication system, the overriding concern is that the sender, the message, the receiver, the channel, and the feedback loop be considered. Organizational communication is an intricate, well-balanced system, so that disorientation in any one part of it will throw the other elements and the entire system off-balance.

NOTES

1. Charles W. Nelson, *The Leadership Inventory Analyzer,* (Chicago: Industrial Relations Center, University of Chicago, 1965), pp. 6-7.

2. Russel Ackoff, "Towards a Behavioral Theory of Communication," Management Science 4 (1957-58), pp. 218-234.

3. A.H. Johnson, *The Wit and Wisdom of Alfred North Whitehead* (Boston: Beacon Press, 1947), p. 6.

4. Richard Steiner, "Communication Complexity and Quality: A New Perspective," *Journal of Technical Working and Communication* 44 (Fall 1974), pp. 265-278.

Chapter 9

EVALUATING HUMAN SERVICE PROGRAMS

INTRODUCTION

Evaluation of human service programs, although often deemed an impossibility, has grown in importance and by mandate. A number of methods for assessing human service program performance will be presented in Chapter 9. Delineated prior to discussion of actual evaluation techniques are the benefits of performance assessments for human service organizations, levels of evaluation methodology, the cyclical nature of performance-measurement systems, and common reasons for low utilization of service-program assessments.

The traditional evaluation methodologies and the validity criteria governing their utilization are presented first. Productivity- or performance-measurement evaluation are proposed as alternatives, when traditional techniques are not feasible. Procedural steps and factors considered to develop this objective-oriented evaluation approach are discussed at length. A sample work sheet is included to demonstrate the applicability of the performance-measurement evaluation for human services. This presentation of evaluation methods is intended to point out the need and practical possibilities for assessing performance of human service programs.

ASSESSING PROGRAM PERFORMANCE

Ask any human service manager about the importance of program evaluation and he will give you a litany of responses. On the other hand, ask the same person what the impact of his particular human service effort is, and you will probably receive a moment of silence followed by short bursts of "You can't turn people into numbers! It is too expensive to evaluate! Instruments are not sophisticated enough! Research designs are not applicable! There is no time!" Welfare specialists have shown the least sophistication and rigor in setting standards for the evaluation of human service programs. Human service specialists seem to have an intuitive, generalized conviction that the public will inherently realize the worth of their efforts. There is little wonder, then, why welfare budgets are the first to be cut in times of economic difficulty. If welfare programs are unable to make an explicit, measurable impact, then one may rightly wonder on what basis the welfare specialists might ask the public for resources. One may also wonder whether human service practitioners can justify programs aimed at "improving the quality of life" when the results of massive previous expenditures are unknown.

One of the most talked about, but least-accomplished program activities, is outcome measurement and assessment. However, the need for performance measurement has recently been emphasized by the establishment of federal government guidelines which call for comprehensive planning and program evaluation under Title XX legislation. Consequently, the debate over performance measurement has shifted from "whether it should be done" to "how it should be done."

Assessment is Beneficial

When viewed positively, any validly designed and initiated program-evaluation effort results in certain benefits to the organization. First, it helps to develop a budgetary-allocation system which relates performance to the level of funding. For example, an organization's hand would be greatly strengthened if it could conclusively demonstrate that previous allocations were wisely spent and resulted in overall benefit to the taxpayer. Now, when allocations are requested from legislative bodies, managers must go begging with hat-in-hand for funds. As we are quickly discovering, the community tax base is not infinite or ever-elastic. Consequently, the budget process becomes a "zero sum game," or, what one agency gains, another one loses. Legislatures are forced into making programmatic choices among such items as resurfaced roads, the purchase of fire trucks, and increased home relief aid. The benefits to the populace of roads and fire-fighting equipment are self-evident because the community, in general, experiences some physically measurable gains. However, what benefits accrue to the taxpayer when home relief payments are boosted? Why should legislators vote funds for this activity to the detriment of others? These are the types of questions human service agencies will have to answer if programs are to receive continued citizen and legislative support. The only realistic way to approach this problem is through establishing an assessment system which would aid in the justification of budgetary requests.

Second, evaluation focuses attention on "do able" program activities. Generalized and prosaic statements, such as "improving the quality of life," give way to more practical programmatic and implementable approaches, such as serving the day-care needs of employable AFDC mothers. Planning is more complete because detailed consideration of achievable program objectives includes delineation of the resources (manpower, time, money, equipment) needed to accomplish these tasks. Third, program evaluation provides a basis for objectively determining program priorities. The inclusion of cost-benefit analysis criteria to program-funding decisions helps define relative program benefits and beneficiaries. Hence, assessment data upgrade the decision-making process. This step is especially useful when programs have "expenditure ceilings." Fourth, program appraisal actually builds flexibility into the delivery system because each service area knows what it actually accomplished and in what order of priority. The evaluation process is useful to the manager as it forces specification of control measures and identification of acceptable performance levels. Consequently, there can be a more immediate, accurate response to deviations from set standards.

Fifth, a program-assessment system ensures that clients receive promised services to which they are entitled. After all, it is client satisfaction in successful outcomes that should be of primary concern to the human service manager. Unfortunately, human service administrators too readily tolerate a double standard. For example, if you purchased an air-conditioned automobile, and it was delivered without this modern-day convenience, you would probably demand either that money paid for this option be returned or that the air-conditioner be installed immediately. Look at the flip-side of this problem from a human service perspective. Assume you were funded at the rate of $1 million to rehabilitate 100 addicts and at the end of the funding year only ten proved to be drug-free. Do you turn back 90 percent of the money? Does the public not have the same right to demand that the promised service be delivered? This situation is when the manager opens up the "excuse bag" and says things like "we had start-up problems," "the technology is just not there," or "red tape did us in." None of these possibilities was considered when asking for funds; in fact, according to the proposal, it was the best program since the invention of chocolate ice cream. When the human services are criticized for over-promising, all the public hears is excuses. If the automobile dealer made excuses about the missing air-conditioner, you would probably tell him "it was his problem and not yours" and that "good money was paid for a product which was not delivered." The same rule applies to the delivery of human services. The public and client expect that program promises and objectives be carried out, and they do not want to hear excuses as to their impossibility. If anything, an evaluation system can be a quick cure for foot-in-the-mouth disease, also known as the overpromising and underdelivering syndrome. Finally, an assessment system can conserve public funds by aiding in the selection of delivery system alternatives and methodologies which have a higher probability of meeting desired outcome. This step can be accomplished by fully testing and evaluating the impact of public funds.

In operational terms, a performance-measurement system can be simply defined as the methods of assessing the effectiveness of human service programs in order to achieve desired objectives. Such a definition implies that through the process of program assessment there can be program change and improvement. An assessment system allows organizations to modify current operations based on an objective evaluation of program performance.

Evaluation Levels

Essentially, there are three levels of evaluation methodology which can be applied to program-performance assessment. At the first level, a recipient group makes a program-activity evaluation on how service-able the delivery system is with respect to the groups' individualized needs, based on their personal perspectives. This approach is useful, especially when it is linked to program design. However, as an effective measure of service output, it is inherently weak. For this reason, emphasis is placed on the following two types of evaluation typologies. At the second level, the evaluation represents an appraisal of the program's success in meeting specific, predetermined performance objectives. Such evaluations can be conducted by second-party experts or by the program managers themselves. Typically, this approach focuses on cost-effectiveness factors. At the third level, we come to what is commonly called scientific measurement of performance. As research, it adheres to the basic logic and rules of scientific methodology as closely as possible by utilizing all available techniques for the collection and analysis of data and by employing a variety of research designs. However, while the scientific approach offers the most reliable, valid method for determining program performance, it is perhaps the most difficult to satisfactorily implement.

Evaluation as a Cycle

Performance-measurement systems are not made up of discrete component parts, but are continuous in nature and consist of: (1) a statement of program objectives; (2) performance standards; (3) measuring criteria; (4) target-setting; (5) outcomes; and (6) suggestions for improvement. New program objectives, which necessitate reaffirmation, rejection, or revision of current objectives, may result at the end of the performance measurement process. See Figure 9-1.

Why Evaluation Results Are Not Used

Before delving more deeply into the techniques of program-performance assessment, it might be worthwhile to investigate commonly stated reasons for low utilization of assessment results. First, there is the problem of organizational inertia. Program assessment implies change, and many organizations are either unwilling or unable to implement changes. Second, program administrators and policymakers oftentimes distrust the results of performance studies and rely instead on their own experiences and instincts. Third, design irrelevance can

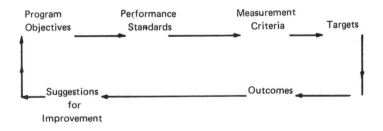

Figure 9.1: THE EVALUATION CYCLE

pose a problem because some performance-measurement systems have little or no relationship to critical program variables or policy issues. Fourth, although a plethora of studies exist, many of the findings are not disseminated to the appropriate decision-makers.[1] Fifth, the numbers provided by a program assessment are not scientific truths. In every case, human judgments are involved in the selection of objectives, criteria, and measurements, and each, thereby, becomes fallible. The data are subject to limitations and inaccuracies. Finally, program-performance measurement cannot by itself directly indicate whether a program was worth the cost. Inevitably, the program will affect different objectives and population segments in different ways. Also, the political process legitimately enters into decisions, especially as it has an impact on program priorities. Elected government officials who are accountable to the public must eventually consider the total array of program information and make decisions on a broader base than just productivity measurements.

What to Evaluate

One of the most difficult decisions a novice evaluator must make is to decide what is to be evaluated. Program measurement is a complex problem because it can involve the evaluation of four separate, distinct operations: effort, efficiency, effectiveness, and technology. Program-effort evaluation is an assessment of organizational energy expended with little regard for its overall client impact. It seeks the answers to such questions as "How many?" and "How much?" In this type assessment, one typically looks at the organization's present or anticipated capacity to service a client population; for example, the number of professionals on staff, amount of funds expended, geographic locations serviced, number of clients served, and so forth. Nevertheless, while these items are important indicators of program potentiality, they in no way measure an operation's relative success in meeting program objectives.

Effort evaluations were commonly used in OEO-funded community action programs where many of us were exposed in statements such as "we employ over 300 community residents who might otherwise be on welfare," or "we spend $3 million a year within the total community." While such facts are nice to know, they have no bearing on output. Managers usually resort solely to effort evaluations when they have inherently weak programs or when they do not have the technology or expertise needed to conduct more valid assessments.

While effort evaluations are indicators of a program's potentiality to perform, they provide little data on cost or actual goal attainment.

Hence, there is a need to look at delivery in terms of cost factors. Put simply, program cost or efficiency is the relationship of output to input or a unit measurement of quantity. Efficiency measurement represents an answer to such questions as, "How much does it cost?" "Are there less expensive ways to attain the results?" "Is the program worth the cost?" It is concerned with the evaluation of alternative methods in terms of costs (money, time, personnel, and public acceptance). For example, in the case of a nutrition program for elderly citizens, it is possible to arrive at the average cost per meal by dividing the operating budget by the total number of meals served. The efficiency ratio is simply a measurement of how much it costs to produce a unit of output. It tells nothing about the standards and quality of the service provided. Hence, questions like "How nutritious were the meals?" are still left unanswered.

Costs can vary greatly among programs. The only way to determine whether the program is worth the expense is through effectiveness evaluations. While efficiency evaluations concentrate on quantity, effectiveness measurement attempts to assess quality or overall program performance. Typically, such assessments are more difficult to achieve since they represent a relationship between output to standards. The intention of such evaluation is to focus on program results rather than on cost or effort. For instance, how much is accomplished when compared to stated objectives? The primary difficulty encountered here is the development of quality standards to measure against.

Effectiveness criteria are some of the most powerful evaluation tools available and can help provide answers to some very real, pressing delivery questions. In addition, when combined with efficiency, data-quality assessment allows cost-effectiveness considerations to be objectively viewed. For example, take this hypothetical dilemma: suppose you needed a kidney transplant and a suitable donor were available. Similarly, assume all expenses were to be paid out-of-pocket. Let us further assume two hospitals in the area were equipped to perform such service with one hospital's charging $6000 and the other $8000. What we have is a straightforward efficiency measurement, with one hospital charging 25 percent more than the other. Armed only with this information, most would logically select the least expensive alternative. What if additional facts were to be added, such as the fact that on the national average 85 percent survive the procedure and live five years or longer? Now, suppose at the $6000 hospital the survival rate is 72 percent and at the $8000 hospital it is 87 percent. Does this alter your thinking? In this case, perhaps it should. What has been added are quality or effectiveness considerations. Consequently, before hard programmatic decisions can be made, one should have knowledge of both operational efficiency and effectiveness.

Next, we come to evaluation of program technology. The basic concern here is the assessment of various alternative methodologies which can be applied when attempting to solve specific social problems. It is incumbent upon a good manager to seek data that either support or contradict current program technology. If a program is achieving objectives in an efficient manner, than specification of how it is accomplished should be made to allow for technology transfers to other delivery sectors. On the other hand, if a program is not meeting expectations, a delineation of technology weakness should be made to allow for change.

There are three main component parts to technology evaluations: first, delivery characteristics, or what type systematic approach has been created to solve a defined social dysfunction. For example, assume there was a program objective calling for a reduction in unwanted pregnancies among teenage girls currently receiving aid to dependent children. There are several types of programs which can be operationalized to reduce this problem. Three major types come immediately to mind: (a) education-counseling programs, (b) utilization of birth-control devices, and (c) abortion. The basic decision a manager would have to make is which program is most cost-effective. Before this decision can be made, the manager must make a detailed investigation of the remaining two components: evaluation of program environment and service population. Both are crucial to successful delivery of services.

The success of any applied program technology often depends upon a community's willingness to accept the particular approach. The planners must take into account the social, political, religious, and economic characteristics of an area prior to program implementation. Utilization of birth-control devices and abortions, for example, while an effective "solution" for unwanted pregnancies, might be strongly resisted in certain areas for religious reasons, thus curtailing the program's ability to achieve its stated mission. Consequently, it is essential that program technology be compatible with community climate and its limits of acceptance; hence, it is important to evaluate environmental characteristics.

The third component part is the evaluation of program or service population. Just as certain programs function better in particular social environments, so will specific programs have greater success rates with different types of population groupings. For example, the odds are that more highly educated females who come from intact family systems with strong physical, social, and economic support would respond more favorably to an education-counseling effort to reduce "unwanted" pregnancies than would poorly educated females who come from broken families with low socioeconomic backgrounds. Through the process of selective client admissions, a program can easily appear to be a success, when in reality, the deck has been stacked, resulting in a distorted view of program functioning.

How to Evaluate

Before we describe the techniques of program evaluation, it is essential to point out that continuum exists, as demonstrated in Figure 9-2. Based on needs, money, resources, and staff qualifications, it is up to the administrator to decide where on the continuum the evaluation effort will fall. The "quick and dirty" approach will yield data with limited expenditure of organizational resources, but there is always the nagging thought that the evaluations are useless, or even worse, point in the wrong direction. On the other hand, a lengthy, rigorously designed research study can be undertaken, and this study, too, can yield inconclusive data or be more expensive than the actual worth of programmatic decisions made from it.

We are going to present an assortment of methodologies from the evaluation continuum. It is up to the manager, based on organizational and programmatic consideration, to select the design which optimizes the agency's ability to deliver and evaluate human services.

Subjective/Intuitive ━ ━ ━ ━ ━ ━ ━ ━ ━ ━ Objective/Analytical
(Quick and Dirty)   (Rigorous and
                                                                      Empirically
                                                                      Derived)

Figure 9.2: **THE EVALUATION CONTINUUM**

Traditional Evaluation

From a traditional perspective, designs or plans of action have been classified according to three criteria. First, there is the true experimental design. This type evaluation is typically conducted in a laboratory or highly controlled, nonnatural setting. Second, there is the nonexperimental approach, also known as the descriptive sample survey, correlational study, or survey technique. Third, there is the controlled-field experiment, which is similar to an experimental design in terms of control, but it is executed under more natural environmental conditions.

As indicated earlier, each design has strengths and weaknesses—the one selected depends on what is to be evaluated, at what stage the program is, and on what types of organizational resources are available. At any rate, prior to implementation, a plan of action which consists of a specific approach and measurement procedures must be developed. The purpose of the plan is to help identify the client impacts, good or bad, directly traceable to the program and to separate these from other forces at work in the environment. Consequently, the evaluation model calls for the gathering of observations according to a plan commonly called a "research design"; it also calls for analyzing collected data by using appropriate statistical procedures.

Controlled Experiments

When investigating designs for use in program evaluations, one should be aware of two potentially limiting criteria. The first is internal validity. It refers to the worth or logic of the proposed evaluation plan and the types of built-in control procedures used to enable the direct delineation of cause and effect. The concept of "cause and effect" is crucial to the understanding of program evaluation. It implies that the results achieved are directly linked to the programmatic activity. For example, is the rise and fall of welfare rolls a direct function of the program's ability to deliver services and rehabilitate people, or is it caused by extraneous environmental variables, such as the economy, political climate, social values, and so forth? If you can directly relate social service caseload size to the delivery of programs, then there exists a cause-effect relationship.

Presently, the only way to achieve or delineate cause-effect relationships is through using highly controlled experimental designs. However, in order to execute an experimental design the following requirements must be present: (1) an independent variable that is manipulatable by the organization; (2) subjects or clients assigned in a random fashion to treatments or program modalities; (3) ability to measure and observe dependent variables or outcomes resulting from program implementation.

Survey Design

While true experimental research designs always satisfy the ability to delineate cause-effect relationships, there are some notable weaknesses in this approach. Such problems are typically associated with the nonnatural environment needed for controlled conditions. Some of the major problems experienced with this design include: awareness of being measured and observed, need for client cooperation with the evaluator, clients forced into specific treatment modalities, impact of the measuring instruments, and researcher bias.

The highly structured evaluation environment, while attaining internal validity, often falters on the external validity dimension. External validity refers to the generalizability of the evaluation study to a wider situation. For example, polling organizations, such as Gallup and Roper, are able to make highly accurate estimates of general public opinion on a various range of issues by utilizing sophisticated survey techniques. Consequently, it would likewise be possible by using similar methodologies to test a "new type of grant dissemination system" prior to massive national implementation. It has been done on several occasions. The ability to make generalized statements of program applicability to larger physical or social units is made possible through random sampling. Random sampling is used to ensure representativeness of the participating client populations.

Another factor needed to ensure external validity is a natural, realistic evaluation environment. While the major strength of survey designs is their generalization, their primary fault lies in their inability to isolate cause-effect interrelationships. In other words, survey designs allow for alternative explanations. For instance, based on correlational studies, many social service managers would like to take credit for decreases in caseloads where they do occur and directly attribute such reductions to program activity. However, most of these conclusions are arrived at through correlational or survey evaluations which would allow for alternative explanations for the reason why this reduction occurred: increased economic activity, building of a new industrial plant in the area, change in the law or eligibility requirements, or outflow of population. Consequently, since other factors might have entered the equation, it is very difficult to attribute the reduction in client loads directly to the delivery of social services. Other types of activities occur to complicate the picture. They include influences on clients which are not directly attributable to the program, such as outside psychiatric assistance, locating a job, husband returning home, and so forth. Similarly, individual clients change, i.e., they get older and no longer are eligible for certain assistance, move away to another jurisdiction, or decide the hassle is not worth it. There is also a problem associated with measuring instruments. Clients, while not lying, attempt to provide answers they feel evaluators want to hear or that make the clients appear in the best light possible. This situation is called instrument/evaluator interaction and bias.

Experimental and survey designs differ in two major respects: the sample from which client populations are drawn and the type of exposures. In program evaluations which use experimental designs, clients from the same population are randomly assigned to different treatment modalities; with survey-style evaluations we let self-selection or individual choice determine the experimental groups. Hence, exposure to programs is forced in the experimental approach and left to individual decision in survey designs.

Controlled-Field Experiment

A highly acceptable alternative to the more traditional experimental- and survey-evaluation designs is called the controlled-field experiment. This approach combines the advantages of both the experiement and survey, while it minimizes their disadvantages. It is strong in internal and external validity. Basically, a controlled-field experiment is a highly controlled design conducted in a natural setting. Here, clients are presented with the opportunity for exposure and are not artificially forced to accept certain types of activities, as with laboratory experiments. Through the use of accurately implemented- and executed-field experiments, evaluators are able to derive valid cause and effect relationships because these conditions exist: realism in the evaluation setting for generalizability, acceptable research design for internal validity, and unobtrusive measurements.[2]

It is important to reinforce the point that any prerequisite for good program evaluation is a plan of action which outlines procedures to be followed and techniques to be utilized. As an evaluation strategy, it is far better to expend extra effort upfront to ensure viability of the evaluation design rather than doing shoddy work and paying for it later in terms of poorly organized, unusable evaluation results.

An Example of the Controlled-Field Design

In all probability, a lot of this discussion sounds like so much "mumbo jumbo." If proposed evaluation designs are to have any value to the manager, there has to be a way of both operationalizing these approaches and utilizing the data for program change and improvement. Perhaps, a demonstration of how a controlled-field design can be implemented would be valuable. A basic concern in terms of social service delivery focuses on the need for accuracy in determining income-maintenance eligibility. As a partial response to this need, separation of services came about in the hope that trained specialists (social welfare examiners), with their major job function as eligibility determination, would be able to reduce eligibility errors and ferret out fraud.

There has been considerable debate about the type employee to be utilized in this position. There are two schools of thought. One views the social welfare examiner as a "super clerk" who needs no more than a high school education. The other school believes that the examiner should be prepared to make professional determinations and should have at least a college degree. The basic consideration thus centers on qualifications needed for the welfare-examiner position. Many of us probably have opinions on the subject and, in fact, make daily decisions based on our prejudices. Would it not be valuable, however, if we could objectively determine which type of employee, the "clerk" or the "professional," actually performed better in terms of reducing income-maintenance ineligibility (providing resources not legally entitled to clients, or over- and underpayments)? For the sake of this example, let us assume that the primary hypothesis is: Professionally educated social welfare examiners will perform better in terms of reducing ineligibility rates among client populations who apply for income maintenance assistance rather than nonprofessionally trained workers.

A highly valid evaluation of this issue can be conducted if these guidelines are followed:

1. Identify the eligible client population; for example, all individuals who request assistance and are willing to complete the application process.

2. Randomly assign each of these applicants to either a professionally educated worker or a nonprofessionally (clerk) educated social welfare examiner.

3. After the application cycle has been completed and eligibility determination made, audit all applications for eligibility.

4. Using a statistical technique known as analysis of variance, compare the ineligibility rates for those clients exposed to professionals as compared to clerks. This technique should provide the answer to which category of employee performs better in terms of reducing ineligibility.

By following these simple steps you will have satisfied the most rigorous of evaluation methodologies. The process is shown diagrammatically in Figure 9-3.

This type of action evaluation enables the organization to determine the cause (worker qualifications), effect (ineligibility rate), and outcomes because: First, there is realism for external validity in the evaluation situation. It is common practice for clients who need monetary assistance to go to a welfare office and apply for aid. Clients are not aware they are part of an evaluation study, since, for all intents and purposes, the regular application procedure is followed. Hence, we have a natural environment. Second, there is an adequate evaluation design for internal validity. An independent variable (worker qualifications) is under the control of the evaluator and is manipulatable. In addition, there is random assignment and distribution of treatments of the independent variable to random groups of subjects. Third, there is observation or measurement of the dependent variable (variation in

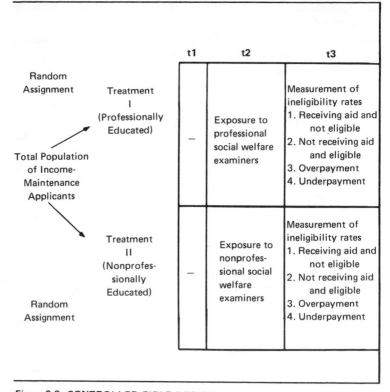

Figure 9.3: CONTROLLED-FIELD DESIGN

eligibility rates) for treatment groups. Finally, this evaluation design can be easily and inexpensively executed.

The statistical manipulations needed to analyze results are not highly complex. In essence, the hypothesis asks the question, "Are there systematic effects on income-maintenance ineligibility rates because of the client's exposure or nonexposure to professionally trained social welfare examiners?" Consequently, an attempt is being made to discover whether a relationship exists between worker qualifications and ineligibility rates. The dependent variable is the rate of ineligibility measured by a post audit. For the sake of analysis, assume that the average ineligibility rate for Treatment I (professionally trained) is 5.7 cases and the average for Treatment II (nonprofessionally trained) is 5.8 Using a fixed-effects analysis of variance, the means can be displayed as in Table 9-1.

Without going into the actual manipulations, assume that the differences are insignificant. In that case, we can neither accept nor reject our original hypothesis. Nonetheless, we have been provided with some very valuable program information. What we have is conclusive evidence, which demonstrates that the professionally trained worker provides no significant programmatic benefit, at least as it relates to ineligibility rates when compared to the nonprofessionally trained social welfare examiner. If pay schedules for the two type employees were identical, then the staffing pattern makes no difference. If the nonprofessionally trained worker received a lower level salary, then the data, at least in terms of efficiency, would indicate a switchover. This situation assumes efficiency is the sole program criteria that is being considered. On the other hand, if the evaluation findings indicated ineligibility rates were significantly lower for the professional, then a movement toward staffing this category of employee might be in order.

Evaluations conducted in this manner are real, visual, and do indicate areas of program strength or weakness in a manner that enables managers to identify potential remedies. Perhaps it is important to reinforce the factor which makes this type of evaluation model function; that is,

Table 9.1: MEANS POST-TREATMENT SCORES

	Ineligibility Scores
Treatment Group I (professionally trained)	5.7
Treatment Group II (nonprofessionally trained)	5.8

randomization. In this case, randomization is not used to secure representation for some larger population. Instead, it has the purpose of equating or distributing potential client deviations among the treatment groups used.

The major obstacle to the application of this type design in the human service setting lies more in the reluctance of service managers to authorize using the design than in difficulties associated with implementation. Human service managers hesitate to allow randomization to be used as a means of allocating individuals to treatments. This concern appears to be unwarranted, since randomization does not necessarily imply that individuals will not be treated. It is possible under this type evaluational approach to alternate the kinds and types of programs, staff, and services in order to compare their relative effectiveness. In the present example, we randomly assigned potential clients to either professionally or nonprofessionally trained social welfare examiners in order to see if there were a causative relationship between staff qualifications and ineligibility rates. This step was accomplished without denying legal services to the public. Hence, what has been provided is a neat, economical, and valid evaluation design that can provide programmatically useful results which have statistical power and significance.

An Alternative to Traditional Evaluation

If the more traditional or "scientific" approach to evaluation is not feasible, or called for, alternative courses of action are possible. Lately, there has been increasing emphasis on productivity measurement to be used as an evaluation methodology. Although similar in many ways to the more traditional approach, productivity measurement focuses on setting, then on measuring the achievement of program objectives. In fact, the performance-audit approach combines traditional methodology with a management-by-objectives format. A well-functioning organizational performance-measurement system could prove to be one of the most valuable, important management tools devised to date. An organization without performance-audit capability is like a ship without a navigation system; it keeps going—but no one knows where. While performance measurement is an intuitively simple process to conceptualize, it is, in reality, quite difficult to implement successfully. The performance-audit approach, as developed here, is predicated on a series of four sequential events:

1. Individual program managers review the nature and goals of their specific programs and their operating agency. A determination of anticipated key program results and objectives are made. These

should be consistent with the overall mission of the agency. A time frame for the achievement of these objectives is set.

2. Operating agency personnel carefully review their mission in order to clarify areas of responsibility and individual program accountability. A serious attempt should be made to map out interrelationships among various programming levels which have impact on affected jurisdictions. Such a process allows for the identification of program overlaps, gaps in coverage, differences in understanding, and gaps in accountability. The objectives of each and every funded program should relate directly to those established for the organization as a whole. Based upon these negotiations and reviews, objectives may be modified so they are consistent with environmental, organizational, and funding constraints. Once these actions are taken the proposed objectives take on the force of contractual obligations between the program manager and the organization.

3. The program operator is given the resources needed to reach the agreed-to proposed targets and objectives. Of course, each operating unit should be allowed considerable latitude to select methods and types of resources and techniques within budgetary limits in order to achieve agreed-upon results.

4. At the end of the specified time period, program performance is appraised on the basis of measured results. Consideration should be given to the way in which the operating agency worked toward objectives and to whether they were achieved. Notations of significant deviations from contractual objective obligations form the basis for programmatic changes or include the possibility of objective modifications.

One of the most difficult, crucial procedures in the performance-measurement system is the development and quantification of objectives. In order to clarify some terminology, an objective is a specific result, product, or service to be accomplished within a definite time frame. A goal, on the other hand, refers to the long-term missions responsibility of an organization or agency. For instance, in the case of a maternal care program, a goal might be the delivery of adequate health care to low-income pregnant women through the provision of pre- and post-natal medical services, nutritional care, and education. An example of a program objective would be to ensure that all low-income pregnant women who receive AFDC support from the county will have access to two nutritionally sound meals each day, with full implementation to be accomplished within six months.

A primary reason for implementing a performance-measuring system is to improve program delivery. Here are some guidelines and considerations that will assist in the setting of program objectives. Generally speaking, there are three types of program objectives: those focusing on behavioral change, information transfer, and skills development. As you might expect, behavioral objectives are not only the most difficult to achieve, but also the most difficult to measure. Programs aimed at reducing juvenile delinquency, altering racial attitudes, or reducing welfare dependency are attempting to bring about significant behavioral restructuring of the person and the community.

Hence, such programs have already built in their own failure mechanisms. It is not to say that programs seeking significant human changes will not work, but that the nature and content of such efforts often do not square with programmatic reality. There is no reason to ensure failure. The program manager who sets unrealistic objectives is often his own worst enemy. Consequently, in terms of success—and nothing works better than success—it is probably better to focus on skills and information-transfer objectives. Information-transfer objectives seek to increase awareness, exposure, interest, and obtain some type of overt action. For example, you can make famale AFDC clients aware of birth-control techniques, but you cannot force them not to have children. Often the best you can do is provide incentives or disincentives for this activity. One information-transfer objective might be to counsel 100 women in the various techniques of birth control. Skills objectives, on the other hand, focus on increasing competency at specific tasks, such as plotting basal body temperature charts and using these as a techniques for birth control.

Whenever you are setting objectives, these should be kept in mind:

1. Program objectives should be both *attainable* and *challenging*. Performance measurement is a results-oriented approach. As such, there is no inherent need to increase stress within the organization. If objectives are seen to be unrealistic, they will be either totally disregarded, subverted, or misreported.

2. Objectives should be keyed to specific time targets and completion dates.

3. Each objective should be stated in terms of the specific results to be achieved; thus, it will serve as an action guide.

4. Each objective should be accompanied by the measurement criteria that will be used to measure performance.

5. Objectives should focus on major areas of achievement and not on the more routine program tasks.

In addition, different degrees of program objectives can be identified. The first category is "program-maintenance objectives." Such objectives detail adequate or acceptable levels of program performance. A second category is that of "push objectives." These are the kinds of objectives that would, if achieved, indicate extremely high levels of output and outstanding performance. Such objectives are often concerned with handling greater areas of program responsibility without concurrent budget increases. There are also long- and short-range objectives. A long-range objective is one that will not be accomplished within the initially funded program year, while a short-range objective is expected to be satisfied within the funding period.

There are several basic problems associated with objective setting. One is that some programs obtain good results of stated objectives at the expense of desirable objectives that did not happen to be on the list of targets. Similarly, there is the problem of suboptimization. This problem occurs when programs attempt to maximize the output of certain objectives without being aware of the consequences for other targets. It might be the objective of the nutrition program for pregnant women to reduce costs by 10 percent. This objective can be accomplished by reducing the size of individual servings; however, such action might also decrease the meal's nutritional value. Consequently, one objective—that of reducing costs—would be met at the expense of another—maintaining nutritional balance. Another problem commonly occurs when objectives are pursued despite events which indicate the desirability of a change in targets.

The Performance Standard

In order to be able to judge whether objectives were achieved, performance standards must be devised. Earlier, the objective example was given as "the insurance that all low-income, pregnant women on social welfare receive nutritional meals each day." A performance standard provides a yardstick to determine whether this objective was satisfied. For instance, in terms of a meal's nutritional value, a performance standard might be that each day's meals should conform to required nutritional standards for pregnant women as established by the American Society of Dietitians. When developing performance standards, it is suggested that four steps be followed:

1. Identify specific objectives or subobjectives.

2. Agree upon a standard which reflects successful achievement.

3. Establish a "region of tolerance" above and below the standard; an actual level of performance within that region is by definition acceptable. Performance levels outside the region suggest the need

to examine the objective more closely and perhaps take programmatic action.

4. Maintain performance records. As a general rule, in setting up a performance-measurement system, it is not advisable to overly increase the load in the measurement system, but rather, to rely on the existing data base.

Performance standards are designed to measure program performance and past and future trends. Standards should be devised with certain qualities in mind:

1. Standards should be meaningful and understandable.

2. Standards should be sensitive to variation in activities measured.

3. Assumptions underlying the indicators should be justifiable and intuitively reasonable.

4. Standards should consist of clearly derived component parts.

5. Each component part should make an independent contribution to variations in objectives measured.

6. Standards should be derivable from data that are available or easily obtainable.

7. Standards should be designed whenever possible for multiple organizational use.

8. Standards should be chosen so that personnel responsible for recording and transmitting data respect the need for accuracy.[3]

Performance standards developed in this fashion can provide the basis of a program feedback and control system which serves all elements of an organization by allowing the tracking of performance trends as shown in Figure 9-4. The trends revealed by performance and flow charts can become a key element in the performance-measurement process. They constitute a "missing link" in many social service programs.

Outcome Measurement

You have to measure—there is no other way. Once objectives have been settled upon, targets set, and standards developed, the next step is the actual measurement of program performance. Human service agencies, for many reasons, have shied away from productivity or performance-measuring systems. It is often claimed that service-oriented objectives cannot be adequately measured. In order to fully understand performance measurement, there must be an understanding of the basic production principle that states that any organization transforms re-

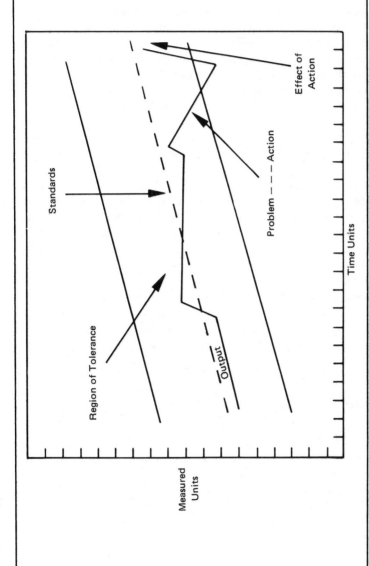

Figure 9.4: PERFORMANCE TRENDS

225

sources into some kind of product which is expected to meet some quality standards. The process is represented in this manner in Figure 9-5.

For instance, in the case of the nutrition program for pregnant women, resources such as manpower, money, equipment, and materials are the inputs. The management and administrative process coordinates, controls, plans, and communicates in order to link and mold the materials, manpower, and financial resources into productive teams and units. These teams and units then can perform the primary task of producing output which, in the case of the nutrition program, is a healthy mother and child. This process is diagrammed in Figure 9-6.

As a word of caution, some problems in measurement and interpreting time-series data should be noted. First, large relative gains come easier from a low starting point than from data approaching a ceiling. For example, if a social agency processed 100 clients in one year and 200 the next, this represents a 100-percent increase in productivity. However, a similar agency processing 1000 clients one year and 1100 the next would post only a 10-percent productivity increase. In reality, it is the second agency that is doing best, at least in terms of numbers. Second, absolute differences often given an opposite impression of that conveyed by relative difference. For instance, if a youth agency received a current budget of $10,000 per year to counsel 100 youths, it represents a unit cost of $100 per client. Assume the agency then requested $20,000 for the next fiscal year and increased their counseling load to 400 youths. This figure would represent a 100-percent increase in budget, but a 50-percent decrease in the unit cost. Third, quantities in a time series often require standardization before interpretation can be ventured. It is the old "apples" and "bananas" comparison. Finally, measurements should not be substituted for policy; meaning, numbers should not alone determine organizational direction.[4]

Put Up—Or Shut Up

An operating unit, agency, or program which can demonstrate and predict the results of its mission will be in a more competitive position when funds are being allocated because they are able to justify needs with hard facts rather than subjective whining. Prospects for additional resources will further increase if the agency shows a real capability to allocate internal resources in order to continually improve yield.

There are several factors which hamper the development of performance-measurement systems in social agencies: (1) not knowing what to measure; (2) inability to agree on quality and quantity standards; (3)

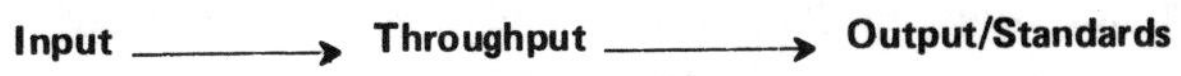

Input ⟶ Throughput ⟶ Output/Standards

Figure 9.5

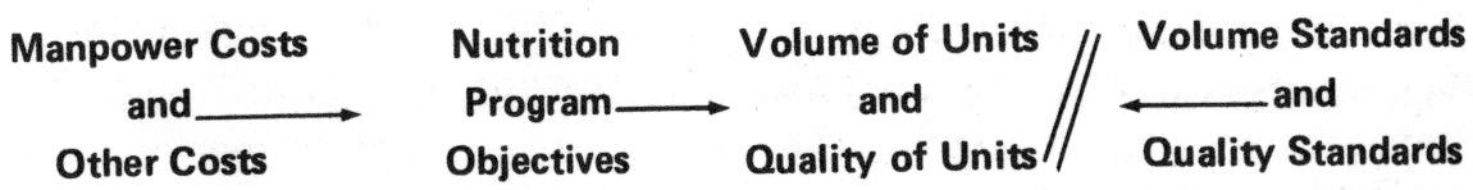

| Manpower Costs and Other Costs | ⟶ | Nutrition Program Objectives | ⟶ | Volume of Units and Quality of Units | // | Volume Standards and Quality Standards ⟵ |

Figure 9.6

an overly technical approach; (4) misuse of measurement indicators; and (5) lack of management understanding of the uses of overall indices and of the need for different indicators for different organizational levels. However, even when technical problems have been worked out, there are policy implications which discourage full implementation. For example, the budget process may encourage a program manager to spend all available funds to demonstrate need and justify continuation or increase. Also, across-the-board reductions penalize tight, well-managed programs and benefit those which have built-in slack. Finally, individuals might be reluctant to divert already scarce funds for the design and implementation of the system, even though prospects for increased productivity are evident.

Getting Down to Business

In order to combine these somewhat ambiguous words, concepts, and ideas together, and to show the practical applicability of program-performance measurement, a sample work sheet has been included. The Program Performance Work Sheet is completed in this manner: First, key program objectives are listed and described. Second, a standard of performance is established. In other words, the quality and quantity standards are recorded. These standards become the yardstick against which successful achievement of the goal is measured. Third, the means of measuring performance on this particular objective must be developed. It should be simple, inexpensive, and require little additional effort on the part of the staff. Fourth, a target or completion date is set. Fifth, the outcome is listed and recommendations for future actions are made. The sample program used to illustrate performance evaluation is fictional; however, the objectives were selected with an eye toward reality. For the sake of argument, assume a local department of social services has decided to measure the performance of a teenage foster-care program. The model program-performance work sheet is explained in Figures 9-7, 9-8, and 9-9.

The outcome and suggestion columns are not completed since the data were not actually evaluated. However, had this been a "live" program-performance evaluation, some very real, vital information would have been gained. Such a performance-measurement system will provide agencies with a more topical, intuitively reasonable method for measuring and improving program output. In addition, a performance-measurement system can be thought of as a planning and control system which can be a powerful agent for program change and development.

What has been demonstrated is a technique for program evaluation. The human service manager should not hesitate to take advantage of

Program Title:	Foster Care		Operating Agency:		Department of Social Services	
Unit of Government:	Local and County		Funding Period:		July 1 – June 30	

Key Program Objectives	Performance Standard	Measurement Used	Target-Completion Date	Outcome	Suggestions for Improvement
Place children in homes that have proper physical safeguards	Homes must meet all local building and fire codes; if found lacking, charges must be removed within 15 days	Housing-and fire-inspection reports, also case record review	30 days		
Provide children with proper nutritional care	Meals should conform to minimum dietary requirements for teenagers as devised by the American Society of Dietitions	Evaluation and review of proposed menu plans on a monthly basis	90 days		
Assure that children receive appropriate care in a healthful and positive social environment	Quarterly home visits with semi-annual evaluations of care	Progress report stating how child's need for care, training, and treatment is being met	60 days		
Foster-home environment should provide an opportunity for academic growth	Children with previous academic difficulties should be able to demonstrate increased competence on standardized mathematics and comprehension tests	Standardized test score prior to foster care– standardized test score during foster care–growth rate	120 days		

Figure 9.7: PROGRAM-PERFORMANCE WORK SHEET

229

Program Title: _____   Operating Agency: _____

Unit of Government: _____   Funding Period: _____

Key Program Objectives	Performance Standard	Measurement Used	Target-Completion Date	Outcome	Suggestions for Improvement
Expedite discharge of child identified as one who is no longer in need of foster-care services	It should take no longer than 3 days to return child to family care once he is certified to be discharged	Case records average time to return child in Time 1 compared to average time to return child in Time 2	30 days		
Provide legal support payments to those eligible on a timely basis	Payments should conform to all legal guidelines and requirements as determined by law and should be paid on the 15th and 30th of each month when children are under care	Financial audits	180 days		

Figure 9.8: PROGRAM-PERFORMANCE WORK SHEET

Program Title: _____

Unit of Government: _____

Operating Agency: _____

Funding Period: _____

Key Program Objectives	Performance Standard	Measurement Used	Target-Completion Date	Outcome	Suggestions for Improvement
Reduce incidences of juvenile delinquency	Juvenile delinquency rate amongst children in foster care should not exceed local average for that age group	Juvenile arrest records	360 days		
Provide supportive services to parents of foster children	Parents of foster children should receive on a weekly basis supportive counseling services	Case records and regular feedback from supportive units	90 days		
Speed successful entry of child back into family unit	Reduce average time in foster care by 20 percent and/or the chances of having to renew placement	Average number of days in placement during Time 1 compared to average number of days in Time 2; percentage of children needing placement after being returned to family in t_1, t_2	60 days		

Figure 9.9: PROGRAM-PERFORMANCE WORK SHEET

either this or some similar assessment methodology. Of course, many welfare practitioners are not opposed to oversimplified development objectives, perhaps because vaguely defined program objectives preclude the setting of operational criteria and performance standards. The absence of well-defined and measurable objectives means the manager cannot be pinned down or be held responsible for program performance because he has failed to measure up to standards. In short, the welfare administrator has a way out. On the other hand, the public, top management, and funding bodies do not welcome glib generalities. Hence, human service programmers should be seeking ways of providing performance data to bolster claims and requests for support and funds.

Conclusion

What has been proposed here are several methods for evaluating program performance; others are available. Before they can be used, human service managers must be convinced of their utility, necessity, and practicality. Evaluation, as stated earlier, provides a number of organizational benefits. The techniques discussed do not exhaust the possible methods of human service program evaluation, and no one method can be universally applied. Although not easy or comfortable for human service managers, evaluation has become an organizational necessity. However, as the preceding discussions show, program-performance assessment is not beyond practical application in the human services.

NOTES

1. Joseph Wholey et al. *Federal Evaluation Policy* (Washington: The Urban Institute, 1971), p. 50.

2. Jack Haskins, "The Controlled Field Experiment," Syracuse University (Mimeographed), 1967.

3. Iwao Moryiama, "Problems in Measurement of Health Status," *Indicators of Social Change*, edited by Eleanor Sheldon and Wilbert Moore (New York: Russell Sage Foundation, 1968), p. 593.

4. Eleanor Sheldon and Wilbert Moore, eds., *Indicators of Social Change* (New York: Russell Sage Foundation, 1968), p. 9.

BIBLIOGRAPHY

BIBLIOGRAPHY

Chapter 1

Managing for Achievement in the Human Services or Where Have We Gone Wrong

Abels, Paul. "The Managers Are Coming! The Managers Are Coming!" *Public Welfare* 31 (April 1973): 13-15.

Anthony, Robert N. and Herzlinger, Regina. *Management Control in Nonprofit Organizations.* Homewood, Ill.: Richard D. Irwin, 1975.

Baker, R.J.S. "Organizational Theory and the Public Sector." *The Journal of Management Studies* 6 (February 1969):15-32.

Bennis, Warren G. *The Unconscious Conspiracy—Why Leaders Can't Lead.* New York: American Management Assn., 1976.

Bennis, Warren G., ed. *American Bureaucracy.* Chicago: Aldine 1970.

Black, Guy. "Systems Analysis in Government Operations." Management Science 14 (October 1967): B-41-58.

Boulding, Kenneth E. "General Systems Theory, the Skeleton of Science." Management Science 3 (April 1956): 197-208.

Buchanan, Bruce II. "Government Managers, Business Executives, and Organizational Commitment." Public Administration Review 35 (July-August 1975): 339-347.

Burkhead, Jesse, and Miner, Jerry. *Public Expenditure.* Chicago: Aldine, 1971.

Carden, Gerlad E. *The Dynamics of Public Administration.* Hinsdale, Ill.: Dryden Press, 1971.

Charlesworth, James C., ed. *Theory and Practice of Public Administration: Scope, Objectives, and Methods.* Philadelphia: American Academy of Political and Social Sciences, 1968.

Clark, Kenneth, and Hopkins, Jeanette. *A Revelant War Against Poverty.* New York: Harper & Row, 1968.

Drucker, Peter F. *The Practice of Management.* New York: Harper & Row, 1970.

Galbraith, John Kenneth. *Economics and the Public Purpose.* New York: Houghton-Mifflin, 1973.

Gruber, M. "Total Administration." Social Work 19 (May 1974): 625-636.

Hall, Richard. *Organizations: Structure and Process.* Englewood Cliffs, N.J.: Prentice-Hall, 1972.

Hasenfeld, Yeheskel, and English, Richard A., eds. *Human Service Organizations.* Ann Arbor: University of Michigan Press, 1974.

Henry, Nicholas. "Paradigms of Public Administration." Public Administration Review 35 (July-August 1975): 378-386.

———*Public Administration and Public Affairs.* Englewood Cliffs, N.J.: Prentice-Hall, 1975.

Johnson, Richard A.; Kast, Freemont, E.; and Rosenzweig, James E. *The Theory and Management of Systems.* 3rd ed. New York: McGraw-Hill, 1973.

Kahn, Herman, and Bruce-Briggs, B. *Things to Come: Thinking about the Seventies and Eighties.* New York: MacMillan, 1972.

Kast, Fremont E., and Rosenzweig, James E. *Organization and Management: A Systems Approach.* New York: McGraw-Hill, 1974.

Levin, Gilbert, and Roberts, Edward B. *The Dynamics of Human Service Delivery.* Cambridge, Mass.: Ballinger, 1976.

Levin, Gilbert; Roberts, Edward B.; and Hirsch, Gary B. *The Persistent Poppy.* Cambridge: Ballinger, 1975.

Lewis, Harold. "Management in the Nonprofit Social Service Organization." Child Welfare 54 (September 1975): 615-623.

Litterer, Joseph A. *The Analysis of Organizations.* New York: John Wiley, 1965.

Manser, Gordon. "Further Thoughts on Purpose of Service." Social Casework 55 (July 1974): 421-427.

Maurer, John G. *Readings in Organization Theory: Open-Systems Approaches.* New York: Random House, 1971.

Meyer, Marshall W. *Bureaucratic Structure and Authority: Coordination and Control in 254 Governmental Agencies.* New York: Harper & Row, 1972.

Morse, Phillip M., and Bacon, Laura W., eds. *Operations Research for Public Systems.* Cambridge, Mass.: MIT Press, 1967.

Moynihan, Daniel. *Maximum Feasible Misunderstanding.* New York: Free Press, 1969.

Mullis, S. "Management Applications to the Welfare System." Public Welfare 33 (1975): 31-34.

Murray, M.A. "Comparing Public and Private Management: An Exploratory Essay." Public Administration Review 35 (July-August 1975): 364-371.

Perrow, Charles. "The Analysis of Goals in Complex Organizations." *Human Service Organizations.* Edited by Yeheskel Hasenfeld and Richard A. English. Ann Arbor: University of Michigan Press, 1974.

Rossi, Peter H., and Lyall, Katharine C. *Reforming Public Welfare.* New York: Russell Sage Foundation, 1976.

Schoderbek, Peter P., ed. *Management Systems.* 2nd ed. New York: John Wiley, 1971.

Stewart, Rosemary. *The Reality of Organizations.* London: MacMillan, 1970.

Susman, Gerald I. *Autonomy at Work: A Sociotechnical Analysis of Participative Management.* Praeger Special Studies in U.S. Economic, Social, and Political Issues. New York: Praeger, 1976.

Trecker, Harleigh B. *Social Work Administration.* New York: Association Press, 1971.

Zurcher, Louis. *Poverty Warriors.* Austin, Tex.: University of Texas Press, 1970.

Chapter 2

Selecting to Achieve

Albrecht, R.; Glaser, E.; and Marks, J. "Validation of a Multiple-Assessment Procedure for Managerial Personnel." Journal of Applied Psychology 48 (December 1964): 351-360.

Beech, C. "The Assessment Center: A Promising Approach to Evaluation." The Canadian Personnel and Industrial Relations Journal (November 1972): 35-38.

Berger, Lance A. "Dispelling a Mystique: Practical Management Manpower Planning." Personnel Journal 55 (June 1976): 296-300.

Bray, Douglas. "The Assessment Center Method of Appraising Management Potential." The Personnel Job in a Changing World, Edited by F.W. Blood, New York: American Management Assn., 1964.

Bray, Douglas and Moses, J. "Personnel Selection." Annual Review of Psychology 23 (1972): 546-576.

Byham, William C. "Assessment Center for Spotting Future Managers." Harvard Business Review 48 (July-August 1970): 150-160.

Byham, William, and Wettengel, Carol. "Assessment Centers for Supervisors and Managers." Public Personnel Management 3 (September-October 1974): 352-364.

Cohen, B.; Moses, S.; and Byham, W. "Validity of Assessment Centers: A Literature Review." Journal of Industrial and Organizational Psychology, (Summer 1973).

Cowan, John, and Kartz, Molly. "Internal Assessment Center: An Organization Development Approach to Selecting Supervisors." Public Personnel Management 5 (January-February 1976): 15-23.

Donovan, J.J., ed. Recruitment and Selection in the Public Service. Chicago: Public Personnel Administration, 1968.

Drake, John D. Interviewing for Managers. New York: American Management Assn., 1972.

Famularo, Joseph J., ed. Handbook of Modern Personnel Administration. New York: McGraw-Hill, 1972.

Hinrichs, J. "Comparison of 'Real Life' Assessments of Management Potential with Situational Exercises, Paper and Pencil Ability Tests, and Personality Inventories." Journal of Applied Psychology 53 (1969): 425-432.

Jackson, A. Recruiting, Interviewing, and Selecting: A Manual for Line Managers. New York: McGraw-Hill, 1972.

Jaffee, Cabot L. Effective Management Selection. Reading, Mass.: Addison-Wesley, 1971.

Kraut, Allen I. "A Hard Look at Management Assessment Centers and Their Future." Personnel Journal 51 (May 1972): 317-326.

Lipsett, Laurence. "Selecting Personnel Without Tests." Personnel Journal 51 (September 1972): 648-654.

Lopez, Felix M. Evaluating Employee Performance. Chicago: Public Personnel Administration, 1968.

McDermott, A. "Merit Systems Under Fire." Public Personnel Management 5 (July-August 1976): 225-233.

Morrisey, George L. *Management by Objectives and Results in the Public Sector.* Reading, Mass.: Addison-Wesley, 1976.

Mosher, Frederick C. *Democracy and the Public Service.* New York: Oxford University Press, 1968.

Mure, Winfred. "Identification and Development of Tomorrow's Managers." Personnel Journal 51 (January 1972): 46-50.

Rosen, Bernard. "A Civil Service Perspective." Civil Service Journal 15 (April-June 1975): 21-23.

"Commentary: The Positive Value of Merit." Civil Service Journal 14 (January-March 1974): 18-19.

Savas, E.S., and Ginsburg, S.G. "The Civil Service: A Meritless System?" Public Interest 32 (Summer 1973): 70-86.

Schlesinger, Kenneth. "Performance Improvement: The Missing Component of Appraisal Systems." Personnel Journal 58 (June 1970): 274-275.

Shafritz, J. "Political Culture—The Determinant of Merit System Viability." Public Personnel Management 3 (January-February 1974): 39-43.

Slevin, Dennis P. "The Assessment Center: Breakthrough in Management Appraisal and Development." Personnel Journal 51 (April 1972): 255-263.

Smith, James W. "Merit Compensation: The Ideal and Reality." Personnel Journal 1 (May 1972): 313-316.

Stahl, Glenn O. *The Personnel Job of Government Managers.* Chicago: Public Personnel Association, 1971.

Steiner, Richard. "New Use for Assessment Centers—Training Evaluation." Personnel Journal 54 (April 1975): 236-237.

Steiner, Richard. "Assessment Center-New York State Style." Public Executive Project, State University of New York at Albany (mimeographed), September 1975.

Thomas, John S. "So Mr. Mayor, You Want to Improve Productivity." Prepared for the National Commission on Productivity and Work Quality, 1974.

Yazer, Edward. "Assessment Centers: The Latest Fad?" Training and Development Journal 30 (January 1976): 41-44.

Chapter 3

Developing the Performing Manager

Argyris, Chris. *Integrating the Individual and the Organization.* New York: John Wiley, 1964.

Bowen, Charles, Jr. "Let's Put Realism into Management Development." Harvard Business Review 51 (July-August 1973): 80-87.

Farnsworth, Terry. *Developing Executive Talent, A Practical Guide.* New York: McGraw-Hill, 1976.

Gorham, William A. "Selecting Employees for Upward Mobility." Civil Service Journal 16 (October-December 1975): 23-24.

Hazer, John T. "Job Satisfaction: A Possible Integration of Two Theories." Training and Development Journal 30 (July 1976): 12-20.

Herzburg, Frederick. *Work and the Nature of Man.* Cleveland: World Publishing, 1966.

———*The Motivation to Work.* New York: John Wiley, 1959.

Hill, Alfred W. "Career Development—Who is Responsible?" Training and Development Journal 30 (May 1976): 14-15.

Horton, Forest W. Jr. *Reference Guide to Advanced Management Methods.* New York: American Management Assn., 1972.

Jun, Jong S. "Management by Objectives in the Public Sector." Public Administration Review 36 (January-February 1976): 1-5.

Levinson, Harry. *The Exceptional Executive.* Cambridge, Mass.: Harvard University Press, 1968.

———. "Asinine Attitudes Toward Motivation." Harvard Business Review 51 (January-February 1973): 70-76.

Levoy, Robert P. "How to Keep Staff Morale and Motivation in High Gear." Personnel Journal 51 (December 1972): 913-918.

Likert, Rensis. *The Human Organization.* New York: McGraw-Hill, 1967.

Maslow, Abraham. *Motivation and Personality.* New York: Harper & Row, 1954.

Morrisey, George L. *Appraisal and Development Through Objectives and Results.* Reading, Mass.: Addison-Wesley, 1972.

Mosher, Frederick. "The Public Service in the Temporary Society." Public Administration Review 31 (January-February 1971), 47-58.

Musolf, Lloyd. "Separate Career Executive Systems: Egalitarianism and Neutrality." Public Administration Review 31 (July-August 1971): 409-419.

Newell, Gale E. "How to Plan a Training Program." Personnel Journal 55 (May 1976): 220-226.

Passett, Barry A. *Leadership Development for Public Service.* Houston: Gulf Publishing, 1971.

Pomerteau, Raymond. "The State of Management Development in the Federal Service." Public Personnel Management 3 (January-February 1974): 23-28.

Rehfuss, John A. "Executive Development: Executive Seminar Center Style." Public Administration Review 30 (September-October 1970): 553-568.

Revans, Reginald W. *Developing Effective Managers.* New York: Praeger, 1971.

Schein, Edgar H. "The Individual, the Organization, and the Career." Journal of Applied Behavioral Science 7 (July-August 1971): 401-427.

Simpson, Karl F. "Management Development: Full Spectrum Training." Training and Development Journal 29 (March 1975): 16-24.

Singer, Edwin, and Ransden, John. *Human Resources: Obtaining Results from People at Work.* New York: McGraw-Hill, 1972.

Stahl, Glenn O. *The Personnel Job of Government Managers.* Chicago: Public Personnel Assn., 1971.

Taylor, B., and Lippett, G.L. eds. *Management Development and Training Handbook.* New York: McGraw-Hill, 1976.

VanDersal, William. *The Successful Manager in Government and Business.* New York: Harper & Row, 1974.

Wagman, Barry L. "An Approach to Measuring Productivity of Staff Functions." Public Personnel Administration 3 (September-October 1974): 425-430.

Chapter 4

Building Effective Organizations

Argyris, Chris. *Integrating the Individual and the Organization.* New York: John Wiley, 1964.

————*On Organizations of the Future.* Beverly Hills: Sage Publications, 1973.

Backoff, Robert. "Operationalizing Administrative Reform for Improved Governmental Performance." Administration and Society 6 (May 1974): 73-106.

Beckhard, Richard. *Organization Development: Strategies and Models.* Reading, Mass.: Addison-Wesley, 1969.

Bennis, Warren G.; Benne, Kenneth D.; Chin, Robert; and Corey, Kenneth E., eds. *The Planning of Change.* New York: Holt, Rinehart & Winston, 1976.

Burns, Tom, and Stalker, G.M. *The Management of Innovation.* London: Tavistock Publications, 1961.

Campbell, John P.; Dunnette, Marvin D.; Lawler, Edward, III; and Weich, Karl E., Jr. *Managerial Behavior, Performance and Effectiveness.* New York: McGraw-Hill, 1970.

Cohen, Michael, and Collins, John. "Some Correlates of Organizational Effectiveness." Public Personnel Management 3 (Nov./Dec. 1974): 493-499.

Cribben, James J. *Effective Managerial Leadership.* New York: American Management Assn., 1972.

Drucker, Peter F. "Managing the Public Service Institution." Public Interest 33 (Fall 1973): 43-60.

"What Results Should You Expect? A Users' Guide to MBO." Public Administration Review 1 (Jan./Feb. 1976): 12-19.

Ghorpade, Jaisingh. *Assessment of Organizational Effectiveness.* California: Goodyear Publishing, 1971.

Gouldner, Alvin W., and Miller, S.M., ed. *Applied Sociology.*   New York: Free Press, 1965.

Gouldner, Alvin W. "Theoretical Requirements of the Applied Social Sciences." American Sociological Review, 22 (February, 1975).

Hage, Jerald, and Aiken, Michael. *Social Change in Complex Organizations.* New York: Random House, 1970.

Harrison, Roger. "Understanding Your Organization's Character." Harvard Business Review 50 (May/June 1972): 119-128.

Hollingsworth, A.T., and Hass, Jane W. "Structural Planning in Organizational Development: An Often Neglected Aspect." Personnel Journal 5 (December 1975): 613-615.

Huse, Edgar F. *Organizational Development and Change.* St. Paul, Minn.: West Publishing, 1975.

Kaufman, Herbert. "The Natural History of Human Organization." Administration and Society 7 (Aug. 1975): 131-149.

Levinson, Harry. *Organizational Diagnosis.* Cambridge, Mass.: Harvard University Press, 1972.

Lippit, Gordon L. *Organizational Renewal,* New York: Appleton-Century-Crofts, 1965.

Likert, Rensis. *The Human Organization.* New York: McGraw-Hill, 1967.

Mack, Ruth P. *Planning on Uncertainty.* New York: John Wiley-Interscience, 1971.

McGregor, Douglas. *The Professional Manager.* Edited by Caroline McGregor and Warren G. Bennis. New York: McGraw-Hill, 1967.

Miller, Stuart J. "Measuring Perceptions of Organizational Change." Journal of Research in Crime and Delinquency 11 (1974): 180-194.

Morgan, John S. *Managing Change.* New York: McGraw-Hill, 1972.

Nadler, David A. "Differential Effects of Multiple Interventions in an Organization." Journal of Applied Behavioral Science 11 (October-November-December 1975): 348-366.

Perrow, Charles. *Organizational Analysis: A Sociological View.* Belmont, Calif.: Wards-Worth Publishing, 1970.

Porter, David O., and Olsen, Eugene A. "Some Critical Issues in Government Centralization and Decentralization." Public Administration Review 1 36 (January-February 1976): 72-83.

Price, James L. *Organizational Effectiveness: An Inventory of Propositions.* Homewood, Ill.: Richard D. Irwin, 1968.

Redden, W.J. *Management Effectiveness.* New York: McGraw-Hill, 1970.

Rubin, Irwin; Polvnick, Mark; and Fry, Ron. "Initiating Planned Change in Health Care Systems." Journal of Applied Behavioral Science 10 (1974): 107-124.

Skogan, Wesley G. "Efficiency and Effectiveness in Big-City Police Departments." Public Administration Review 3 6 (May/June 1976): 278-285.

Topliss, Eda P. "Organizational Change As Illustrated by a Case-Study of a Geriatric Hospital." British Journal of Sociology 25 (1974), 356-364.

Tosi, Henry L., and Carroll, Stephen J. *Management: Contingencies, Structure, and Process.* Chicago, Ill.: St. Clair Press, 1976.

U.S. General Accounting Office. *Comptroller General's Report to the Congress, Social Services: Do They Help Welfare Recipients Achieve Self-Support or Reduced Dependency?,* June 27, 1973; pp. 1-6.

Whelan, Noel. "Organization Change in the Public Sector." Administration 22 (Autumn 1974): 205-220.

Chapter 5

Organizing For Service Delivery

Argyris, Chris. *Management and Organizational Development.* New York: McGraw-Hill, 1971.

Beckhard, Richard. *Organizational Development: Strategies and Models.* Reading, Mass.: Addison-Wesley, 1969.

Bowers, D.; Franklin, J.; and Pecorella, P. "Matching Problems, Precursors and Interventions in OD: A Systemic Approach." Journal of Applied Behavioral Science 11 (October/November/December 1975): 391-409.

Burke, W. Warner. "OD in Transition." Journal of Applied Behavioral Science 12 (January/February/March 1976): 22-43.

Copeland, William C. "Laboratory for Public Welfare Administrative Systems Development." (mimeographed) Minneapolis, 1976.

Culbert, S. and Reisel, J. "Organization Development: An Applied Philosophy for Managers of Public Enterprise." Public Administration Review 31 (March/April 1971): 159-169.

Dalton, Gene W.; Lawrence, Paul R.; and Lorsch, Jay W. *Organizational Structure and Design.* Homewood, Ill.: Richard D. Irwin, Dorsey Press, 1970.

Drucker, Peter. *Management: Tasks, Responsibilities, Practices.* New York: Harper & Row, 1974.

"Yes! Smith's Welfare Cuts Are Defensible." *Empire State Report.* 2 (June 1976).

French, Wendell, and Bell, Cecil H., Jr. *Organization Development.* Englewood Cliffs, N.J.: Prentice-Hall, 1973.

Gellerman, William. "Organization, Decentralization and the Individual." Decentralization: Citizen Participation in Urban Development 3 (1974): 233-253.

Hall, Richard H. *Organizations: Structure and Process.* Englewood Cliffs, N.J.: Prentice-Hall, 1972.

Hays, Samuel. "Reorganizing For Fun and Profit." *School of Social Welfare and The Public Executive Project.* State University at Albany (1975).

Hollingsworth, A.T., and Hass, Jane. "Structural Planning in Organizational Development: An Often Neglected Aspect." Personnel Journal 5 (December 1975): 613-15.

Huse, Edgar. *Organization Development and Change.* St. Paul, Minn.: West Publishing, 1975.

Huse, Edgar and Bowditch, James. *Behavior in Organizations: A Systems Approach to Managing.* Reading, Mass.: Addison-Wesley, 1973.

Huse, Edgar and Beer, Michael. "Eclectic Approach to Organizational Development." Harvard Business Review 49 (September/October 1971): 103-12.

Kahn, Robert. "Organizational Development: Some Problems and Proposals." Journal of Applied Behavioral Science 10 (October/November/December 1974): 485-502.

Kingdon, Donald Ralph. *Matrix Organization: Managing Information Technologies.* London: Tavistock Publications, 1973.

Lawrence, Paul R., and Lorsch, Jay W., eds. *Studies in Organization Design.* Homewood, Ill.: Richard D. Irwin-The Dorsey Press, 1970.

Lowenstein, Edward; Rice, Barbara; Swyer, Richard; Goran, Leonard; and Rosh, David. "The Managment of Organizational Change." Public Welfare 31 (Winter 1973): 48-57.

Mulles, Scott. "Management Applications to the Welfare System." Public Welfare 33 (Fall 1975): 30-34.

New York State Department of Social Services. *Annual Report* (1974).

Office of the Secretary U.S. Department of Health, Education and Welfare. *Poverty Study Task Force.* (September 1976).

Partin, J. Jennings, ed. *Current Perspectives in Organization Development.* Reading, Mass.: Addison-Wesley, 1973.

Patti, Reno and Resnick, Herman. "Changing the Agency From Within." Social Work 17 (July 1972): 48-57.

Selfridge, Richard and Sokalik, Stanley. "A Comprehensive View of Organization Development." Michigan State University Business Topics 23 (Winter 1975): 46-61.

Warrick, D.D. "Applying OD to the Public Sector." Public Personnel Management 5 (May/June 1976): 186-190.

Wax, John. "Power Theory and Institutional Change." Social Service Review 45 (September 1971), 274-288.

Weissman, Harold. *Overcoming Mismanagement in the Human Service Profession.* San Francisco: Josey-Bass, 1973.

Chapter 6

Generating Production—Not Conflict

Ackoff, Russel. "Structural Conflicts Within Organizations." *Operations Research and the Social Sciences.* Edited by J.R. Lawrence, New York: Tavistock Publications, 1966.

Aldrich, H. "Organizational Boundaries and Inter-Organizational Conflict." Human Relations 24 (August 1971): 279-93.

Boulding, Elise, ed. *Conflict Management in Organizations.* A report of a seminar conducted by the Foundation for Research on Human Behavior in cooperation with the Center for Research on Conflict Resolution. Ann Arbor, Michigan: University of Michigan, 1961.

Boulding, Kenneth. *Conflict and Defense: A General Theory.* New York: Harper Torch Books, 1962.

Brewer, Harry D. "Dealing with Complex Social Problems: The Potential of 'Decision Seminar'." in *Political Development and Change.* Edited by Harry D. Brewer and Ronald D. Brunner. New York: Free Press, 1975.

Gillespie, D.F. *et al.* "Collective Stress and Community Transformation." Human Relations 27 (October 1974): 767-78

Goodin, Robert E. "The Logic of Bureaucratic Back Scratching." Public Choice 21 (Spring 1975): 53-67.

Green, Stephen. "Professional/Bureaucratic Conflict: The Case of the Medical Profession in the National Health Service." Sociological Review 23 (February 1975): 121-141.

Hardy, Dennis. "A Servant of Two Masters." Built Environment 3 (July 1974): 366-367.

Hershey, Cary S., "Limits of Federal Protest." Public Administration Review 34 (July/August 1974): 359-368.

———"Responses of Federal Agencies to Employee Risk-Taking." Bureaucrat 2 (Fall 1973): 285-293.

Jandt, Fred E. *Conflict Resolution Through Communication.* New York: Harper and Row, 1973.

Kahn, Robert L. and Boulding, Elise, eds. *Power and Conflict in Organizations.* New York: Basic Books, 1964.

Kahn, Robert L., *et al. Organizational Stress: Studies in Role Conflict and Ambiguity.* New York: John Wiley, 1964.

Kahn, Robert L., ed. *Power and Conflict in Organizations,* New York: Basic Books, 1964.

Labovitz, Sanford and Miller, Jon. "Implications of Power, Conflict and Change in an Organizational Setting." Pacific Sociological Review 17 (April 1974): 214-239.

Lawrence, Paul R. and Lorsch, Jay W. *Organization and Environment.* Homewood, Ill.: Richard D. Irwin, 1969.

Likert, Rensis, and Likert, Jane Gibson. *New Ways of Managing Conflict.* New York: McGraw-Hill, 1976.

McMahon, Anne and Camilleri, Santo F. "Rank-and-File Participation in Organizational Decision-Making: A Model and Some Preliminary Evidence." Pacific Sociological Review 18 (October 1975): 387-420.

McNeil, Elton. *The Nature of Human Conflict.* Englewood Cliffs, N.J.; Prentice-Hall, 1965.

Miewald, Robert. "Conflict and Harmony in the Public Service." Public Personnel Management 3 (November/December 1974): 531-535.

Pettigrew, Andrew. "Decision-Making as a Political Process." in *The Politics of Organizational Decision-Making.* London: Tavistock Publications, 1974, pp. 16-31.

"The Disparity of Demands in an Innovative Decision Process." in *The Politics of*

Organizational Decision-Making. London: Tavistock Publications, 1974, pp. 168-228.

Rapoport, Anatol. *Fights, Games, and Debates.* Ann Arbor: University of Michigan Press, 1970.

Randinelli, Dennis. "The Dynamics of Policy Making." in *Urban and Regional Development Planning: Policy and Administration.* Ithaca, N.Y.: Cornell University Press, 1975, pp. 186-211.

Schein, Edgar. "In Defense of Theory Y." Organizational Dynamics 4 (Summer 1975): 17-30.

Schelling, Thomas. The Strategy of Conflict. Oxford: Oxford University Press, 1960.

Segal, Morley. "Organization and Environment: A Typology of Adaptability and Structure." Public Administration Review 34 (May/June 1974): 212-220.

Smith, Alexander. *The Comparative Policy Process.* Santa Barbara, Calif.: Clio Press, 1975.

Sorensen, James and Sorensen, Thomas. "The Conflict of Professionals in Bureaucratic Organizations." Administrative Science Quarterly 19 (March 1974): 98-106.

Spector, Paul. "Relationships of Organizational Frustration with Reported Behavioral Reactions of Employees." Journal of Applied Psychology 60 (October 1975): 635-637.

Stene, Edwin. "Conflict, Compromise, and Cooperation: A Model of Organization Theory." Administrative Change 1 (December 1973): 1-11.

Vickers, Geoffrey. "Institutional and Personal Roles." in *Making Institutions Work.* New York: John Wiley, 1973, pp. 105-122.

Vickers, Geoffrey. "The Management of Conflict." in *Making Institutions Work.* New York: John Wiley, 1973, pp. 137-156.

Vroom, Victor H., and Yetton, Phillip W. *Leadership and Decision-Making.* Pittsburgh, Pa.: University of Pittsburgh Press, 1973.

Chapter 7

Surviving to Achieve: The Role of Public Relations

Bates, Don. "Non-Profit Public Relations." Public Relations Journal 32 (August 1976): 24-25, 32-33.

Berelson, Bernard. *Reader in Public Opinion and Communication.* New York: Free Press, 1966.

Bernays, Edward L. *The Engineering of Consent.* Oklahoma: University of Oklahoma Press, 1955.

Burger, Chester. "How to Meet the Press." Harvard Business Review 53 (July-August 1975): 62-70.

Cainfield, B.R., and Moore, H.F. *Public Relations.* Homewood, Ill.: Richard D. Irwin, 1973.

Center, Allen H. "What About the State of the Art?" Public Relations Journal 32 (January 1976): 30-31.

Cutlip, Scott M., and Center, Allen H. *Effective Public Relations.* 4th ed. Englewood Cliffs, N.J.: Prentice-Hall, 1971.

Cutlip, Scott M., ed. *Public Opinion and Public Administration.* Montgomery, Alabama: Bureau of Public Administration, 1965.

Darrow, Richard W. *The Dartnell Public Relations Handbook*. Chicago: Dartnell Corp., 1967.

Deutsch, Karl W. *The Nerves of Government: Models of Political Communication and Control*. New York: Free Press of Glencoe, 1963.

Etzioni, Amatai. "Alternative Conceptions of Accountability: The Example of Health Administration." Public Administration Review 35 (May-June 1975): 279-286.

Fenn, Dan H. Jr. "Executives as Community Volunteers." Harvard Business Review 49 (March-April 1971): 4-9, 12-16, 156-157.

Fisher, William Jr. "Social Agencies: A New Challenge for Public Relations." Public Relations Quarterly 4 (April 1959): 14-21.

Forrestal, Dan J. "Placing Public Relations in Perspective." Public Relations Journal 30 (March 1974): 6-8, 34.

Gordon, George. *Persuasion: The Theory and Practice of Manipulative Communication*. New York: Hastings House, 1971.

Harris, Huntington. "Community of Interest—A Concept of Public Relations," Quarterly Review of Public Relations 6 (Spring 1961): 2-8.

Helm, Lewis M. "HEW: Going Public." Public Relations Journal 30 (May 1974): 28-29.

Hoffman, Jack J., and Osborn, Richard. *How to Improve the Public Image*. Washington, D.C.: Education, Training, and Research Science, Corp., 1971.

Kepler, Edwin C. "The New Scope of Community Relations." Quarterly Review of Public Relations 6 (Winter 1961): 23-30.

Kitaeff, A. "Public Service T.V. Spots Can Work for You." Public Relations Journal 31 (December 1975).

Lerbinger, Otto, and Sullivan, Albert J., eds. *Information, Influence, and Communication*. New York: Basic Books, 1965.

Levy, Harold P. "Are Social Work's Public Relations Poor Relations?" Public Relations Journal 5 (June 1949): 26-32.

———*A Study in Public Relations*. New York: Harper, 1956.

———*Public Relations for Social Agencies*. New York: Harper, 1956.

Lundborg, Louis B. *Public Relations in the Local Community*. New York: Harper, 1950.

Marston, J.E., "A Strategy for Public Relations," *Public Relation's Journal*, 31 (September 1975).

Rosenberg, M.L., and Brody, R. "The Threat or Challenge of Accountability." Social Work 19 (March 1974): 344-350.

Schmidt, Frances, and Weiner, Harold N., eds. *Public Relations in Health and Welfare*. New York: Columbia University Press, 1960.

Steiner, Richard. "PR for PA." The Bureaucrat 2 (Winter 1974): 462-467.

Tropp, E. "Expectation, Performance, and Accountability." Social Work 19 (February 1974): 139-148.

Wagner, Gary. "Closing the Annual Report Credibility Gap." Public Relations Journal 29 (March 1973): 14-15.

Wolfe, Nancy Beals. "Public Relations Begins at Home." Public Relations Journal 19 (June 1973): 8-10.

Chapter 8

Communicating Within the Organization

Anderson, John. "What's Blocking Upward Communications?" Personnel Administration 31 (January 1968): 5-7, 19-20.

Blake, Robert, and Mouton, Jean. *The Managerial Grid*. Houston: Gulf Publishing, 1964.

Bormann, Ernest; Howell, William; Nicholas, Ralph; and Shapiro, George. *Interpersonal Communication in the Modern Organization*. Englewood Cliffs, N.J.: Prentice-Hall, 1969.

Boyd, Bradford B. "An Analysis of Communication Between Departments–Roadblocks and By-Passes." Personnel Administration 28 (November 1965): 33-38.

Carney, Thomas F. *Content Analysis: A Technique for Systematic Inference from Communications*. Winnipeg: University of Manitoba Press, 1972.

Davis, Keith. *Human Relations at Work: The Dynamics of Organizational Behavior*. 3rd ed. New York: McGraw-Hill, 1967.

Goldhaber, Gerald M. *Organizational Communication*. Dubuque, Iowa: William C. Brown Co., 1974.

Greiner, Larry. "What Managers Think of Participative Leadership." Harvard Business Review 51 (March/April 1973): 111-117.

Haney, William V. "A Comparative Study of Unilateral and Bilateral Communication." Academy of Management Journal 7 (June 1964): 128-136.

–––*Communication and Organizational Behavior*. Homewood, Ill.: Richard D. Irwin, 1973.

Highsaw, Robert B., and Bowen Don L., eds. *Communication in Public Administration*. University, Ala.: University of Alabama, Bureau of Public Administration, 1965.

Huseman, Richard C.; Logue, Cal M.; and Freshley, Dwight L. *Readings in Interpersonal and Organizational Communication*. 2nd ed. Boston: Holbrook Press, 1974.

Kelly, Joseph F. *Computerized Management Information Systems*. New York: MacMillan, 1970.

Krain, Mark. "Communication as a Process of Dyadic Organization and Development." Journal of Communication 23 (December 1973): 392-408.

Leese, Joseph. "The Bureaucratic Colander." Personnel Journal 53 (October 1974): 757-760.

Mears, Peter. "Structuring Communication in a Working Group." Journal of Communication 24 (Winter 1974): 71-78.

Melcher, Arlyn J., and Beller, Ronald, "Toward a Theory of Organization Communication: Consideration in Channel Selection." Academy of Management Journal 10 (March 1967): 39-52.

Meltzer, Morton F. *The Information Center: Management's Hidden Asset*. Binghamton: American Management Assn., 1967.

Menning, Jack H., and Wilkinson, Clyde W. *Communicating Through Letters and Reports*. rev. ed. Homewood, Ill.: Richard D. Irwin, 1972.

Mortensen, David C., and Sereno, Kenneth K. *Foundation of Communication Theory*. New York: Harper & Row, 1970.

Nemec, Richard. "Internal Communications–A Scary Science." Public Relations Journal 29 (December 1973): 6-8, 27-28.

Nwankwo, Robert L. "Communication as Symbolic Interaction: A Synthesis." Journal of Communication 23 (June 1973): 195-213.

Quinn, Robert E. "The Impacts of a Computerized Information System on the Integration and Coordination of Human Services." Public Administration Review 36 (March-April 1976): 166-174.

Rafe, Stephen C. "Credibility–Key to Communications Success." Public Relations Journal 28 (June 1972): 14-17.

Redding, William C. *Communication Within the Organization.* New York: Industrial Communication Council, 1972.

Simon, Herbert A. "Applying Information Technology to Organization Design." Public Administration Review 33 (May-June 1973): 268-277.

Terzian, Carl R. "Going to Communicate? Try Speaking!" Public Relations Journal 32 (May 1976): 16-19.

Tessen, Abraham; Rosen, Sidney; and Batchelor, Thomas. "Some Message Variables and the MUM Effect." Journal of Communication 22 (September 1972): 239-256.

Thayer, Lee. *Communication and Communication Systems.* Homewood, Ill.: Richard D. Irwin, 1968.

Vardaman, Gordon, and Vardaman, Patricia Black. *Communication in Modern Organizations.* New York: John Wiley, 1973.

Wade, Larry L. "Communications in a Public Bureaucracy." Journal of Communication 18 (March 1968): 18-25.

Zwerman, Williams L., and Lee, Blaine M. "Developing a Facilitation System for Horizontal and Diagonal Communications in Organizations." Personnel Journal 54 (July 1975): 400-402.

Chapter 9

Evaluating Human Service Programs

Baker, Jerome. "Measuring Cost Effectiveness in Human Services." Canadian Welfare 51 (January-February 1975): 5-6.

Banner, David K. "Problems in the Evaluation of Social Action Programs." ITCC Review 3 (April 1974): 19-31.

Becker, Marshall; Drachman, Robert; and Kirscht, John P. "A Field Experiment to Evaluate Various Outcomes of Continuity of Physician Care." American Journal of Public Health 64 (November 1974): 1062-1070.

Bolin, David C., and Kivens, Laurence. "Evaluation in a Community Mental Health Center: Huntsville, Alabama." Evaluation 2 (No. 1, 1974): 26-35.

Campbell, D.T., and Stanley, J.C. *Experimental and Quasi-Experimental Design for Research.* Chicago: Rand McNally, 1963.

Caro, F.G. *Readings in Evaluation Research.* New York: Russell Sage Foundation, 1971.

Chafetz, Morris E. *"Monitoring an Evaluation at NIAA"* Evaluation 2 (No. 1, 1974): 49-52.

Chommie, P.W., and Hudson, J. "Evaluation of Outcome and Process." Social Work 19 (November 1974): 682-687.

Eppley, David. "How Effective Are Social Services?" Social and Rehabilitation Record 2 (September 1975): 10-13.

Fanshel, Sol. "The Welfare of the Elderly: A System Analysis Viewpoint." Policy Sciences 6 (September 1975): 343-357.

Franklin, Jack L., and Thrasher, Jean H. *An Introduction to Program Evaluation.* New York: John Wiley, 1976.

Galvin, D.E. "Program Evaluation in Michigan VR Service." Social and Rehabilitation Record 1 (November 1974): 28-31.

Gearing, Frances Rowe. "Methadone Maintenance Treatment Five Years Later— Where Are They Now." American Journal of Public Health Supplement 64 (December 1974): 44-50.

Golfarb, Robert S. "Learning in Government Programs and the Usefulness of Cost Benefit Analysis: Lessons from Manpower and Urban Renewal History." Policy Sciences 6 (September 1975): 281-299.

Guttentag, Marcia, and Snapper, Kurt. "Plans, Evaluations and Decisions." Evaluation 2 (No. 1, 1974): 58-74.

Haskins, J.B. *The Controlled Field Experiment.* Syracuse: Syracuse University Press, 1967.

Hatry, Harry; Winnie, R.E.; and Fish, D.M. *Practical Program Evaluation for State and Local Government Officials.* Washington D.C.: The Urban Institute, 1973.

Havens, Harry S. "Measuring the Unmeasurable: Program Evaluation in an Unquantified World." Bureaucrat 5 (April 1976): 53-64.

Lifsey, Jeremy A. "Politics, Evaluations, and Manpower Programs." *Management and Policy Science in American Government.* Edited by White, Radnor, and Tansik, Lexington, Mass.: D.C. Heath, 1975, pp. 245-259.

Mayer, M.F. "Program Evaluation as a Part of Clinical Practice: An Administrator's Position." Child Welfare 54 (June 1975): 379-394.

Mosher, Loren; Menn, Alma; and Mathews, Susan M. "Soteria: Evaluation of a Home-Based Treatment for Schizophrenia." American Journal of Ortho-psychiatry 45 (April 1975): 455-467.

Nance, Kathy Newton, and Pillsbury, Jolie Bain. "An Evaluation System for Decision Making." Public Welfare 34, (Spring 1976): 45-52.

Olkon, Sheldon H. "Linking Planning with Evaluation in Community Mental Health." Community Mental Health Journal 11 (Winter 1975): 359-370.

Pillsbury, Jolie Bain, and Nance, Kathy Newton. "An Evaluation Framework for Public Welfare Agencies." Public Welfare 3 (Winter 1976): 7-51.

Ratcliffe, Donald. "Cost-Benefit Analysis and the Personal Social Services." Policy and Politics 2 (March 1974): 237-247.

Rivlin, Alice M. *Systematic Thinking for Social Action.* Washington, D.C.: The Brookings Institution, 1971.

Robin, Gerald, "The In-School Neighborhood Youth Corps Program." Evaluation 2 (No. 1, 1974): 53-57.

Rossi, P., and Williams, W. *Evaluation, Social Programs.* New York: Seminar Press, 1972.

Selltiz, Claire; Wrightsman, Lawrence; and Cook, Stuart. *Research Methods in Social Relations.* New York: Holt, Rinehart, & Winston, 1976.

Sheldon, E., and Morre, W., eds. *Indicators of Social Change.* New York: Russell Sage Foundation, 1967.

Skipper, James K., Jr., and McCaghy, Charles H. "Evaluation of a Short-Term Treatment Program for Police Case Inebriates." Social Science 49 (No. 4, 1974): 220-227.

Smith, William. "Evaluation of the Clinical Services of a Regional Mental Health Center." Community Mental Health Journal 11 (No. 1, 1975): 45-57.

Suchman, E. *Evaluation Research.* New York: Russell Sage Foundation, 1967.

Weiss,Carol H. "Alternative Models of Program Evaluation." Social Work 19 (November 1974): 675-681.

Weiss, Carol H. *Evaluation Research.* Englewood Cliffs, N.J.: Prentice-Hall, 1972.

Wheeler, Gerald R. "Evaluating Social Programs: The Case for a State GAO." Policy Studies Journal 3 (Summer 1975): 390-397.

Zymelman, Manuel. *The Economic Evaluation of Vocational Training Programs.* World Bank Staff Occasional Papers No. 21. Balimtore: John Hopkins University Press, 1976.

INDEX

249

ABOUT THE AUTHOR

RICHARD STEINER is a Visiting Associate Professor of Management at the School of Social Welfare, State University of New York at Albany. He is also Co-Director of the school's comprehensive Continuing Education Program and Project Director of its Management and Organizational Development component. A management consultant to numerous public sector organizations, and an Adjunct Professor at the School of Management, Rensselaer Polytechnic Institute, Dr. Steiner has also held senior administrative positions in human service agencies. He is the author of a number of articles that seek to merge sound and modern management practice with the reality of human service programming.

Dr. Steiner is a specialist in preparing professional staff for management positions in the human services and an experienced organizational development workshop leader. A transplanted New York City resident, he currently resides with his family in Saratoga County. Dr. Steiner received his B.A. degree in political science from Brooklyn College and his M.A. and Ph.D. degrees in communications from the Newhouse School of Public Communications at Syracuse University.